# The New International

# WEBSTER'S STANDARD THESAURUS

TRIDENT REFERENCE PUBLISHING

2006 EDITION

LARGE PRINT EDITION

# THE NEW INTERNATIONAL
# WEBSTER'S STANDARD THESAURUS

Published by

## TRIDENT REFERENCE PUBLISHING

**aback** *adv.* **BACKWARD:** back, behind, rearward; **UNEXPECTED:** suddenly, unawares, unexpectedly

**abandon** *n.* **ENTHUSIASM:** impetuosity, spontaneity; **IMMORALITY:** shamelessness, wantonness

**abandon** *v.* **GIVE UP:** forgo, forswear, quit, relinquish; **DESERT:** forsake, leave, resign, vacate

**abandonment** *n.* abdication, renunciation, repudiation, resignation, surrender

**abase** *v.* debase, degrade, disgrace, dishonor, humble, humiliate

**abased** *adj.* degraded, disgraced, dishonored, humbled, humiliated, lowered

**abasement** *n.* degradation, deterioration, disgrace, dishonor, groveling, humiliation, lowering, shame

**abash** *v.* confound, confuse, disconcert, embarrass, humble, humiliate, mortify, shame

**abashed** *adj.* ashamed, chagrined, confused

**abasing** *adj.* abusive, insulting, offensive

**abate** *v.* **LESSEN:** decline, decrease diminish, ease, ebb, fade, lower, moderate, slacken, relieve, slow; **DISCOUNT:** allow, deduct, rebate, remit, subtract

**abatement** *n.* **LESSENING:** alleviation, decrease, mitigation, slackening, subsidence; **ENDING:** cessation, remission, suppression, termination

**abbreviate** *v.* abridge, condense, contract, cut, reduce, shorten, truncate

**abbreviation** *n.* abridgement, brief, compendium, condensation, shortening, truncation

**abdicate** *v.* abandon, cede, disavow, disclaim, disown, relinquish, renounce, resign, secede

1

**abdomen** *n.* belly, breadbasket, gut, midsection, paunch, potbelly, stomach, tummy

**abduct** *v.* capture, kidnap, seize, shanghai

**abecedarian** *n.* beginner, novice

**aberrant** *adj.* **DEVIATING:** divergent, errant, irregular, straying; **ODD:** abnormal, peculiar, queer, strange, unnatural, unusual, weird

**aberrational** *adj.* curious, odd, peculiar, strange

**abet** *v.* advance, aid, assist, back, condone, favor, further, help, promote, sanction, support

**abettor** *n.* accessory, accomplice, ally, associate, cohort, confederate, conspirator

**abeyance** *n.* cessation, deferral, discontinuance, hiatus, moratorium, suspension

**abhor** *v.* despise, detest, hate, loathe

**abhorrence** *n.* aversion, disgust, dislike, distaste, hatred, loathing, horror, repugnance

**abhorrent** *adj.* abominable, despicable, detestable, disgusting, loathsome, offensive, nauseating, odious, repugnant, repulsive, revolting, shocking, vile

**abidance** *n.* compliance, continuance

**abide** *v.* **DWELL:** inhabit, live, reside, stay; **WAIT:** attend, await, remain, stay, tarry; **ENDURE:** allow, bear, remain, stand, suffer

**abiding** *adj.* enduring, lasting, permanent, steadfast

**ability** *n.* aptitude, bent, capability, capacity, competence, dexterity, expertise, facility, faculty, knack, proficiency, qualification, skill, skillfulness, talent

**abject** *adj.* base, contemptible, degrading,

despicable, disheartening, ignominious, miserable, poor, sorry

**abjection, abjectness** *n.* churlishness, degradation, humiliation, meanness, nastiness

**abjuration** *n.* abnegation, denial, disavowal, rejection, renouncement, renunciation

**abjure** *v.* forswear, recant, recall, renounce, retract, withdraw

**ablaze** *adj.* BURNING: aflame, blazing, fiery, flaming; FERVENT: ardent, eager, excited, exhilarated, intense

**able** *adj.* CAPABLE: adequate, apt, competent, efficient, fit, qualified; SKILLFUL: accomplished, adroit, dexterous, expert, gifted, ingenious, proficient, talented

**able–bodied** *adj.* fit, healthy, robust, strong

**abloom** *adj.* blossoming, flowering, sprouting

**ablution** *n.* cleansing, purification, purging, washing

**abnegation** *n.* abjuration, denial, disavowal, rejection, renouncement, renunciation

**abnormal** *adj.* aberrant, anomalous, curious, deviant, irregular, odd, peculiar, unnatural

**abnormality** *n.* anomaly, curiosity, irregularity, malformation, nonconformity, peculiarity, perversion

**abode** *n.* domicile, dwelling, habitat, house, residence

**abolish** *v.* abrogate, annul, cancel, eliminate, end, eradicate, extinguish, nullify, obliterate

**abolishment** *n.* annulment, cancellation, elimination, eradication, nullification

**abolition** *n.* annulment, cancellation, dissolution, elimination, eradication, repeal, revocation

**abominable** *adj*. abhorrent, contemptible, despicable, detestable, disgusting, hateful, horrible, loathsome, offensive, repugnant

**abominate** *v*. abhor, despise, detest, hate, loathe

**abomination** *n*. **HORROR:** loathing, revulsion; **WICKEDNESS:** amorality, depravity, evil, immorality

**aboriginal** *adj*. domestic, indigenous, local, native, original, primitive

**abort** *v*. annul, cancel, destroy, fail, interrupt, miscarry, nullify, scrap, stop, terminate

**abortion** *n*. **CESSATION:** cancellation, interruption, termination; **MONSTROSITY:** abnormality

**abortive** *adj*. fruitless, futile, ineffectual, unavailing

**abound** *v*. overflow, pour, swarm, swell, teem

**abounding** *adj*. abundant, lavish, luxuriant, plentiful

**about** *adv*. **CONCERNING:** referencing, regarding; **APPROXIMATELY:** almost, around, close, near, nigh

**above** *adv*. **HIGHER:** atop, beyond, over, overhead; **GREATER:** preeminent, superior, surpassing

**aboveboard** *adj*. candid, frank, guileless, honest, open, overt, sincere, straightforward

**abrading** *adj*. annoying, harsh, nasty, offensive

**abrade** *v*. **WEAR:** chafe, corrode, erode, grind, rub, scrape; **IRRITATE**: anger, annoy, bother, gall, irk

**abrading** *n*. abrasion, attrition, erosion

**abrasion** *n*. blemish, bruise, cut, scrape, scratch

**abrasive** *adj*. annoying, exasperating, grating, harsh, jarring, nasty, offensive, rasping, shrill, strident

**abreast** *adj.,* *adv.* **BESIDE:** against, aligned; **INFORMED:** apprised, familiar

**abridge** *v.* abstract, compress, condense, curtail, cut, decrease, diminish, lessen, reduce, restrict, shorten

**abrogate** *v.* abolish, annul, cancel, invalidate, nullify, repeal, rescind, revoke, void

**abrupt** *adj.* **SUDDEN:** quick, sharp, unexpected; **CURT:** blunt, boorish, brusque, discourteous, hasty, impatient, rude; **STEEP:** craggy, hilly, precipitous, sheer

**abruptness** *n.* brevity, curtness, shortness, terseness

**abscessed** *adj.* inflamed, painful, ulcerated

**abscission** *n.* deletion, eradication, excision, removal

**abscond** *v.* bolt, depart, escape, flee

**absconder** *n.* cheat,

charlatan, rogue, swindler

**absence** *n.* **LACK:** dearth, default, defect, deficiency, need, want; **AWAY:** nonattendance, truancy

**absentee** *n.* defector, delinquent, deserter, fugitive, escapee, runaway, truant

**absent–minded** *adj.* forgetful, oblivious, preoccupied, unmindful

**absolute** *adj.* **PERFECT:** certain, definite, faultless, ideal, sure, unconditional, unquestionable, utter, whole;

**AUTHORITARIAN:** autocratic, despotic, dictatorial, imperious, peremptory, strict, tyrannical

**absolution** *n.* acquittal, clearance, exoneration, vindication

**absolvable** *adj.* excusable, forgivable, inconsequential, justifiable, minor, pardonable, permissible, venial

**absolve** *v.* acquit, clear, discharge, excuse, exonerate, forgive, free, justify, liberate, pardon, release

**absorb** *v.* **INCORPORATE:** amalgamate, assimilate, consume, devour, engulf; **ENGROSS:** engage, employ, occupy; **UNDERSTAND:** grasp, assimilate, learn, sense

**absorbed** *adj.* **INCORPORATED:** assimilated, digested, dissolved, permeated; **ENGROSSED:** enthralled, immersed, intent, involved, preoccupied, rapt

**absorbent** *adj.* permeable, penetrable, porous, spongy

**absorbing** *adj.* engaging, enthralling, exciting, fascinating, interesting

**absorption** *n.* absent-mindedness, preoccupation, reflection, reverie

**abstain** *v.* avoid, decline, eschew, forgo, refrain, shun

**abstinence** *n.* avoidance, forbearance, moderation, self–denial, sobriety, temperance

**abstinent** *adj.* abstemious, continent, moderate

**abstract** *adj.* **THEORETICAL:** conceptual, ideal, hypothetical; **ISOLATED:** apart, separate, special, unrelated; **COMPLEX:** complicated, deep, difficult, obscure

**abstract** *n.* abridgment, brief, compendium, condensation, digest, distillation, outline, summary

**abstract** *v.* **REMOVE:** disjoin, dissociate, isolate, separate, withdraw; **CONDENSE:** abbreviate, abridge, digest, distill, edit, outline, summarize

**abstruse** *adj.* complex, difficult, intricate, involved

**absurd** *adj.* asinine, foolish, irrational,

inane, ludicrous, pre-
posterous, ridiculous,
silly

**abundance** *n.* bounty,
extravagance, full-
ness, profusion, pros-
perity, wealth

**abundant** *adj.* copious,
abounding, flowing,
fruitful, opulent, pro-
fuse, plentiful, prodi-
gal, prolific, teeming

**abuse** *n.* misuse, defilement, desecration,
mistreatment, profa-
nation, subversion,
violation

**abuse** *v.* MISUSE: attack, desecrate, harm,
hurt, injure, maltreat,
mistreat, wrong;
BERATE: assail, de-
nounce, disparage,
insult, malign, re-
proach, revile, scold

**abusive** *adj.*
AGONIZING: insuf-
ferable, intolerable,
painful, unbearable,
unendurable;
DISCOURTEOUS: rude,
sarcastic, slanderous,
truculent, vituperative

**abut** *v.* adjoin, border,
touch, verge

**abysmal** *adj.* bottom-
less, deep, im-
measurable, pro-
found, unfathomable

**abyss** *n.* chasm, gorge,
gulf, hole, perdition

**academic** *adj.*
SCHOLARLY: collegiate,
erudite, learned, let-
tered, literary, scho-
lastic, schooled;
TRADITIONAL: con-
ventional, conserva-
tive, established, for-
malistic;
THEORETICAL: con-
jectural, speculative,
suppositional

**academician** *n.* intellectual, egghead,
scholar

**academics** *n.* courses,
studies

**academy** *n.* college,
conservatory, school

**accede** *v.* acquiesce,
agree, allow, assent,
comply, consent,
permit, sanction

**accelerate** *v.* hasten,
expedite, quicken,
throttle

**acceleration** *n.* dispatch, hastening,
quickening

**accent** *n.* **MODULATION:** beat, inflection, emphasis, rhythm; **SIGNIFICANCE:** importance, prominence

**accent, accentuate** *v.* emphasize, stress, underscore

**accept** *v.* **RECEIVE:** embrace, take, welcome; **ACQUIESCE:** accede, acknowledge, allow, assent, concede, concur, grant; **BELIEVE:** affirm, maintain, trust; **UNDERSTAND:** appreciate, conclude, construe

**acceptable** *adj.* adequate, agreeable, permissible, pleasant, pleasing, satisfactory, sufficient

**acceptance** *n.* concent, acknowledgement, agreement, assent, capitulation, concurrence, recognition

**accepted** *adj.* **ACCREDITED:** accustomed, acknowledged, allowed, recognized; **SETTLED:** admitted, affirmed, endorsed

**accessible** *adj.* approachable, attainable, available, convenient, obtainable, reachable

**accessory** *adj.* added, contributing, extra

**accessory** *n.* abettor, accomplice

**accident** *n.* **MISHAP:** casualty, misadventure, pileup, wreck; **CHANCE:** coincidence, fortune

**accidental** *adj.* **UNEXPECTED:** casual, chance, fortuitous, odd, random, unintentional, unplanned; **INCIDENTAL:** insignificant, minor, nonessential, secondary, subsidiary

**acclaim** *n.* applause, approval, enthusiasm, fame, plaudits, praise, recognition

**acclaim** *v.* applaud, celebrate, commend, laud, praise

**acclamation** *n.* acclaim, accolades, applause, approval, jubilation, plaudits, praise

**acclimate** *v.* accommodate, adapt, adjust, conform

**acclimatize** *v.* acclimate, adapt, adjust, conform

**acclivity** *n.* ascent, incline, slope, upgrade

**accolade** *n.* acknowledgement, esteem, praise, tribute

**accommodate** *v.* **AID:** abet, assist, oblige, provide, serve, supply; **ENTERTAIN:** board, house, lodge, quarter; **ADJUST:** adapt, conform, fit, harmonize, reconcile, temper; **RECEIVE:** contain, have, hold

**accommodating** *adj.* kind, gracious, helpful, obliging

**accompaniment** *n.* addition, accessory, adjunct, appendage, appurtenance

**accompany** *v.* **ATTEND:** chaperon, convey, escort, follow, join, see, show, usher; **APPEND:** augment, complement, complete, enhance, supplement

**accomplice** *n.* accessory, affiliate, associate, confederate, conspirator, partner

**accomplish** *v.* achieve, attain, complete, do, effect, execute, fulfill, make, manage, perform, realize

**accomplished** *adj.* skillful, able, cultivated, expert, proficient, talented

**accomplishment** *n.* achievement, attainment, exploit, feat, fulfillment, success

**accord** *n.* agreement, conformity, consent, harmony, peace, unanimity

**accord** *v.* **AGREE:** accommodate, adapt, affirm, coincide, concur, correspond; **BESTOW:** allow, deign, grant, concede, yield

**accordance** *n.* accord, agreement, coincidence, concordance, conformity, harmony

**accost** *v.* address, approach, confront, greet, meet, proposition, solicit, waylay

**account** *n.* **NARRATIVE:** anecdote, chronicle, description, exposé, journal, narration, recital, report, story, tale; **REASON:** excuse, grounds, motive; **WORTH:** advantage, benefit, estimation, importance, profit, reputation

**account** *v.* **EXPLAIN:** describe, justify; **REGARD:** consider, count, credit, deem, estimate, hold, judge, reckon, think

**accountable** *adj.* answerable, culpable, liable, responsible

**accredit** *v.* certify, endorse, pass, ratify, recognize, sanction, support, uphold, validate, warrant

**accrual, accruement** *n.* accumulation, expansion, growth, increase, recovery, return, yield

**accumulate** *v.* accrue, amass, collect, cumulate, gather, heap, garner, increase, stockpile, store

**accuracy** *n.* exactness, precision, sureness

**accurate** *n.* careful, correct, exact, factual, faithful, flawless, precise, proper, right, true, unerring

**accursed** *adj.* doomed, bewitched, condemned, damned, haunted, ill-fated

**accusation** *n.* allegation, charge, complaint, denunciation, indictment, insinuation, slur, smear

**accuse** *v.* arraign, arrest, blame, charge, denounce, implicate, impute, incriminate, indict, involve

**accustom** *v.* familiarize, habituate, inure, season

**ace** *n.* champion, expert, genius, master, specialist, virtuoso

**acerbate** *n.* heighten, increase, intensify, worsen

**acerbic** *adj.* bitter, harsh, rough, sharp, sour

**ache** *n.* agony, pain, pang, spasm, twinge

**ache** *v.* hurt, pain, suffer, throb

**achievable** *adj.* attainable, feasible, obtainable

**achieve** *v.* accomplish, effect, fulfill, finish, reach, attain, gain, get, realize, secure

**achy** *adj.* aching, bruised, painful

**acid** *adj.* biting, cutting, sarcastic, sardonic, scornful, sharp, vitriolic

**acknowledge** *v.* admit, agree, allow, appreciate, approve, avow, concede, confess, confirm, declare, endorse, grant, ratify, recognize, reply, respond

**acknowledgment** *n.* ACCEPTANCE: affirmation, corroboration, recognition; RESPONSE: answer, call, greeting, letter, nod, note, reaction, reply, thanks

**acme** *n.* apex, peak, summit, top, zenith

**acolyte** *n.* aide, assistant, helper, subordinate

**acquaint** *v.* inform, accustom, advise, familiarize, reconnoiter, introduce, present

**acquaintance** *n.* friend, associate, colleague, companion, crony, pal

**acquainted** *adj.* conversant, familiar, introduced

**acquiesce** *v.* assent, accede, accept, agree, comply, concur, consent, submit, yield

**acquire** *v.* appropriate, attain, earn, obtain, gain, procure, secure

**acquisitive** *adj.* avaricious, grasping, greedy

**acquisitiveness** *n.* covetousness, greed

**acquit** *v.* absolve, exonerate, pardon, release

**acquittal** *n.* absolution, amnesty, deliverance, discharge, dismissal, exoneration, pardon, vindication

**acreage** *n.* grounds, land, property, spread, terrain

**acrid** *adj.* astringent, biting, bitter, caustic, harsh

**acrimonious** *adj.* acerbic, caustic, irascible, testy

**acropolis** *n.* bastion, citadel, blockhouse, fort, fortification, redoubt, stronghold

**across** *adv.* athwart, crosswise, over, transversely

**act** *n.* **EXPLOIT:** accomplishment, deed, feat, performance; **DECREE:** edict, law, order, resolution, statute, writ; **PERFORMANCE:** routine, sketch, stint, turn

**act** *v.* **DO:** accomplish, conduct, operate; **SUBSTITUTE:** represent, officiate, serve; **PERFORM:** appear, dramatize, impersonate, pretend, play, simulate

**acting** *adj.* deputy, officiating, surrogate, temporary

**acting** *n.* depiction, performance, role impersonation

**action** *n.* **MOTION:** activity, maneuver, movement; **FEAT:** accomplishment, exercise, transaction; **BEHAVIOR:** conduct, response; **MACHINE:** apparatus, contrivance, mechanism; **CONFLICT:** battle, contest, encounter, engagement, skirmish; **LAWSUIT:** case, claim, litigation, proceeding, process, suit

**activate** *v.* animate, begin, initiate, stimulate

**active** *adj.* animated, busy, dynamic, energetic, functioning, industrious, lively, living, mobile, moving, operative, spirited, tireless, working

**actively** *adv.* energetically, spryly, vigorously

**activist** *n.* agitator, firebrand, malcontent, radical, reformer, revolutionary

**activity** *n.* action, motion, movement, pastime

**actor** *n.* artist, entertainer, impersonator, mime, performer, player, thespian, trouper

**actual** *adj.* **FACTUAL:** certain, genuine, definite, true; **EXISTING:** concrete, material, real, tangible

**actually** *adv.* indeed, really, truly

**actuate** *v.* drive, impel, move, propel, push

**acuity** *n.* discernment, discrimination, insight, perception, perspicacity, sharpness, shrewdness

**acumen** *n.* cleverness, discernment, insight, intelligence, keenness, sagacity, shrewdness

**acute** *adj.* **POINTED:** keen, sharp; **IMPORTANT:** critical, crucial, intense, serious; **PERCEPTIVE:** astute, clever, discerning, intelligent, keen, penetrating

**adage** *n.* cliché, maxim, motto, proverb, saying, slogan

**adamant** *adj.* firm, fixed, insistent, obstinate, resolute, set, steadfast, stubborn, unbending, unyielding

**adapt** *v.* acclimatize, accustom, adjust, conform, fashion, fit, modify, reconcile, shape, tailor, temper

**adaptable** *adj.* docile, flexible, pliable, pliant, tractable, versatile

**adaptation** *n.* **ACCLIMATIZATION:** acculturation, conversion, revising; **DEVICE:** apparatus, appliance, contraption, contrivance, gadget, mechanism

**add** *v.* **AFFIX:** annex, append, attach, augment, connect, supplement, unite: **CALCULATE:** compute, figure, increase, sum, tally, total

**addendum** *n.* addition, adjunct, annexation, appendix, attachment, augmentation, codicil, rider

**addict** *n.* buff, devotee, fan, hound, junkie, lover

**addicted** *adj.* chronic, dependent, fanatical, fixated, habituated, hooked, inclined, obsessed

**addictive** *adj.* compelling, irresistible, overpowering

**additional** *adj.* added, auxiliary, collateral, extra

**addle** *v.* cloud, confound, confuse, obfuscate

**addled** *adj.* befuddled, bewildered, confounded, confused, dazed, disconcerted, flustered, muddled

**add–on** *n.* improvement, modernization, supplement

**address** *n.* **SPEECH:** discourse, lecture, oration, sermon; **LO-CATION:** dwelling, house, lodging, residence

**adept** *adj.* able, capable, competent, expert, proficient, skilled

**adequacy** *n.* acceptability, plenty, sufficiency

**adequate** *adj.* ample, enough, satisfactory, suitable

**adhere** *v.* **STICK:** attach, cleave, cling, fasten, hold; **CONFORM:** comply, follow, heed, obey

**adherent** *n.* advocate, devotee, disciple, fan, follower

**adhesive** *n.* cement, epoxy, glue, mucilage

**adjacent** *adj.* abutting, adjoining, bordering, close, contiguous, near, nearby, neighboring, touching

**adjoin** *v.* abut, append, border, butt, meet, neighbor, touch, verge

**adjourn** *v.* defer, discontinue, dissolve, recess, interrupt, postpone, suspend

**adjournment** *n.* break, continuance, deferment, intermission, pause, postponement, recess

**adjudicate** *v.* arbitrate, decide, mediate, settle

**adjudication** *n.* determination, judgment, finding, ruling, verdict, sentence

**adjudicator** *n.* arbiter, judge, mediator, referee

**adjunct** *n.* accessory, addition, attachment

**adjure** *v.* ask, appeal, beg, beseech, entreat, implore, petition, plead, request, supplicate, urge

**adjust** *v.* adapt, alter, calibrate, correct, modify, regulate, tune, temper, true

**adjustable** *adj.* flexible, malleable, tractable, variable

**adjustment** *n.* **ALTERATION:** modification, setting; **COMPENSATION:** allotment, compromise, reconciliation, redress, remuneration, settlement

**adjutant** *n.* aide, assistant, attaché, deputy, helper

**ad–lib** *adj.* improvised, spontaneous, unrehearsed

**administer** *v.* **MANAGE:** control, direct, execute, oversee, supervise; **DISPENSE:** distribute, give, parcel

**administrative** *adj.* bureaucratic, executive, governmental, official, managerial

**admirable** *adj.* commendable, excellent, meritorious, noble, praiseworthy, splendid, superb, worthy

**admiration** *n.* approbation, awe, esteem, fondness, regard, respect, veneration

**admire** *v.* esteem, honor, regard, respect, revere, venerate

**admirer** *n.* **FAN:** devotee, enthusiast, follower, supporter; **BEAU:** adorer, suitor, sweetheart, wooer

**admissible** *adj.* allowable, lawful, legal, legitimate

**admission** *n.* **ACCESS:** admittance, entrée, entrance, entry; **AFFIRMATION:** acknowledgment, confirmation, disclosure

**admit** *v.* ACCOM-MODATE: allow, grant, permit; AFFIRM: concede, disclose, divulge, expose, reveal

**admittance** *n.* access, admission, entrance

**admonish** *v.* caution, counsel, exhort, reprove, warn

**admonition** *n.* COUNSEL: advice, caution, warning; REBUKE: censure, reprimand, reproach, scolding

**ado** *n.* bother, bustle, commotion, fuss, stir

**adolescence** *n.* puberty, pubescence, teens, youth

**adolescent** *adj.* childish, immature, juvenile, youthful

**adolescent** *n.* minor, teen, teenager, youth

**adopt** *v.* APPROPRIATE: assume, borrow, espouse, utilize; RATIFY: approve, confirm, endorse, sanction

**adorable** *adj.* charming, cute, darling, delightful, enchanting, lovable, precious

**adoration** *n.* devotion, idolatry, veneration, worship

**adore** *v.* cherish, esteem, idolize, love, revere, venerate, worship

**adorer** *n.* admirer, beau, suitor, sweetheart, wooer

**adorn** *v.* beautify, bedeck, decorate, embellish, garnish, festoon, ornament, trim

**adroit** *adj.* adept, dexterous, expert, handy, quick, resourceful, skillful

**adulation** *n.* adoration, glorification, laudation, praise, worship

**adult** *adj.* developed, grown, mature, ripe

**adulteration** *n.* contamination, pollution, taint

**adulterer** *n.* debaucher, lecher, libertine, philanderer, rake, reprobate

**adulterous** *adj.* dissolute, immoral, licentious, lustful

**adultery** *n.* cuckoldry, fornication, infidelity

**adulthood** *n.* majority, maturity

**advance** *v.* **PROGRESS:** go, move, proceed, update; **BROACH:** introduce, propose, present, suggest; **PROMOTE:** encourage, foster, propound; **OFFER:** lend

**advanced** *adj.* aged, elderly, futuristic, precocious, radical, seasoned, unconventional

**advancement** *n.* betterment, elevation, preference, progression, promotion

**advantage** *n.* benefit, edge, gain, leverage, profit

**adventure** *n.* undertaking, experience, exploit

**advantageous** *adj.* beneficial, expedient, favorable, lucrative, profitable, worthwhile

**advent** *n.* appearance, arrival, coming

**adventure** *n.* escapade, exploit, feat, happening, quest, undertaking, venture

**adventuresome, adventurous** *adj.* bold, courageous, daring, enterprising, gallant

**adversarial** *adj.* antagonistic, hostile, unfriendly

**adversary** *n.* antagonist, enemy, foe, opponent

**adverse** *adj.* antagonistic, conflicting, contrary, hostile, negative, unfavorable

**adversity** *n.* affliction, distress, hardship, misery, misfortune, sorrow, trouble

**advertise** *v.* broadcast, exhibit, expose, proclaim, promote, publicize, show

**advertisement, advertising** *n.* blurb, broadside, endorsement, handbill, pitch, poster, plug

**advice** *n.* counsel, guidance, lesson, suggestion

**advisable** *adj.* advantageous, desirable, expedient, politic, prudent, sensible, sound

**advise** *v.* admonish, caution, counsel, consult, forewarn, inform, notify, recommend

**advised** *adj.* cautious, circumspect, deliberate

**adviser, advisor** *n.* attorney, consultant, counsel, counselor, elder, expert, guide, instructor, lawyer, mentor, patriarch, teacher, tutor

**advocacy** *n.* adoption, belief, espousal, promotion

**advocate** *v.* advance, bolster, champion, further, promote, recommend, support

**aesthete** *n.* collector, connoisseur, dilettante

**aesthetic, aesthetical** *adj.* artistic, discriminating, elegant, pleasing, polished, refined, tasteful

**affable** *adj.* agreeable, amiable, civil, cordial, courteous, friendly, gracious, obliging, pleasant, sociable

**affair** *n.* CONCERN: business, pursuit; ROMANCE: liaison, relationship, tryst, rendezvous; GATHERING: event, function, party

**affect** *v.* INFLUENCE: alter, change, modify, sway, stir, transform; PRETEND: assume, dissemble, fake, feign

**affectation** *n.* artificiality, pose, pretense

**affection** *n.* devotion, fondness, friendship, liking, love, regard, respect, tenderness, warmth

**affectionate** *adj.* attentive, devoted, loving, tender

**affianced** *adj.* betrothed, pledged, plighted

**affidavit** *n.* affirmation, deposition, oath, testimony

**affiliate** *n.* agent, associate, colleague, partner

**affiliation** *n.* alliance, association, coalition, confederation, connection, federation, pact, union

**affinity** *n.* ATTRACTION: affection, closeness, fondness; SIMILARITY: correspondence, likeness, resemblance

**affirm** *v.* DECLARE: assert, claim, maintain, state, swear, testify; CONFIRM: approve, endorse, ratify

**affirmative** *adj.* concurring, confirming, endorsing, supporting

**affix** *v.* add, append, attach, bind, connect, fasten

**afflict** *v.* ail, beset, distress, torment

**affliction** *n.* distress, hardship, misfortune, suffering

**affluence** *n.* abundance, prosperity, wealth

**afford** *v.* allow, grant, permit, provide, sustain

**affront** *v.* insult, abuse, offend, provoke, slight

**aficionado** *n.* buff, devotee, fan, hound, lover

**afield** *adv.* amiss, astray, awry

**afoot** *adj.* WALKING: hiking, marching; FORTHCOMING: brewing, happening, hatching, progressing

**aforementioned** *adj.* earlier, former, preceding, prior

**afraid** *adj.* anxious, apprehensive, disquieted, fearful, frightened, scared, shocked, terrified

**after** *adj., adv.* afterward, following, later, subsequent

**aftereffect** *n.* consequence, outcome, result

**afterthought** *n.* addendum, addition, appendix

**agape** *adj.* ASTONISHED: aghast appalled confounded dismayed horrified shocked; AJAR: open

**age** *n.* PERIOD: eon, epoch, era, generation, time; STAGE: adolescence, adulthood, childhood, infancy

**age** *v.* decline, deteriorate, develop, mature, mellow, ripen, season

**ageless** *adj.* classic, timeless, traditional

**agenda** *n.* aims, goals, program, calendar, list, plan

**agent** *n.* **MEDIUM:** agency, cause, instrument, means, method, vehicle; **REPRESENTATIVE:** ambassador, attorney, broker, factor, intermediary, proxy

**agglomerate** *v.* amass, concentrate, consolidate

**aggrandize** *v.* **ENLARGE:** amplify, expand, extend, increase; **ACCLAIM:** boast, exaggerate, extol, praise

**aggravate** *v.* **WORSEN:** deepen, exacerbate, heighten, increase, intensify; **PROVOKE:** anger, annoy, exasperate, irritate

**aggravating** *adj.* bothersome, disquieting, disturbing

**aggravation** *n.* **AFFLICTION:** annoyance, irritation; **WORSENING:** deepening, heightening

**aggregate** *adj.* combined, complete, entire, total

**aggressive** *adj.* **HOSTILE:** belligerent, combative, contentious, pugnacious; **ASSERTIVE:** determined, dynamic, energetic, enterprising, forward, pushy

**aggressor** *n.* attacker, intruder, invader, trespasser

**aggrieve** *v.* disturb, harass, irritate, trouble, worry

**aggrieved** *adj.* harmed, hurt, injured

**aghast** *adj.* appalled, horrified, shocked

**agile** *adj.* **QUICK:** brisk, deft, lithe, lively, nimble, sprightly, vigorous; **BRIGHT:** clever, keen, smart

**agility** *n.* dexterity, liveliness, nimbleness

**agitate** *v.* **STIR:** churn, mix, toss, tumble; **DISTURB:** discomfit, disquiet, fluster, perturb, trouble, unsettle, upset; **DEBATE:** argue, dispute

**agitator** *n.* activist, firebrand, rabble–rouser, radical

**agnostic** *n.* doubter, non–believer, skeptic, unbeliever

**agonize** *v.* struggle, suffer, writhe, toss

**agony** *n.* anguish, distress, misery, pain, suffering, torment

**agree** *v.* **COINCIDE:** correspond, equal, harmonize, match, suit; **COMPROMISE:** contract, resolve, settle; **CONSENT:** accede, acquiesce, allow, assent, concede

**agreeable** *adj.* **PLEASING:** amiable, congenial, gracious, pleasant, polite; **SUITABLE:** acceptable, satisfactory

**agreement** *n.* **COVENANT:** bargain, compact, contract, deal, pact, settlement, understanding; **ACCORD:** compromise, harmony, peace, unity

**ahead** *adj., adv.* before, earlier, preceding

**aid** *n.* **ASSISTANCE:** backing, charity, help, relief, support; **HELPER:** aide, assistant, colleague, supporter

**aid** *v.* assist, facilitate, help, serve, support, sustain

**ailment** *n.* illness, affliction, infirmity, sickness

**air** *n.* atmosphere, breeze; tune; affectation, manner

**air** *v.* ventilate; announce

**alarm** *v.* warn; frighten

**alert** *adj.* ready, aware, attentive, intelligent, wary

**alert** *v.* caution, inform, warn

**alien** *adj.* foreign, strange, unfamiliar

**alienation** *n.* animosity, disaffection

**allay** *v.* calm, alleviate

**allegation** *n.* accusation, assertion, claim

**allege** *v.* assert, attest, declare

**alleviate** *v.* abate, ease, relieve, lessen, soften

**alliance** *n.* union, treaty, marriage

**allocate** *v.* allot, designate

**allow** *v.* approve, grant, let, permit, sanction

**allure** *v.* tempt, attract

**ally** *n.* associate, backer, confederate

**alms** *n.* charity, dole, donation

**aloof** *adj.* cool, detached, distant, reserved

**alter** *v.* change, modify, adjust

**altercate** *v.* contend, oppose, quarrel, bicker

**alternate** *n.* replacement, substitute

**alternative** *n.* choice, option

**altruism** *n.* benevolence, charity, kindness

**amateur** *n.* beginner, neophyte, novice

**amaze** *v.* astonish, dumfound, stupefy

**amazement** *n.* awe, shock, surprise

**ambassador** *n.* diplomat, emissary, envoy, minister

**ambiguous** *adj.* indistinct, puzzling, unclear, vague

**ambitious** *adj.* determined, industrious

**ambivalent** *adj.* uncertain, wavering

**ameliorate** *v.* alleviate, improve, rectify

**amenable** *adj.* agreeable, docile, pliable, responsive

**amend** *v.* improve, change, correct

**amenity** *n.* courtesy, consideration, pleasantness

**amiable, amicable** *adj.* friendly, affable, agreeable, congenial, kindly, genial

**amiss** *adj.* wrong, faulty, erroneous, imperfect, awry

**amity** *n.* goodwill, regard, friendliness, affection

**amnesty** *n.* pardon, liberation, reprieve

**among** *prep.* amid, amongst, amidst

**amount** *n.* **TOTAL:** sum; **PRICE:** expense, output, outlay; **QUANTITY:** bulk, mass, number

**ample** *adj.* sufficient, plenty, adequate, enough

**amplify** *v.* increase, augment, magnify

**amulet** *n.* charm, talisman

**amuse** *v.* entertain, divert, cheer, enliven

**amusement** *n.* entertainment, recreation, pastime

**analyze** *v.* dissect, examine, investigate

**anarchy** *n.* disorder, turmoil, chaos

**ancestor** *n.* forebear, progenitor, forefather

**ancestry** *n.* lineage, heritage, parentage

**ancient** *adj.* old, antiquated, antique, aged

**anecdote** *n.* story, tale, incident, episode

**anger** *n.* ire, wrath, rage, fury, exasperation, irritation

**anger** *v.* infuriate, annoy, irritate enrage

**angle** *n.* PLAN: plot, scheme, maneuver; VIEWPOINT: outlook, standpoint, perspective; INTERSECTION: crotch, elbow, fork

**angry** *adj.* enraged, furious, infuriated, irate, raging, cross, annoyed, displeased, riled, hostile

**anguish** *n.* pain, wretchedness, agony

**angular** *adj.* intersecting, crossing, crotched, forked

**animate** *v.* activate, vitalize, arouse, energize

**animosity** *n.* hatred, dislike, enmity, displeasure

**annex** *v.* add, incorporate, append, attach, affix.

**annihilate** *v.* destroy, demolish, exterminate

**annotate** *v.* comment, explain, interpret

**announcement** *n.* declaration, publication, statement, bulletin, notice, communiqué, release

**annoy** *v.* bother, irritate, pester, trouble

**annoyance** *n.* irritation, pique, displeasure, nuisance, discontent, dissatisfaction, impatience,

**annul** *v.* invalidate, repeal, revoke, cancel

**anoint** *v.* sprinkle, consecrate

**anonymous** *adj.* unsigned, nameless, unknown

**answer** *v.* **REPLY:** respond, retort, acknowledge, refute, rebut; **EXPLAIN:** solve, elucidate, clarify

**answerable** *adj.* responsible, liable

**antagonism** *n.* hatred, enmity, hostility, opposition

**antic** *n.* prank, joke, trick, frolic, caper

**anticipate** *v.* expect, forecast, predict, assume, await

**antipathy** *n.* aversion, dislike, hatred, repulsion

**antiquated, antique** *adj.* old, outmoded, out–of–date

**antiseptic** *adj.* clean, germ–free, sterilized, pure

**antithesis** *n.* contrasting, reverse

**antitoxin** *n.* vaccine, antibody, serum

**anxiety, anxiousness** *n.* concern, trouble, misgiving

**anxious** *adj.* **EAGER:** desirous, zealous, fervent; **APPREHENSIVE:** concerned, troubled

**apathetic** *adj.* unemotional, unconcerned, indifferent.

**ape** *v.* imitate, mimic, copy, impersonate.

**aperture** *n.* opening, hole, slot

**aphorism** *n.* motto, proverb, saying

**apologetic** *adj.* regretful, contrite, remorseful, sorry

**appall** *v.* horrify, amaze, dismay, shock

**apparel** *n.* clothes, attire, suit, dress

**apparent** *adj.* open, visible, clear, manifest, obvious

**apparition** *n.* ghost, manifestation, phantom, spirit

**appeal** *n.* **PLEA:** request, petition, entreaty, prayer, supplication; **ATTRACTIVENESS:** charm, glamour

**appeal** *v.* **REQUEST:** beg, urge, petition; **FASCINATE:** attract, interest, engage

**appear** *v.* **EMERGE:** rise, loom, arrive, recur, materialize, show; **SEEM:** resemble

**appearance** *n.* bearing, demeanor, features

**appease** *v.* satisfy

**append** *v.* add, affix, attach, supplement

**appendix** *n.* supplement, attachment

**appetite** *n.* hunger, thirst, craving, longing, desire

**appetizing** *adj.* savory, tasty, delectable, delicious

**applaud** *v.* approve, cheer, clap, acclaim

**applicable** *adj.* suitable, appropriate, usable, fit

**applicant** *n.* petitioner, claimant, candidate.

**application** *n.* **USE:** employment, utilization; **ATTENTION:** devotion, zeal, diligence; **PETITION:** entreaty, appeal; **INSTRUMENT:** form, requisition

**apply** *v.* **REQUEST:** petition, beg; **UTILIZE:** employ, practice, exploit; **PERTAIN:** involve, affect

**appoint** *v.* name, select, designate

**appointment** *n.* **DESIGNATION:** selection, nomination, choice; **ENGAGEMENT:** meeting, rendezvous, date

**appraise** *v.* assess, price, assay, rate

**appreciable** *adj.* considerable, sizable, tangible, large

**appreciate** *v.* **THANK:** acknowledge; **ESTEEM:** honor, praise, admire

**appreciative** *adj.* grateful, obliged, satisfied, thankful

**apprehend** *v.* **ARREST:** detain, seize; **COMPREHEND:** understand, perceive, grasp

**apprehension** *n.* **FOREBODING:** trepidation, dread, misgiving, fear; **UNDERSTANDING:** comprehension; **ARREST:** capture, seizure, detention

**apprentice** *n.* beginner, student, learner

**apprise** *v.* notify, teach, warn

**approach** *n.* ACCESS: avenue, path, entrance, gate, way; PLAN: method, program, procedure

**approbation** *n.* approval, regard

**appropriate** *adj.* suitable proper, suited, fitting, fit

**appropriate** *v.* SEIZE: secure, usurp, take; SET APART: allocate, assign, reserve, apportion, budget, allot

**appropriation** *n.* stipend, grant, fund, allotment, allowance, allocation, contribution, support

**approval** *n.* REGARD: esteem, favor, admiration; SANCTION: endorsement, consent, permission

**approve** *v.* authorize, endorse, ratify, confirm, sanction, accredit, allow, advocate

**approximate** *adj.* inexact, imprecise, close

**appurtenance** *n.* adjunct, accessory

**apropos** *adj.* applicable, appropriate, befitting

**apt** *adj.* APPROPRIATE: apropos, suitable, fitting; INCLINED: probable, prone, liable, likely; QUICK: adept, clever, bright, intelligent, talented

**aptitude** *n.* ability, capability, competence, capacity

**arbitrary** *adj.* OPTIONAL: discretionary, unscientific; WHIMSICAL: capricious, fanciful, inconsistent; AUTOCRATIC: willful, tyrannical,

**arbitrate** *v.* settle, adjust, reconcile, negotiate

**arch** *n.* arc, curve, vault, bend, arching, archway

**archaic** *adj.* antiquated, old, obsolete

**architect** *n.* planner, designer, draftsman, artist

**archive** *n.* repository, vault, museum

**ardent** *adj.* fervent, impassioned, zealous, enthusiastic

**arduous** *adj.* hard, laborious, difficult, strenuous

**argue** *v.* dispute, contend, wrangle, bicker, debate

**argumentative** *adj.* hostile, contentious, factious

**arid** *adj.* parched, desert, dried, dry, barren

**arise** *v.* **GET UP:** rise, stand; **ASCEND:** mount, climb, rise

**aristocracy** *n.* nobility, elite, gentry

**aristocratic** *adj.* noble, refined, well–bred

**arm** *n.* limb, member, appendage, projection, branch

**armistice** *n.* treaty, cease–fire, truce

**aroma** *n.* smell, fragrance, perfume, odor

**arouse** *v.* awaken, stir, excite, stimulate

**arraign** *v.* accuse, summon

**arrange** *v.* order, regulate, systematize, organize

**arrest** *v.* apprehend, capture, imprison, incarcerate

**arrival** *n.* **ENTRANCE:** appearance, landing, debarkation; **NEWCOMER:** visitor

**arrive** *v.* land, disembark, reach, appear, attain

**arrogance** *n.* insolence, audacity, haughtiness, pride

**art** *n.* representation, illustration, abstraction, creation

**artery** *n.* **BLOOD VESSEL:** aorta, capillary, vein; **MAIN CHANNEL:** highway, line, route, canal, roadway

**artful** *adj.* crafty, cunning, clever, adroit, ingenious

**article** *n.* **WRITING:** essay, editorial, commentary; **ITEM:** object, substance, commodity, thing

**articulate** *v.* **SPEAK:** enunciate, pronounce, verbalize; **JOIN:** combine, connect, link

**artifact** *n.* antique, heirloom, relic

**artifice** *n.* ruse, scheme, trick

**artificial** *adj.* synthetic, counterfeit, false, imitation

**artistic** *adj.* imaginative, creative, cultured, sensitive, elegant, harmonious

**artistry** *n.* workmanship, skill, proficiency

**artless** *adj.* innocent, rough, unskilled

**arty** *adj.* affected, ostentatious

**ascend** *v.* soar, rise

**askance** *adv.* suspiciously, disapprovingly

**aspect** *n.* **APPEARANCE:** looks, countenance, face, features; **VIEW:** perspective, regard, slant, viewpoint

**asperity** *n.* roughness, harshness

**aspiration** *n.* desire, yearning, inclination, ambition

**assail** *v.* assault, attack

**assailant** *n.* antagonist, foe, enemy

**assassin** *n.* murderer, slayer, butcher, killer

**assassinate** *v.* **MURDER:** kill, slay, slaughter; **SLANDER:** defame, denigrate, libel

**assault** *n.* **ATTACK:** charge, advance, onslaught

**assay** *v.* test, analyze

**assemble** *v.* **CONVOKE:** convene, mobilize, gather; **CONSTRUCT:** erect, join, unite

**assent** *n.* approval, consent, permission, agreement

**assert** *v.* state, say, affirm, declare

**assertion** *n.* affirmation, statement, declaration

**assess** *v.* **TAX:** charge, exact; **ESTIMATE:** judge, reckon, guess

**asset** *n.* property, holdings, possessions, capital

**assiduous** *adj.* painstaking, diligent

**assign** *v.* **ALLOCATE:** allot, earmark; **APPOINT:** commission, name, select, deputize, charge, elect

**assimilate** *v.* **ABSORB:** digest, osmose; **UNDERSTAND:** grasp, learn, sense

**assistance** *n.* comfort, support, compensation, help

**assistant** *n.* aid, deputy, helper, flunky

**associate** *n.* comrade, peer, henchman, colleague, friend, ally, confederate, collaborator, teammate

**associate** *v.* relate, link, connect, join, compare

**association** *n.* **RELATIONSHIP:** friendship, community, camaraderie, membership; **RECOLLECTION:** impression, remembrance; **ORGANIZATION:** union, club

**assortment** *n.* variety, combination, group, collection

**assume** *v.* suppose, theorize, postulate, hypothesize, conjecture, imagine, surmise, opine, estimate, speculate, infer

**assurance** *n.* **GUARANTY:** support, pledge, promise; **CONFIDENCE:** trust, certainty, faith

**assure** *v.* **GUARANTEE:** aver, attest; **CONVINCE:** prove, persuade, induce

**astonish** *v.* shock, amaze, astound, surprise, stun

**astonishment** *n.* amazement, bewilderment, wonder

**astute** *adj.* perceptive, shrewd

**asunder** *adv.* apart, divided, separated, disjoined

**atmosphere** *n.* sense, impression, taste, character

**atone** *v.* compensate, pay

**atrocious** *adj.* cruel, offensive

**atrocity** *n.* **BRUTALITY:** wickedness, barbarity, cruelty; **OFFENSE:** outrage, horror, crime

**attach** *v.* **ADHERE:** join, connect, append, add; **ATTRIBUTE:** associate, impute, ascribe, give

**attachment** *n.*
AFFECTION: fondness, liking, devotion; ACCESSORY: adjunct, annex, addition

**attack** *n.* ASSAULT: raid, onslaught, siege, invasion, incursion; LIBEL: slander, denunciation; ILLNESS: seizure, breakdown

**attacker** *n.* aggressor, assailant, antagonist, invader

**attain** *v.* achieve, accomplish, reach, gain

**attempt** *v.* endeavor, strike, venture, try

**attend** *v.* heed; minister; frequent, visit, revisit, haunt

**attention** *n.* regard, vigilance, heed, alertness, diligence, thoroughness, recognition

**attentive** *adj.* considerate, thoughtful

**attest** *v.* testify, certify

**attitude** *n.* BEARING: air, demeanor; DISPOSITION: inclination, nature, temperament, mood

**attorney** *n.* lawyer, barrister, counsel

**attract** *v.* DRAW: pull, drag, bring; ALLURE: entice, lure, charm, fascinate

**attraction** *n.* EVENT: spectacle, display, demonstration; ALLUREMENT: enticement, appeal

**attractive** *adj.* engaging, beautiful, handsome

**attribute** *n.* peculiarity, quality, characteristic, trait

**attribute** *v.* ascribe, impute, give

**audacious** *adj.* bold, daring, shameless

**audible** *adj.* perceptible, discernible

**audience** *n.* interview; spectators, patrons

**audit** *n.* checking, scrutiny, inspection, examination

**auditorium** *n.* hall, theater, playhouse, amphitheater

**augment** *v.* increase, enlarge, expand, magnify

**auspices** *n. pl.* protection, aegis, patronage, omen

**austere** *adj.* stern, harsh, hard, ascetic, severe, plain

**authentic** *adj.* genuine, real, true, actual

**authenticate** *v.* verify, confirm, validate, prove

**author** *n.* writer, journalist, columnist, playwright, poet, novelist, essayist

**authority** *n.* **COMMAND:** jurisdiction, power; **SPECIALIST:** expert, veteran, professional

**authorization** *n.* sanction, signature, permission

**authorize** *v.* **ALLOW:** permit, tolerate, suffer; **APPROVE:** sanction, ratify, affirm, endorse

**autocratic** *adj.* domineering, aggressive, absolute

**autograph** *n.* signature, handwriting

**automatic** *adj.* **MECHANIZED:** computerized, self–regulating, automated; **INVOLUNTARY:** instinctive, spontaneous

**autonomous** *adj.* self–governing, independent, free

**auxiliary** *adj.* **SUBSIDIARY:** secondary, subordinate; **SUPPLEMENTARY:** reserve, supplemental, spare, extra

**available** *adj.* accessible, convenient, feasible, handy, obtainable, possible

**avarice** *n.* acquisitiveness, greed

**aver** *v.* assert, claim, declare, swear

**average** *adj.* ordinary, medium, mediocre, common

**averse** *adj.* disinclined, opposed

**aversion** *n.* abhorrence, disgust, dislike, loathing

**avocation** *n.* hobby, sideline

**avoid** *v.* evade, shun, elude, dodge, withdraw,

**avow** *v.* affirm, assert, declare, swear

**awake** *adj.* alert, attentive, vigilant; conscious

**awake, awaken** *v.* stir, arise, waken, arouse

**award** *n.* citation, honor, scholarship, prize, judgment

**award** *v.* grant, confer, bestow, give

**aware** *adj.* conscious, knowledgeable, cognizant

**awareness** *n.* alertness, keenness, attentiveness, perception, apprehension

**awe** *n.* fright, wonder, reverence

**awesome** *adj.* striking, moving, exalted, grand

**awkward** *adj.* clumsy, bungling, gawky, floundering, ungainly, unwieldy, inept

**axiom** *n.* adage, maxim, proverb

**babble** *n.* chatter jabber, twaddle, nonsense.

**babel** *n.* bedlam, clamor, commotion

**baby** *adj.* juvenile, childish, small

**backlash** *n.* repercussion, reaction, recoil

**badge** *n.* marker, emblem, pin, medal, insignia, shield, symbol, medallion, crest

**baffle** *v.* perplex, confuse, puzzle, bewilder

**baggage** *n.* luggage, gear, trunk, valise, suitcase,

**bail** *v.* dip, scoop, empty, drain

**bait** *v.* LURE: entice, attract, draw; TEASE: provoke, torment, anger, nag, bother

**balance** *n.* REMAINS: excess, surplus, residue, remainder; EQUILIBRIUM: symmetry, equivalence, parity

**balance** *v.* equalize, even, compensate, adjust, coordinate, equate, match, harmonize

**balcony** *n.* gallery, verandah, terrace

**baleful** *adj.* noxious, harmful

**balk** *v.* refuse, demur, desist

**balky** *adj.* contrary, obstinate, perverse, stubborn

**ball** *n.* **SPHERE:** globe, spheroid, orb, globule, pellet, pill; **DANCE:** promenade, reception

**ballad** *n.* carol, chant, song

**ballot** *n.* tally, ticket, poll, vote

**balm** *n.* **OINTMENT:** salve, lotion, dressing, medicine; **SOLACE:** comfort, relief, refreshment, remedy

**ban** *n.* taboo, prohibition, limitation, refusal

**ban** *v.* forbid, prohibit, outlaw, prevent

**banal** *adj.* dull, trite, hackneyed, prosaic, trite

**bandage** *n.* compress, cast, gauze, dressing

**bandage** *v.* tie, swathe, truss, bind, fasten.

**bandit** *n.* highwayman, thief, brigand, robber

**bang** *n.* **REPORT:** blast, detonation; **BLOW:** hit, cuff, whack; **THRILL:** enjoyment, kick, excitement

**banish** *v.* exile, deport, expel, expatriate, ostracize, outlaw, isolate

**bank** *n.* shore, ledge, embankment, edge

**bankrupt** *adj.* failed, broke, insolvent

**banner** *n.* flag, colors, pennant, emblem; headline

**banquet** *n.* feast, repast, festivity, dinner

**bar** *n.* **STICK:** boom, crosspiece, rod; **OBSTRUCTION:** hindrance, hurdle, obstacle, barrier; **SALOON:** dive, tavern, lounge, cabaret, pub; **LAWYERS:** counselors, barristers, solicitors, jurists, attorneys, advocates; **STRIP:** stripe, ribbon, band

**bar** *v.* **OBSTRUCT:** barricade, blockade, impede; **BAN:** forbid, prevent, stop; **CLOSE:** shut, lock, seal

**barbarian** *n.* savage, brute, beast

**barbaric** *adj.* inhuman, brutal, fierce, cruel

**bare** *adj.* **UNCOVERED:** bald, naked; **PLAIN:** unadorned, simple, modest; **EMPTY:** barren, void, unfurnished

**bare** *v.* divulge, reveal, uncover, expose

**bargain** *n.* DISCOUNT: reduction, giveaway, steal UNDERSTANDING: agreement, compact, pact, contract, deal;

**bargain** *v.* barter, buy, sell, negotiate

**barrel** *n.* cask, keg, vat, receptacle, container

**barren** *adj.* childless, fallow, unproductive, fruitless

**barricade** *n.* obstacle, obstruction, barrier, blockade

**barrier** *n.* obstruction, hindrance, obstacle, hurdle, restriction, restraint, impediment, barricade

**barter** *v.* trade, bargain, swap, buy, sell

**base** *n.* BOTTOM: footing, foundation; BASIS: principle; HEADQUARTERS: terminal, harbor, station

**bashful** *adj.* retiring, reserved, timid, modest, shy

**basic** *adj.* fundamental, essential, central, primary

**basin** *n.* bowl, pan, tub, container

**basis** *n.* foundation, justification, reason, background, source, authority, principle, grounds

**bask** *v.* relax, enjoy, wallow

**bathe** *v.* soap, scour, scrub, wash.

**battery** *n.* beating, assault, mugging

**bauble** *n.* ornament, trifle, trinket

**bazaar** *n.* market, fair

**beach** *n.* shore, seaside, sand, coast

**beached** *v.* stranded, marooned, aground, abandoned

**beacon** *n.* signal, flare, beam

**beam** *n.* timber, brace, rafter, stringer, joist, girder, support, trestle, post

**beam** *v.* TRANSMIT: broadcast, send; SHINE: radiate, glitter, glare; SMILE: grin, laugh, smirk

**bear** *v.* TOLERATE: undergo, endure; SUPPORT: sustain

**bearable** *adj.* endurable, tolerable

**beastly** *adj.* brutal, savage, coarse, depraved, loathsome, vile, foul, base, disgusting, vulgar

**beat** *adj.* weary, fatigued, tired, exhausted

**beat** *v.* **HIT:** whip, flog, spank, scourge, buffet, bash; **PULSATE:** pound, thump, pulse, throb; **MIX:** whip, knead; **WORST:** overcome, conquer, defeat

**beautiful** *adj.* lovely, attractive, appealing, charming, enticing, elegant, gorgeous, exquisite, alluring

**beckon** *v.* summon, signal, motion

**becoming** *adj.* attractive, handsome, comely, fair

**bedlam** *n.* pandemonium, clamor, confusion, noise

**befall** *v.* occur, happen

**beg** *v.* entreat, implore, beseech, supplicate, solicit, plead, petition, request, ask

**beggar** *n.* panhandler, moocher, bum

**begin** *v.* initiate, start, inaugurate, launch, mount, create, institute, introduce, originate, found, establish, commence, arise

**beguile** *v.* charm, deceive

**behavior** *n.* conduct, performance

**behold** *v.* observe, regard, view

**belief** *n.* opinion, feeling, conviction

**believable** *adj.* trustworthy, creditable, convincing

**believe** *v.* trust, accept, think

**believer** *n.* convert, adherent, apostle, disciple, follower

**bellicose** *adj.* hostile, aggressive

**belligerent** *adj.* warlike, pugnacious, hostile

**bellow** *v.* howl, call, shout, cry, yell

**beloved** *adj.* cherished, loved, adored, worshipped, idolized, treasured, favored

**beloved** *n.* fiancé, sweetheart, lover

**below** *prep.* **BENEATH:** underneath, under; **INFERIOR:** subject, subordinate

**bend** *v.* turn, twist, contort, coil, curl, loop, curve

**beneficial** *adj.* advantageous, helpful, useful

**benefit** *v.* help, aid, serve, profit

**benevolence** *n.* altruism, charity, kindness

**bent** *adj.* curved, crooked, contorted, twisted

**bent** *n.* leaning, tendency, propensity, inclination

**bequeath** *v.* grant, give

**beseech** *v.* ask, implore

**best** *adj., adv.* first, greatest, finest, incomparable, unrivaled, unequaled, inimitable, foremost

**best** *v.* overcome, defeat, worst

**bestow** *v.* bequeath, present, offer, give, endow

**betray** *v.* **DOUBLE-CROSS:** delude, trick, deceive; **REVEAL:** divulge, disclose

**betrayal** *n.* treason, treachery, disloyalty

**bewail** *v.* complain, gripe, grumble, lament

**bewilder** *v.* confound, disconcert, puzzle, confuse.

**bewildered** *adj.* confused, muddled, dazed, puzzled, baffled, disconcerted, stupefied, befuddled, confounded

**bewitch** *v.* charm, enchant, fascinate, captivate

**bias** *n.* prejudice, partiality, preference, inclination

**bicker** *v.* squabble, argue, quarrel

**bid** *n.* proposal, proposition, declaration, suggestion

**bigoted** *adj.* biased, dogmatic, opinionated, prejudiced

**billow** *v.* surge, swell

**bind** *n.* dilemma, predicament

**bind** *v.* **SECURE:** attach, adhere, fasten; **JOIN:** unite, connect; **BANDAGE:** dress, treat; **CONTAIN:** shackle, fetter, leash, restrict, hitch, yoke, tether; **OBLIGATE:** oblige, compel, force

**biography** *n.* memoir, journal, autobiography, life

**bit** *n.* **FRAGMENT:** piece, crumb, particle, morsel, flake, scrap; **TRIFLE:** iota, mite

**bite** *n.* **MOUTHFUL:** taste, morsel, nibble; **WOUND:** sting, laceration

**biting** *adj.* **TANGY:** sharp, keen, sour; **SARCASTIC:** caustic, acrimonious, bitter

**bitter** *adj.* **ACRID:** astringent, acid; **INTENSE:** harsh, severe; **SARCASTIC:** acrimonious, caustic, biting

**bizarre** *adj.* unusual, unexpected, fantastic, grotesque

**blackmail** *n.* extortion, tribute, protection

**blame** *v.* charge, condemn, denounce, disparage

**bland** *adj.* insipid, flat, dull, tasteless

**blanket** *n.* quilt, robe, comforter, featherbed, throw, cloak, covering

**blanket** *v.* cover, envelop, conceal, bury

**blast** *v.* explode, dynamite, detonate; denounce

**blatant** *adj.* clear, obvious, plain

**blaze** *n.* conflagration, combustion, burning, fire

**bleak** *adj.* dreary, desolate, bare, cheerless, barren

**bleary** *adj.* blurred, fuzzy

**bleed** *v.* hemorrhage, gush, spurt, flow

**blemish** *n.* flaw, defect, stain, imperfection, dent

**blemish** *v.* damage, deface, mar

**blend** *n.* mixture, combination, compound, amalgam

**blight** *n.* disease, withering, mildew, decay

**blind** *adj.* **OBTUSE:** unseeing, unaware; **CLOSED:** obstructed, blocked; **RANDOM:** accidental, unplanned, aimless

**blindly** *adv.* wildly, frantically, heedlessly, carelessly, recklessly, aimlessly, indiscriminately

**bliss** *n.* joy, rapture, ecstasy, happiness

**blithe** *adj.* gay, lighthearted, vivacious

**blizzard** *n.* snowstorm, tempest, blast, gale

**block** *n.* **CHUNK:** slab, cake, clod, hunk; **BARRIER:** obstruction, hindrance, obstacle

**block** *v.* **IMPEDE:** prevent, hinder, restrict; **TACKLE:** check, stop

**blockade** *n.* barrier, barricade, bar, barrier

**bloom** *n.* **FLOWER:** blossom, floweret; **GLOW:** blush, flush

**blossom** *n.* flower, bloom, floweret, bud

**blot** *n.* flaw, stain, smudge, blemish

**blotch** *n.* stain, blemish

**blow** *n.* hit, wallop, rap, clout, buffet

**blow** *v.* **FLUTTER:** waft, whisk, flap, wave; **SPEND:** waste, squander

**blue** *adj., n.* despondent, depressed, melancholy, sad

**bluff** *n.* **BANK:** hill, cliff, precipice; **DECEPTION:** trick, ruse, delusion

**bluff** *v.* fool, mislead, trick, deceive

**blunder** *n.* mistake, lapse, oversight, error

**blunt** *adj.* **DULL:** unsharpened, round; **ABRUPT:** brusque, curt, bluff, rude

**bluster** *v.* brag, boast

**board** *n.* **PLANK:** lath, strip, lumber; **MEALS:** food, fare, provisions; **REGULATORS:** council, cabinet, committee

**boast** *n.* brag, pretension, self–satisfaction, bravado

**boast** *v.* gloat, swagger, swell, brag, strut, flaunt

**boastful** *adj.* bragging, pretentious, bombastic

**body** n. CHASSIS: fuselage, hull, skeleton; GROUP: society, organization; ANATOMY: physique, figure, trunk, build; CORPSE: cadaver, carcass, mummy, remains; COLLECTION: reservoir, supply, variety

**bog** n. marsh, swamp

**boil** v. cook, steep, seethe, stew, simmer

**boisterous** adj. rowdy, uproarious, noisy, loud, rude

**bold** adj. DARING: courageous, intrepid, fearless; IMPERTINENT: brazen, audacious, presumptuous, rude; PROMINENT: strong, clear, plain, definite

**boldness** n. audacity, self–reliance, courage

**bombastic** adj. high–sounding, pompous

**bond** n. LINK: attachment, connection, affiliation; DEBENTURE: security, warranty; BAIL: surety, guaranty

**bonus** n. reward, compensation, payment, incentive

**boor** n. yokel, lout, clown, bumpkin, churl, oaf, boob

**boost** n. ASSISTANCE: aid, help; INCREASE: addition, hike

**boost** v. PUSH UPWARD: raise, hoist; INCREASE: raise, heighten, expand; SUPPORT: promote, encourage

**booth** n. stall, counter, nook, corner, stand

**border** n. EDGE: hem, end, trim, fringe, margin; BOUNDARY: frontier, perimeter

**bore** v. DRILL: ream, perforate; WEARY: fatigue, tire

**boredom** n. apathy, doldrums, listlessness, monotony, tedium, indifference

**botch** v. bungle, blunder, mishandle

**bottom** n. base, foot; depths, bed, floor

**bough** n. limb, arm, fork, branch

**boulder** n. stone, slab, crag, rock

**boulevard** n. street, avenue, highway, road

**bounce** *v.* rebound, ricochet, recoil

**bound** *v.* **LEAP:** spring, vault, jump; **BOUNCE:** ricochet, recoil; **LIMIT:** restrict, confine, circumscribe

**boundary** *n.* border, rim, bounds, extremity, perimeter, extent, periphery, limit

**bounteous** *adj.* abundant, lavish, plentiful

**bounty** *n.* bonus, inducement, reward; profusion

**bouquet** *n.* fragrance, aroma, scent, smell

**bow** *v.* **CURTSEY:** stoop, dip; **YIELD:** submit, surrender, acquiesce, capitulate

**bowl** *n.* dish, vessel, tureen, pot, saucer, crock

**boycott** *v.* ostracize, avoid, strike

**brace** *v.* support, prop, bolster, steady

**brackish** *adj.* salty, disagreeable, tainted

**brag** *v.* boast, swagger, exult, gloat, boast

**braggart** *n.* blowhard, windbag, swaggerer

**braid** *v.* interweave, plait, twine

**brain** *n.* **INTELLECT:** genius, mentality; **SCHOLAR:** egghead, intellectual

**brake** *v.* check, dampen, slow, stop

**branch** *n.* **DIVISION:** office, bureau, extension; **SHOOT:** bough, limb, sprig, twig, arm, fork, growth

**brand** *n.* mark, scar, welt, earmark, trademark

**brand** *v.* blaze, stamp, imprint, mark

**brandish** *v.* wave, flourish, gesture, warn, threaten

**brass** *n.* boldness, impudence, effrontery, rudeness, impertinence, audacity

**bravado** *n.* pretense, bluster

**brave** *adj.* fearless, daring, dauntless, valiant, intrepid, bold, stout, stalwart

**brawl** *v.* fight, quarrel, squabble

**brawn** *n.* power, strength

**brazen** *adj.* bold, brassy, impudent

**breach** *n.* **BREAK:** opening, rupture; **VIOLATION:** infringement, transgression, crime

**breadth** *n.* extent, vastness, size, width

**break** *n.* **BREACH:** fracture, split, rupture; **PAUSE:** intermission, interim; **LUCK:** accident, opportunity

**breakthrough** *n.* finding, discovery, invention

**breath** *n.* inhalation, exhalation, gasp, sigh, wheeze

**breathe** *v.* respire, inhale, exhale, gasp, pant

**breed** *n.* strain, variety, kind, race, type

**breeze** *n.* zephyr, flurry, wind

**brevity** *n.* conciseness, shortness, terseness

**brew** *v.* make, concoct, ferment, mull, cook

**bridge** *n.* **STRUCTURE:** viaduct, pontoon, catwalk, trestle; **LINK:** connection, bond, tie

**bridle** *n.* halter, leash, restraint

**brief** *adj.* momentary, fleeting, concise, abrupt

**brief** *n.* abstract, outline, summary

**bright** *adj.* **QUICK-WITTED:** intelligent, clever, alert; **CLEAR:** sunny, fair; **LIVELY:** cheerful, vivacious; **SHINING:** luminous, lustrous, sparkling, illuminated

**brighten** *v.* lighten, glow; polish, intensify, shine

**brightness** *n.* shine, luster, illumination, light

**brilliant** *adj.* **SPARKLING:** shining, dazzling, gleaming, bright; **TALENTED:** profound, intelligent

**bring** *v.* transport, convey, bear, carry

**brink** *n.* edge, limit, brim, rim

**brisk** *adj.* invigorating, stimulating, active

**briskly** *adv.* energetically, brusquely, nimbly

**bristle** *n.* hair, fiber, quill, point

**brittle** *adj.* fragile, crisp, inelastic, weak

**broad** *adj.* wide, large, extensive, spacious, expansive, roomy

**broadcast** *v.* transmit, announce, air, send

**broaden** *v.* widen, expand, increase, grow

**broad–minded** *adj.* tolerant, progressive, unprejudiced, liberal

**brochure** *n.* handout, circular, pamphlet, folder

**broil** *v.* cook, sear, bake, roast

**broken** *adj.* **INOPERABLE:** busted, faulty; **FRACTURED:** shattered, smashed, damaged, cracked; **INCOHERENT:** muttered, mumbled

**brood** *v.* pine, grieve, fret, sulk, mope, muse, deliberate, worry

**brook** *n.* stream, creek, streamlet, river

**broth** *n.* soup, consommé, bouillon, stock

**browbeat** *v.* intimidate, bully, frighten, threaten

**browse** *v.* skim, peruse, scan, inspect, examine

**bruise** *v.* wound, damage, beat, injure, hurt

**brush** *n.* **THICKET:** undergrowth, shrubbery, grove, hedge, fern, scrub; **TOUCH:** rub, tap, stroke

**brush** *v.* **CLEAN:** sweep, whisk, wipe; **TOUCH LIGHTLY:** stroke, smooth, graze

**brusque** *adj.* abrupt, blunt, curt, terse

**brutal** *adj.* pitiless, harsh, unmerciful, cruel

**brutalize** *v.* degrade, demean

**buckle** *n.* clasp, clamp, harness, fastening, fastener

**budge** *v.* stir, move

**budget** *n.* projection, estimate, allocation, plan, funds

**buffet** *v.* batter, strike, whip

**buffoon** *n.* clown, jester, fool, jerk

**bug** *n.* **INSECT:** beetle, pest, spider, gnat; **MICROORGANISM:** bacillus, virus; **DEFECT:** flaw, fault, annoyance

**bug** *v.* **EAVESDROP:** spy, overhear, wiretap; **ANNOY:** irritate, pester, bother, disturb

**build** *v.* increase; construct, form, erect, make, manufacture, fabricate, fashion, produce, devise

**bulb** *n.* globe, globule, ball, knob

**bulge** *n.* swelling, protuberance, bump, prominence

**bulk** *n.* most, majority

**bulk** *v.* enlarge, expand

**bull** *n.* **NONSENSE:** balderdash, rubbish, trash; **ANIMAL:** steer, calf, ox, cow;

**bulletin** *n.* report, release, notice

**bully** *n.* ruffian, rowdy, tough, rascal

**bully** *v.* intimidate, tease, domineer, harass, threaten

**bum** *n.* derelict, loafer, hobo, tramp, vagrant, beggar

**bump** *n.* **COLLISION:** knock, jounce, jar, nudge; **BULGE:** swelling, projection, protuberance, lump

**bump** *v.* **COLLIDE:** strike, crash, hit; **SOUND:** thud, whack, sock

**bun** *n.* roll, muffin, scone, roll, pastry

**bunch** *n.* cluster, clump, group, sheaf, tuft, shock, bundle, knot, collection

**bungle** *v.* botch, blunder, fumble, mishandle, fail

**bungler** *n.* muddler, numskull, dolt, clod

**burden** *v.* hinder, encumber, hamper, strain, load, tax, try, trouble, oppress

**burglar** *n.* thief, housebreaker, robber, criminal

**burglary** *n.* stealing, robbery, theft

**burial** *n.* interment, funeral

**burlesque** *v.* imitate, mock, satirize

**burly** *adj.* strong, muscular

**burn** *v.* ignite, kindle, incinerate, blaze, scorch

**burnish** *v.* polish, shine, smooth

**burnt** *adj.* scorched, singed, charred, burned

**burrow** *n.* hole, shelter

**burrow** *v.* dig, hide

**burst** *v.* **EXPLODE:** erupt, rupture, disintegrate; **BREAK:** crack, split, fracture, destroy

**bury** *v.* **INTER:** entomb, enshrine, embalm; **HIDE:** cover, conceal, secrete; **DEFEAT:** overcome, conquer

**bush** *n.* bramble, thicket, hedge, shrubbery, plant

**bushy** *adj.* fuzzy, shaggy, tufted, woolly, bristly

**bushed** *adj.* tired, fatigued

**busy** *adj.* active, occupied, diligent, employed, working

**butcher** *v.* **MASSACRE:** slaughter, slay, kill; **RUIN:** mutilate, spoil, botch, destroy

**button** *n.* knob, catch, disk, fastener

**buy** *v.* obtain, purchase, get, procure, gain, shop

**buzz** *v.* hum, drone, whir

**cabaret** *n.* bar, café, nightclub

**cabin** *n.* house, cottage, hut, home, shelter

**cabinet** *n.* advisors, council, bureau, ministry

**cable** *n.* rope, cord, chain, wire

**cacophony** *n.* dissonance, noise

**cadaver** *n.* body, corpse, remains

**cadaverous** *adj.* pale, gaunt

**cadence** *n.* rhythm, meter, flow, beat, measure

**cadge** *v.* beg, freeload

**café** *n.* coffeehouse, restaurant, cafeteria, lunchroom

**cage** *n.* coop, jail, crate, enclosure, pen

**cagey** *adj.* cunning, shrewd, clever

**calamity** *n.* tragedy, cataclysm, catastrophe, disaster

**calculate** *v.* count, measure, reckon, enumerate, determine, forecast, weigh, gauge, compute, cipher

**calculating** *adj.* scheming, shrewd, crafty

**calendar** *n.* schedule, journal, diary, daybook, chronology, logbook, register, almanac, agenda, docket

**calisthenics** *n.* exercise, workout, gymnastics

**callous** *adj.* heartless, indifferent, unfeeling, hardened, insensitive

**callow** *adj.* inexperienced, immature

**calm** *adj.* tranquil, reserved, cool, composed, collected, impassive, aloof, serene, placid

**calm** *v.* tranquilize, soothe, pacify, quiet

**calumniate** *v.* defame, slander, sully, vilify

**camouflage** *v.* conceal, cover, veil, disguise, hide

**campaign** *v.* crusade, electioneer, contend, barnstorm, stump

**canal** *n.* waterway, trench, ditch, channel, duct

**cancel** *v.* invalidate, rescind, repeal, retract, void

**cancerous** *adj.* carcinogenic, virulent, mortal, harmful

**candid** *adj.* sincere, open, frank, honest

**candidate** *n.* nominee, aspirant, office–seeker

**candor** *n.* frankness, honesty

**canny** *adj.* cautious, watchful, shrewd

**canon** *n.* law, principle, standard, decree, rule

**cantankerous** *adj.* quarrelsome, disagreeable

**canteen** *n.* container, jug, flask, bottle

**canvas** *n.* SAILCLOTH: tarpaulin tenting, duck, tarp; PAINTING: portrait, oil, art

**canyon** n. gorge, gulch, gully, ravine, valley

**capability** n. capacity, skill, aptitude, ability

**capable** adj. proficient, competent, able

**capacity** n. limit, size, volume, scope, dimensions

**cape** n. **HEADLAND:** peninsula, point, jetty; **CLOAK:** mantilla, mantle, shawl, wrap, poncho;

**caper** n. **FROLIC:** play, romp; **PRANK:** trick, escapade

**capital** n. assets, cash, estate, property, wealth

**capitalist** n. entrepreneur, investor, financier

**capitulate** v. submit, surrender, yield

**capsize** v. upend, overturn, invert, tip over, upset

**caption** n. heading, title, inscription

**captious** adj. critical, fault–finding

**captivate** v. attract, charm, fascinate, bewitch

**captive** adj. restrained, incarcerated, jailed, bound

**captive** n. prisoner, hostage, convict

**capture** v. take, hold, seize, apprehend, arrest

**care** n. **CONCERN:** worry, anxiety, distress; **CAUTION:** concern, regard, precaution, vigilance; **CUSTODY:** keeping, watching

**careen** v. lean, swerve

**career** n. work, occupation, vocation, job, profession

**careful** adj. deliberate, meticulous, finicky, exacting, painstaking, conscientious, cautious, guarded, discreet, thrifty, wary

**careless** adj. loose, lax, incautious, reckless, indiscreet, imprudent, heedless, negligent, casual, rash

**carelessness** n. unconcern, nonchalance, neglect, negligence, disregard, imprudence, indifference

**caress** *v.* touch, love, embrace, cuddle, pat

**cargo** *n.* freight, baggage, lading, load

**caricature** *v.* mimic, ridicule, satirize

**carnage** *n.* bloodbath, massacre, slaughter

**carnal** *adj.* fleshly, worldly, sensuous, lewd

**carnival** *n.* merrymaking, festival, fair, entertainment

**carouse** *v.* drink, imbibe, party, revel

**carriage** *n.* **BEARING:** presence, look, demeanor, poise, air; **VEHICLE:** buggy, surrey, gig, sulky, hansom

**carry** *v.* **TRANSPORT:** convey, transfer, cart, take, bring, haul, tote; **TRANSMIT:** transfer, relay; **SUPPORT** bear, sustain, shoulder

**cartel** *n.* alliance, coalition, federation

**carve** *v.* fashion, shape, form, chisel, sculpture, cut

**cascade** *v.* cataract, flow, rapids

**cast** *n.* **REPRODUCTION:** facsimile, replica, copy; **ACTORS:** players, company, troupe; **APPEARANCE:** aspect, complexion; **TINGE:** hue, shade, tint, color

**cast** *v.* **THROW:** pitch, fling, hurl; **MOLD:** shape, form

**caste** *n.* position, status, birth

**casual** *adj.* **CHANCE:** unplanned, spontaneous; **BLASÉ:** apathetic, unconcerned, indifferent

**catalog** *n.* directory, index, classification

**catalog** *v.* list, organize

**catastrophe** *n.* disaster, calamity, misadventure, misery, affliction, devastation, tragedy, upheaval

**categorize** *v.* classify, type, arrange

**caucus** *n.* conference, faction

**cause** *n.* **AGENT:** condition, circumstances; **PURPOSE:** goal, motive, foundation, reason; **BELIEF:** principles, conviction, faith

**cause** *v.* originate, provoke, generate, occasion, begin

**caution** *n.* discretion, care, heed, prudence, warning

**cautious** *adj.* circumspect, watchful, wary, careful

**cavil** *v.* criticize, object

**cavity** *n.* pit, depression, basin, hole, hollow

**cavort** *v.* frolic, prance

**cease** *v.* stop, desist, terminate, discontinue, halt

**cede** *v.* relinquish, surrender, yield

**celebrate** *v.* **INDULGE:** feast, carouse, rejoice, revel; **COMMEMORATE:** observe, consecrate, honor

**celebrity** *n.* notable, dignitary, personage, luminary

**celibate** *adj.* unmarried, abstaining

**cement** *n.* adhesive, glue, tar, gum, mortar, paste

**cement** *v.* join, unite, mortar, plaster, connect, fasten

**cemetery** *n.* churchyard, necropolis, catacomb, tomb, vault, crypt, graveyard

**censor** *n.* restrict, suppress, expurgate

**censor** *v.* review; ban

**censorship** *n.* restriction, restraint

**censure** *v.* **BLAME:** criticize, judge, disapprove; **SCOLD:** rebuke, reprove, attack

**census** *n.* count, enumeration, tabulation, tally

**center** *n.* middle, nucleus, core, heart, essence, gist, kernel

**center** *v.* focus, concentrate, centralize

**central** *adj.* middle, midway, equidistant

**cerebral** *adj.* brainy, intelligent

**ceremonial** *adj.* ritualistic, stately, solemn, formal

**ceremonious** *adj.* formal, ritualistic

**ceremony** *n.* function, commemoration, rite, celebration, observance, ritual, formality, custom, tradition

**certain** *adj.* **BEYOND DOUBT:** conclusive, incontrovertible, irrefutable, true, unmistakable; **FIXED:** settled, concluded, definite, determined; **CONFIDENT:** assured, positive, untroubled, confident; **SPECIFIC:** definite, particular, singular, precise, express

**certainly** *adv.* positively, absolutely, unquestionably

**certificate** *n.* document, warrant, credentials, certification, document, warranty, guarantee

**certify** *v.* swear, attest, state, declare, testify

**cessation** *n.* ending, stopping

**chagrin** *n.* embarrassment, setback

**chain** *n.* **LINKS:** series, string, cable, manacle; **SEQUENCE:** succession, progression, continuity

**chain** *v.* connect, secure, fasten hold, bind, restrain

**challenge** *v.* **COMPETE:** defy, denounce, invite, dare, threaten; **QUESTION:** dispute, inquire, ask, doubt

**challenging** *adj.* difficult, intriguing

**champion** *n.* conqueror, victor, hero

**chance** *adj.* accidental, unplanned, unintentional, aimless, incidental, fortuitous

**chance** *v.* risk, venture, stake, hazard, wager, jeopardize, speculate

**change** *v.* **MAKE DIFFERENT:** vary, alter, transform, turn; **BECOME DIFFERENT:** evolve, transform, adapt, moderate, adjust; **EXCHANGE:** displace, supplant, transpose; **DRESS:** undress, disrobe

**changeable** *adj.* **FICKLE:** flighty, unreliable, unstable; **VARIABLE:** unsteady, unsettled, uncertain

**channel** *n.* conduit, duct, gutter, trough, artery

**chant** *n.* recitation, chorus, incantation

**chaos** *n.* confusion, disorder, turmoil, discord

**character** *n.* SYMBOL: mark, sign, figure, emblem; QUALITY: temperament, nature, attribute, characteristic; ECCENTRIC: crank, nut, oddball, weirdo

**characteristic** *n.* attribute, quality, faculty, peculiarity, aspect, distinction, nature, essence, component

**charge** *v.* PRICE: cost; ACCUSE: indict, censure, blame; ATTACK: assail, assault, invade

**charitable** *adj.* generous, philanthropic, forgiving

**charlatan** *n.* cheat, fake, fraud

**charming** *adj.* alluring, appealing, captivating, diverting, enchanting, fascinating, lovable, provocative

**chart** *n.* diagram, plan, map, graph

**chase** *v.* pursue, trail, track, seek, hunt

**chastise** *v.* scold, discipline, spank, punish

**cheap** *adj.* INFERIOR: shoddy, poor; INEXPENSIVE: competitive, reasonable, economical

**cheapen** *v.* depreciate, degrade, spoil, demean

**cheat** *n.* rogue, charlatan, fraud, swindler, chiseler, trickster

**cheat** *v.* defraud, swindle, beguile, deceive

**check** *v.* CONTROL: bridle, repress, inhibit, neutralize, restrain; EXAMINE: review, monitor, investigate

**cheer** *v.* HEARTEN: console, brighten, comfort, encourage, help; APPLAUD:, shout, salute, support, yell

**cheerful** *adj.* HAPPY: gay, merry, joyful; BRIGHT: sunny, sparkling, pleasant

**cherish** *v.* treasure, value, adore, love, protect

**chest** *n.* BREAST: thorax, bosom, peritoneum, ribs; BOX: case, coffer, strongbox, cabinet, crate

**chew** *v.* munch, masticate, nibble, gnaw, eat

**chief** *adj.* leading, first, foremost, main, principal

**chilly** *adj.* brisk, fresh, crisp, cold, cool

**chivalrous** *adj.* courteous, valiant, brave, noble, polite

**choice** *n.* selection, preference, election, favorite, pick

**choke** *v.* asphyxiate, strangle; gag, gasp

**choose** *v.* pick, prefer, appoint, favor, decide

**chop** *v.* cut, mince, fell, whack

**chore** *n.* task, routine, errand, job

**chronic** *adj.* deep-seated, persistent, lingering, protracted, prolonged, recurrent

**chronologic, chronological** *adj.* ordered, classified, sequential, consecutive

**chunk** *n.* lump, piece, mass, part

**churlish** *adj.* crude, vulgar, grouchy, surly

**churn** *v.* stir, beat, mix, agitate

**circle** *n.* disk, ring, loop, orbit, hoop

**circle** *v.* circumscribe, enclose, circulate, surround

**circuitous** *adj.* roundabout, devious

**circular** *adj.* spherical, globular, round

**circulate** *v.* send, report, distribute

**circulation** *n.* rotation, current, flow

**circumference** *n.* perimeter, periphery, boundary

**circumspect** *adj.* cautious, prudent

**circumstance** *n.* situation, condition, contingency, status, occurrence, episode

**circumvent** *v.* avoid, bypass, dodge, elude, evade

**civic** *adj.* civil, urban, municipal, public

**civil** *adj.* formal, polite, courteous, refined

**claim** *v.* **DEMAND:** request, own; **STATE:** assert, insist

**clamor** *n.* outcry, din, discord, noise, uproar

**clan** *n.* family, tribe, group, organization, race

**clandestine** *adj.* covert, furtive, secret, sly

**clarify** *v.* interpret, elucidate, explain

**clash** *v.* conflict, mismatch, contrast, differ

**clasp** *n.* fastener, buckle, pin, clamp

**classic** *n.* masterwork, masterpiece

**classify** *v.* arrange, order, organize, categorize, label, catalogue, tag, sort, index

**clatter** *n.* noise, racket, hubbub

**clause** *n.* provision, condition, codicil, requirement

**clean** *adj., adv.* **PURE:** unadulterated, undefiled, spotless, cleansed; **DISTINCT:** clear–cut, sharp, readable; **THOROUGH:** complete, entire, total, absolute

**clean** *v.* cleanse, wash, scrub, disinfect, polish, sterilize, scour

**clear** *adj., adv.* **OBVIOUS:** explicit, plain, manifest; **TRANSPARENT:** limpid, translucent; **UNCLOUDED:** sunny, bright, fair

**clemency** *n.* leniency, mercy

**clench** *v.* hold, grip, grasp

**clever** *adj.* **SKILLFUL:** apt, expert, adroit, able; **INTELLIGENT:** smart, bright, shrewd

**cliché** *n.* platitude, slogan, banality, triviality, motto

**client** *n.* customer, patient, patron, buyer

**climax** *n.* crisis, peak, culmination, zenith, summit,

**climb** *v.* scale, ascend, surmount, mount

**cling** *v.* hold, adhere, attach, clasp, stick

**clip** *v.* shorten, snip, crop; strike; cheat; fasten

**cloak** *v.* cover, conceal, camouflage

**clog** *v.* obstruct, impede, seal, close, hinder

**cloister** *v.* seclude, protect

**close** *adj.* nearby; like; confining; restrictive, limited,

**close** *n.* ending, conclusion

**close** *v.* END: conclude, finish, terminate; SEAL: shut, clog, block, bar, dam, cork; CONNECT: meet, unite, agree, join; SHUT: slam, fasten, bolt, bar, shutter, lock

**cloth** *n.* fabric, material, stuff, goods

**clothe** *v.* cover, attire, dress, costume

**clothes, clothing** *n.* apparel, raiment, garments, garb, vestments, attire, outfit, toggery, togs, duds

**clown** *n.* fool, buffoon, joker, harlequin

**clumsy** *adj.* ungainly, gawky, inexpert, awkward

**cluster** *n.* group, gathering, batch, clump, bunch

**clutch** *v.* grasp, grab, grip, hold, seize

**clutter** *n.* disarray, jumble, disorder, confusion

**coach** *v.* teach, train drill, instruct

**coagulate** *v.* clot, curdle, congeal, thicken

**coalition** *n.* union, group, association, faction

**coarse** *adj.* ROUGH: crude, unrefined; VULGAR: low, common, base, obscene

**coast** *n.* shore, shoreline, beach, seaboard

**coast** *v.* glide, float, drift, ride

**coax** *v.* cajole, wheedle, inveigle, urge

**cocky** *adj.* overconfident, flamboyant

**codicil** *n.* addendum, addition, appendix, rider

**coerce** *v.* force, compel, impel, constrain

**cogent** *adj.* forceful, compelling

**cogitate** *v.* consider, ponder, reflect

**cognizance** *n.* knowledge, awareness

**coherent** *adj.* comprehensible, intelligible, logical

**coincide** *v.* correspond, match, agree

**coincidence** *n.* chance, happening, accident

**cold** *adj.* **WINTRY:** crisp, cool, freezing, frosty, frigid, nippy, brisk, numbing, raw; **UNFEELING:** reserved, unfriendly, indifferent

**collaborate** *v.* cooperate, conspire

**collapse** *v.* drop, deflate, fall, fail

**collateral** *n.* security, guarantee, pledge, insurance

**colleague** *n.* associate, partner, collaborator

**collect** *v.* **CONSOLIDATE:** amass, accumulate, concentrate; **CONGREGATE:** assemble, flock, gather

**collection** *n.* assortment, accumulation, assemblage, concentration, mess, lot, heap, bunch

**collector** *n.* hobbyist, fancier, hoarder

**collide** *v.* hit, strike, crash; clash, disagree, oppose

**collision** *n.* impact, contact, encounter, crash

**collusion** *n.* conspiracy, plot

**colorful** *adj.* bright, vivid; picturesque, quaint

**colossal** *adj.* large, huge, enormous, immense

**column** *n.* **SUPPORT:** pillar, shaft, pylon, post; **COMMENTARY:** article, editorial

**combat** *n.* conflict, battle, struggle, warfare, fight

**combine** *v.* link, join, fuse, merge, blend, mix, unite

**comedian** *n.* comic, jester, entertainer, actor, clown

**comedy** *n.* farce, satire, burlesque, slapstick

**comely** *adj.* attractive, pleasing

**comfort** *n.* contentment, relaxation, repose, ease

**comfort** *v.* soothe, reassure, console

**comfortable** *adj.*
CONTENTED: relaxed, untroubled, soothed, satisfied; SNUG: cozy, luxurious, rich

**comic, comical** *adj.* funny, silly, humorous, ironic

**command** *v.* ORDER: charge, tell, demand; CONTROL: rule, dominate, master

**commemorate** *v.* honor, memorialize

**commence** *v.* begin, start, originate

**commend** *v.* praise, laud, support, acclaim, approve

**comment** *v.* remark, criticize, mention, interject, say

**commentary** *n.* criticism, analysis, interpretation

**commerce** *n.* trading, marketing, business

**commit** *v.*
PERPETRATE: complete, perform; ENTRUST: delegate, promise, charge, employ, dispatch

**commitment** *n.* responsibility, duty, promise

**commotion** *n.* disturbance, tumult, uproar

**communicate** *v.* inform, tell, confer, talk, converse, chat, write

**communication** *n.* utterance, writing, broadcasting, speaking, interchange

**community** *n.* public, people; village, hamlet

**compact** *adj.* small, light, dense

**compact** *n.* covenant

**compact** *v.* pack, compress

**companion** *n.* comrade, escort, chaperon, bodyguard

**companionship** *n.* brotherhood, fellowship, friendship

**company** *n.* ASSEMBLY: throng, band, gathering; BUSINESS: firm, corporation; GUEST: visitor, caller

**comparable** *adj.*
SIMILAR: akin, relative, alike, like; EQUAL: equivalent, tantamount

**compare** *v.* **LIKEN:** relate, associate, link, contrast, correlate; **EXAMINE:** weigh, analyze

**compassion** *n.* concern, sympathy, pity

**compatible** *adj.* agreeable, congruous, harmonious

**compel** *v.* force, enforce, constrain, coerce

**compelling** *adj.* forceful, impressive

**compensate** *v.* offset, repay, recompense, remunerate

**compete** *v.* strive, struggle, oppose, clash, encounter

**competent** *adj.* qualified, suitable, fit, skilled, able

**competition** *n.* rivalry; contest, meet, game

**compile** *v.* gather, collect, assemble, accumulate, edit

**complacent** *adj.* self–satisfied, egotistic, happy, smug

**complain** *v.* grumble, remonstrate, fret, fuss, gripe

**complaint** *n.* **OBJECTION:** charge, criticism, reproach, accusation; **ILLNESS:** ailment, disease, infirmity

**complete** *v.* execute, consummate, perfect, accomplish, realize, perform, achieve, fulfill, conclude

**complex** *adj.* **MULTIPLE:** combined, compounded; **CONVOLUTED:** intricate, complicated, tortuous, knotty

**complexion** *n.* coloration, tinge, cast, pigmentation

**compliance** *n.* agreement, assent, conformity

**complicate** *v.* confound, jumble, tangle

**complicated** *adj.* intricate, tangled, complex

**compliment** *v.* congratulate, hail, toast, applaud, commend, acclaim, glorify

**composure** *n.* self–control, calmness, poise, aplomb

**compound** *v.* combine, mix

**comprehend** *v.* understand, grasp, discern, perceive

**comprehensive** *adj.* broad, extensive

**comprise** *v.* contain, embrace, embody

**compromise** *v.* settle, agree, conciliate

**compulsive** *adj.* driven, passionate

**compulsory** *adj.* obligatory, requisite, necessary

**compunction** *n.* apprehension, qualm, uneasiness,

**conceal** *v.* cover, screen, secrete, hide

**concede** *v.* acknowledge, grant, yield, admit, allow

**conceit** *n.* arrogance, narcissism, vanity

**concept** *n.* theory, idea, notion, thought

**conceptual** *adj.* theoretical, ideal

**concern** *v.* **PERTAIN:** relate, influence; **BOTHER:** worry

**conciliate** *v.* appease, placate

**concise** *adj.* succinct, brief, short

**conclave** *n.* gathering, meeting, parley

**conclude** *v.* **CLOSE:** terminate, finish, complete, achieve; **DEDUCE:** presume, reason, assume

**concur** *v.* correspond, coincide, agree, equal

**concurrent** *adj.* parallel, coexisting, simultaneous

**condemn** *v.* doom, sentence, damn, convict, punish

**condescending** *adj.* patronizing, disdainful, smug

**condiment** *n.* seasoning, relish

**condition** *n.* **REQUIREMENT:** stipulation, provision; **FITNESS:** tone, shape; **CIRCUMSTANCE:** situation, position, status; **MODIFIER:** limitation, restriction, qualification; **ILLNESS:** ailment, infirmity

**condone** *v.* forgive, disregard, excuse, overlook

**conduct** *n.* behavior, deportment, demeanor, manner

**conduct** *v.* **LEAD:** guide, escort, attend, accompany; **MANAGE:** administer, handle

**confer** *v.* converse, deliberate, discuss

**conference** *n.* meeting, discussion, gathering

**confess** *v.* acknowledge, own, concede, admit

**confession** *n.* disclosure, acknowledgment

**confidant** *n.* friend, adherent, companion

**confident** *adj.* assured, fearless, bold

**confidential** *adj.* secret, classified, intimate, private

**confine** *v.* restrain, restrict; imprison, incarcerate

**confirm** *v.* **RATIFY:** affirm, settle, approve, endorse; **PROVE:** validate, verify, authenticate, explain

**confiscate** *v.* seize, appropriate, impound, usurp

**conflict** *v.* clash, contrast, contend, fight

**conform** *v.* adapt, accommodate, reconcile, agree

**conformity** *n.* **SIMILARITY:** correspondence, resemblance; **OBEDIENCE:** submission, compliance

**confound** *v.* confuse, bewilder, puzzle, perplex

**confront** *v.* brave, defy, repel, dare, face

**confrontation** *n.* battle, strife, dispute

**confuse** *v.* bewilder, befuddle, puzzle, perplex, confound, fluster, disconcert, baffle, mystify

**congeal** *v.* thicken, solidify

**congenial** *adj.* friendly, compatible, harmonious

**congregate** *v.* gather, assemble, convene, meet

**congruous** *adj.* appropriate, suitable, fitting

**conjecture** *n.* guess, opinion, speculation

**connect** *v.* join, link, attach, associate

**connoisseur** *n.* critic, expert, judge

**connotation** *n.* implication, meaning

**conquer** *v.* overcome, subdue, crush, defeat

**conquest** *n.* triumph, success, conquering, victory

**conscience** *n.* duty, morals, shame

**conscientious** *adj.* thorough, fastidious, meticulous, complete, careful, reliable

**conscious** *adj.* awake, aware, sentient, cognizant, discerning, knowing, mindful, understanding

**consecutive** *adj.* ordered, chronological, sequential

**consensus** *n.* agreement, consent, unison, accord

**consent** *v.* acquiesce, agree, allow, approve

**consequence** *n.* EFFECT: outgrowth, end, outcome, result; IMPORTANCE: moment, value, weight

**conservative** *adj.* reserved, conventional

**consider** *v.* contemplate, regard, think, believe

**considerable** *adj.* IMPORTANT: noteworthy, significant; SUBSTANTIAL: abundant, lavish, bountiful, plentiful

**considerate** *adj.* kind, solicitous, polite, thoughtful

**consideration** *n.* THOUGHTFULNESS: attentiveness, kindness; PAYMENT: remuneration, salary, wage

**consistent** *adj.* constant, regular

**console** *v.* comfort, cheer, gladden, encourage

**consolidate** *v.* combine, mix, unify

**consortium** *n.* alliance, union

**conspicuous** *adj.* obvious, striking, prominent, flagrant, noticeable

**conspiracy** *n.* plan, intrigue, collusion, connivance, cabal

**constant** *adj.* unchanging, steadfast, steady, uniform, unvarying, unbroken

**consternation** *n.* confusion, distress

**constituent** *adj.* component, element, ingredient, part

**constitute** *v.* **FOUND:** create, establish, develop, frame; **MAKE UP:** compound, compose

**constraint** *n.* **FORCE:** coercion, compulsion, pressure; **SHYNESS:** restraint, humility, reserve; **CONFINEMENT:** captivity, detention, restriction, arrest

**constrict** *v.* squeeze, contract, tighten

**construct** *v.* build, erect, make, fabricate, create

**constructive** *adj.* helpful, useful, instructive, valuable, effective

**consult** *v.* confer, conspire, counsel, ask

**consume** *v.* **USE:** spend, deplete; **EAT:** absorb, devour

**consummate** *v.* complete, perfect

**consumption** *n.* use, spending, waste,

**contact** *v.* touch, reach, communicate

**contagious** *adj.* communicable, infectious, spreading, epidemic, endemic, catching

**contain** *v.* hold, keep, limit, stop, restrain

**contaminate** *v.* pollute, infect, defile, corrupt, dirty

**contemplate** *v.* study, ponder, consider, muse, think

**contemporary** *adj.* current, fashionable, modern

**contempt** *n.* disdain, disrespect, scorn, derision

**contend** *v.* compete, contest, dispute, fight, argue, claim

**content, contented** *adj.* satisfied, appeased, gratified

**contention** *n.* **ARGUMENT:** quarrel, struggle, competition, dispute; **ASSERTION:** charge, declaration

**contest** *n.* competition, trial, match, challenge, game

**contest** *v.* challenge, compete, oppose

**contingency** *n.* possibility, likelihood

**continual** *adj.* uninterrupted, unbroken

**continue** *v.* **PERSIST:** endure, persevere, progress; **RESUME:** renew, return, reinstate, reestablish

**contort** *v.* twist, deform, distort

**contraband** *n.* plunder, booty

**contract** *v.* **AGREE:** pledge, bargain, obligate; **REDUCE:** diminish, shrink, recede, condense, compress, decrease; **ACQUIRE:** catch, get, incur

**contradiction** *n.* incongruity, inconsistency, opposition, difference, opposite

**contrary** *adj.* **OPPOSED:** antagonistic, hostile; **DISAGREEABLE:** contradictory, unpropitious; **OBSTINATE:** headstrong, stubborn

**contrast** *v.* compare, differentiate, deviate, differ, vary

**contribute** *v.* give, endow, bestow, present, confer, bequest, grant, donate, bequeath, subsidize

**contrive** *v.* create, devise, scheme, improvise, invent

**control** *v.* **CHECK:** constrain, repress, restrain; **DIRECT:** lead, dominate, supervise, head, manage, govern

**controversial** *adj.* disputable, debatable, uncertain

**controversy** *n.* contention, debate, quarrel, difference

**convene** *v.* assemble, congregate, collect, gather

**convenient** *adj.* accessible, available, handy

**convention** *n.* **CUSTOM:** practice, habit, fashion; **GATHERING:** assembly, convocation

**conventional** *adj.* accepted, customary, typical, commonplace, traditional, formal

**conversation** *n.* talk, discussion, discourse, speech

**converse** *v.* speak, talk, visit

**converse** *n.* antithesis, reverse, opposite

**conversion** *n.* change, turn, regeneration

**convert** *v.* alter, transform, change

**convey** *v.* transport, transfer, send

**convict** *n.* felon, criminal, prisoner

**convict** *v.* condemn, sentence, doom

**conviction** *n.* persuasion, confidence, belief, faith

**convince** *v.* persuade, establish, satisfy

**convincing** *adj.* reasonable, plausible, likely

**convivial** *adj.* congenial, gregarious

**cooperate** *v.* conspire, participate, agree

**copious** *adj.* abundant, abounding

**copy** *v.* **REPRODUCE:** duplicate, counterfeit, forge, depict, portray; **IMITATE:** mimic, ape

**cordial** *adj.* friendly, genial, warm–hearted

**core** *n.* essence, gist, heart, center, hub

**corporation** *n.* enterprise, company, business

**corporeal** *adj.* material, tangible

**corpse** *n.* body, remains, cadaver

**correct** *adj.* **ACCURATE:** true, right; **PROPER:** suitable

**correct** *v.* remedy, rectify, amend, repair

**correctness** *n.* **ACCURACY:** precision, exactness; **PROPRIETY:** decency, decorum, fitness

**correlation** *n.* interdependence, equivalence

**correspond** *v.* **COMPARE:** match, resemble, conform; **COMMUNICATE:** write

**correspondence** *n.* **LIKENESS:** conformity, equivalence, similarity; **COMMUNICATION:** message, letter

**corroborate** *v.* confirm, prove, support

**corrupt** *adj.* immoral, underhanded, fraudulent, crooked, nefarious, unscrupulous, dishonest

**corrupt** *v.* debase, pervert, adulterate, taint

**cost** *n.* price, value, expense, charge

**costly** *adj.* expensive, splendid, precious

**costume** *n.* dress, clothing, attire, apparel, garb

**couch** *n.* sofa, lounge, davenport, chair

**council** *n.* group, cabinet, committee

**counsel** *n.* **ADVICE:** guidance, instruction, suggestion; **ADVISER:** lawyer, attorney, barrister

**countenance** *n.* appearance, aspect

**countenance** *v.* approve, endorse

**counter** *v.* react, respond

**counter** *n.* board, shelf, ledge

**counteract** *v.* mitigate, check, hinder

**counterfeit** *adj.* forged, fraudulent

**countermand** *v.* cancel, reverse

**countless** *adj.* innumerable, incalculable, infinite

**coup** *n.* feat, achievement

**couple** *n.* pair, two, set, brace,

**couple** *v.* join, unite, link, copulate

**courage** *n.* valor, boldness, audacity, mettle, stouteheartedness, gallantry, daring

**course** *n.* route, passage, pathway, road

**courteous** *adj.* well-mannered, courtly, affable, polite

**courtesy** *n.* affability, politeness, refinement

**covenant** *n.* agreement, contract

**cover** *v.* **WRAP:** envelop, enshroud, encase; **PROTECT:** shield, screen, shelter; **HIDE:** screen, mask, disguise; **INCLUDE:** embrace, incorporate; **TRAVEL:** traverse; **FLOOD:** drench, engulf; **REPORT:** recount, narrate, relate

**covert** *adj.* secret, hidden, disguised

**cower** *v.* cringe, shrink, quake, tremble, shake, snivel, flinch, quail, grovel

**coy** *adj.* shy, demur, evasive, bashful, humble

**cozy** *adj.* comfortable, secure, sheltered, snug, safe

**crack** *n.* **OPENING:** crevice, fissure, rift; **COMMENT:** retort, jest, joke, remark

**crack** *v.* **BREAK:** cleave, burst, split, sever; **DAMAGE:** injure, hurt, impair; **SOLVE:** answer, decode

**craft** *n.* **TRADE:** occupation, career, work, job; **SKILL:** proficiency, competence, aptitude, ability

**craftsman** *n.* artisan, journeyman, machinist, artist

**craggy** *adj.* rough, steep, irregular

**cramp** *n.* spasm, crick, pang, pain

**cramped** *adj.* confined, restraining, restricted

**crank** *n.* **DEVICE:** bracket, arm, handle; **PERSON:** eccentric, complainer, grouch

**cranky** *adj.* irritable, ill–tempered, disagreeable

**crash** *v.* **FALL:** plunge, tumble; **COLLIDE:** jostle, bump, jolt, hit; **MAKE NOISE:** clatter, bang, smash; **BREAK:** shatter, splinter; **GO UNINVITED:** invade, intrude

**crate** *n.* box, carton

**crater** *n.* depression, hollow, opening, abyss, hole

**craving** *n.* need, longing, yearning, desire

**crawl** *v.* creep, wriggle, squirm, slither, writhe, grovel

**crazy** *adj.* crazed, demented, mad, insane, foolish

**cream** *n.* lotion, cosmetic, jelly, salve, emulsion

**creamy** *adj.* smooth, buttery, rich, soft

**create** *v.* originate, build, fashion, shape, fabricate

**creative** *adj.* imaginative, inventive, artistic, original

**credibility** *n.* likelihood, probability

**credible** *adj.* plausible, believable, reliable

**creed** *n.* belief, doctrine, dogma, faith

**creep** *v.* slither, writhe, crawl

**crestfallen** *adj.* saddened, disheartened

**crevice** *n.* crack, chasm, cleft, slit, gap

**crew** *n.* company, troupe, squad, team

**crime** *n.* transgression, wrongdoing, offense, violation

**criminal** *adj.* illegal, felonious, bad

**criminal** *n.* lawbreaker, felon, crook, gangster, thief

**cringe** *v.* cower, shrink, flinch, quail, wince, crawl

**crisis** *n.* straits, plight, predicament, trauma

**crisp** *adj.* invigorating, brisk, bracing, stimulating; fresh, green

**criterion** *n.* basis, standard, principle

**critic** *n.* **REVIEWER:** commentator, analyst; **FAULTFINDER:** detractor, complainer

**critical** *adj.* **CRUCIAL:** decisive, significant; **DISAPPROVING:** condemning, disparaging; **ANALYTICAL:** perceptive, discerning, observant

**criticize** *v.* **EVALUATE:** study, analyze, examine; **FIND FAULT:** chastise, reprove, reprimand, blame

**crook** *n.* **CRIMINAL:** swindler, thief; **BEND:** notch, fork, angle

**crooked** *adj.* **CURVED:** bowed, twisted, bent; **DISHONEST:** iniquitous, devious, corrupt, nefarious

**crop** *v.* trim, cut, clip

**cross** *adj.* cranky, pettish, critical, irritable

**cross** *v.* **INTERSECT:** divide, traverse, span; **INTERBREED:** mingle, cross–pollinate, mix

**crucial** *adj.* **CRITICAL:** decisive, climatic, deciding; **SEVERE:** trying, taxing, hard, difficult

**crude** *adj.* unrefined, rough, unpolished, coarse

**cruel** *adj.* heartless, malevolent, vicious, savage

**crumb** *n.* piece, fragment, particle, scrap, pinch, bit

**crumble** *v.* decay, disintegrate, collapse

**crumple** *v.* collapse, rumple, crush, crease, wrinkle

**crush** *v.* **SUBDUE:** defeat, overwhelm, annihilate; **BREAK:** smash, pulverize, powder, grind

**cry** *v.* weep, sob, wail, sorrow, grieve

**cuddle** *v.* embrace, snuggle, nestle

**cuddly** *adj.* affectionate, lovable

**cue** *n.* signal, hint, prompt

**cuff** *n.* slap, blow, punch, hit

**cultivate** *v.* nurture, educate, refine, improve, teach

**cultivation** *n.* horticulture, agriculture, gardening

**cultural** *adj.* educational, enlightening, enriching

**culture** *n.* **FOLKWAYS:** convention, custom, mores; **REFINEMENT:** breeding, gentility, manners, polish

**cunning** *adj.* sly, crafty, clever, skillful, ingenious

**cure** *v.* restore, heal, remedy

**curious** *adj.* **UNUSUAL:** strange, odd, queer, unique **INQUISITIVE:** interested, inquiring, questioning;

**current** *adj.* prevailing, contemporary, fashionable

**current** *n.* drift, flow, tide

**curt** *adj.* brusque, brief, concise, terse

**curtain** *n.* hanging, screen, drape, drapery, shutter

**curve** *n.* arc, bow, arch

**curve** *v.* deviate, vow, crook, twist, bend

**custodian** *n.* caretaker, attendant, gatekeeper

**custody** *n.* care, protection, guardianship

**custom** *n.* tradition, practice, convention, ritual

**customary** *adj.* usual, habitual, conventional

**cut** *v.* **REDUCE:** shorten, curtail, lessen, decrease; **SEVER:** separate, cleave; **CROSS:** intersect, pass

**cynic** *n.* skeptic, mocker, scoffer, detractor, critic

**cynical** *adj.* sardonic, unbelieving, sneering, sarcastic

**dainty** *adj.* delicate, fragile, petite, airy

**dally** *v.* dawdle, trifle with, putter, dabble

**dam** *v.* obstruct, check, restrict, restrain

**damage** *v.* injure, scratch, mar, deface, break

**damages** *n.* compensation, reparations, costs, reimbursement, expense

**damp** *adj.* moist, humid, sodden, wet

**danger** *n.* risk, peril, jeopardy, threat, menace

**dangerous** *adj.* perilous, serious, vital, hazardous, risky, deadly, precarious, treacherous, unsafe

**dangle** *v.* hang, droop, sway, suspend

**dare** *n.* challenge, defy

**dare** *v.* **VENTURE:** undertake, endeavor, hazard, risk, try; **DEFY:** confront, oppose, challenge, face

**daring** *adj.* bold, courageous, fearless, brave

**dark** *adj.* **SINISTER:** evil, bad, gloomy, dismal, immoral, corrupt; **UNLIT:** dim, shadowy, somber, indistinct, dusky, murky, gloomy, obscure, shady, hazy

**darken** *v.* cloud, shade, shadow, blacken, shade

**darkness** *n.* **GLOOM:** murkiness, nightfall, night; **EVIL:** wickedness, sin, corruption; **SECRECY:** concealment, obscurity,

**dart** *n.* missile, barb, arrow, weapon

**dart** *v.* shoot, speed, plunge, thrust, hurtle, fling, heave, pitch, dash, spurt, skim, fly

**dash** *n.* sprinkle, scattering, trace

**dash** *v.* **DISCOURAGE:** dampen, dismay, dispirit; **RUSH:** race, sprint, speed, hurry

**dashing** *adj.* adventurous, dapper

**date** *n.* **APPOINTMENT:** rendezvous, engagement, call, visit; **COMPANION:** partner, friend, lover

**date** *v.* **ACCOMPANY:** court, escort, accompany

**dawn** *n.* start, sunrise, daybreak, morning, beginning

**daze** *n.* stupor, bewilderment, distraction, confusion

**daze** *v.* stun, bewilder

**dazzle** *v.* blind, amaze,

**dead** *adj.* **LIFELESS:** deceased, perished, inanimate, defunct; **EXHAUSTED:** wearied, worn, spent, tired; **NUMB:** insensible, anesthetized

**deaden** *v.* anesthetize, dull, chloroform, numb

**deal** *n.* agreement, pledge, pact, contract

**deal** *v.* trade, barter, bargain, buy, sell, distribute

**dealer** *n.* vendor, businessman, merchant

**debar** *v.* exclude, prohibit, restrict

**debate** *v.* discuss, contend, contest, dispute, argue

**debris** *n.* remains, rubble, rubbish, wreckage, trash

**debt** *n.* obligation, liability, mortgage, note

**decadent** *adj.* immoral, wicked, degenerate, bad

**deceit** *n.* misrepresentation, trickery, fraud, duplicity, deception, dishonesty

**deceitful** *adj.* tricky, cunning, insincere, dishonest

**deceive** *v.* mislead, swindle, delude, defraud, victimize, betray, hoodwink, dupe, fleece, bilk

**decent** *adj.* seemly, respectable, proper, virtuous, ethical, trustworthy, upright, good

**deception** *n.* trickery, craftiness, treachery, betrayal, pretense, deceit, duplicity, dishonesty

**decide** *v.* settle, determine, judge, select, pick

**decision** *n.* judgment, resolution, opinion

**decisive** *adj.* conclusive, resolved, final, definitive, absolute, definite, determined

**declaration** *n.* statement, assertion, affirmation, proclamation, affidavit, testimony, announcement

**declare** *v.* state, assert, tell, affirm, maintain, testify, certify, contend, allege, profess, swear

**decline** *v.* **REFUSE:** reject; **DETERIORATE:** degenerate, backslide

**decorate** *v.* adorn, beautify, renovate, brighten, enhance, embellish, elaborate

**decoration** *n.* **EMBELLISHMENT:** adornment, ornamentation; **CITATION:** medal, ribbon

**decorative** *adj.* ornamental, embellishing, beautifying, ornate

**decrease** *v.* lessen, diminish, decline, subside, shrink, reduce, restrain, blunt, curtail

**decree** *n.* proclamation, edict, declaration, pronouncement, judgment

**decrepit** *adj.* worn, aged

**dedicate** *v.* devote, apportion, assign

**dedication** *n.* sanctification, devotion

**deduce** *v.* conclude, infer

**deduction** *n.* **SUBTRACTION:** reduction, decrease, discount; **REASONING:** inference, thought; **CONCLUSION:** answer, judgment

**deed** *n.* **ACTION:** act, commission, accomplishment; **DOCUMENT:** release, agreement, charter, title

**deep** *adj.* comprehensive, acute, penetrating, profound

**default** *n.* failure, neglect, shortcoming, insufficiency

**defeat** *v.* overcome, conquer, vanquish, subdue, overthrow, crush, overwhelm, repulse, decimate

**defect** *n.* imperfection, fault, deficiency, flaw

**defect** *v.* abandon, forsake, desert, leave

**defective** *adj.* imperfect, poor, inadequate, faulty

**defend** *v.* PROTECT: shield, shelter; JUSTIFY: alibi, endorse, support

**defender** *n.* champion, patron, guardian, protector

**defense** *n.* RESISTANCE: protection, security, backing; PLEA: denial, alibi, explanation, justification, proof

**defer** *v.* postpone, delay, suspend

**deference** *n.* regard, veneration, homage, reverence

**deferent, deferential** *adj.* respectful, obedient

**defiant** *adj.* resistant, obstinate, rebellious

**deficient** *adj.* lacking, defective, insufficient, skimpy, meager, inadequate,

**deficit** *n.* shortage, paucity, deficiency, lack

**defile** *v.* corrupt, debase, ravish, violate, molest

**define** *v.* LIMIT: bound, confine, circumscribe, edge; DESCRIBE: designate, characterize, represent, exemplify, explain, name

**definite** *adj.* EXACT: fixed, precise, positive, specific, categorical; DISTINCT: unmistakable, sharp, obvious; POSITIVE: sure, certain

**definition** *n.* meaning, terminology, signification, translation, explanation, description

**definitive** *adj.* conclusive, final, absolute

**deform** *v.* damage, disfigure, deface

**defraud** *v.* hoax, dupe, cheat, deceive

**deft** *adj.* skillful, dexterous

**defy** *v.* resist, oppose, insult, face, dare

**degenerate** *adj.* corrupted, depraved

**degradation** *n.* depravity, corruption, degeneration, evil

**degrade** *v.* disgrace, debase, discredit, diminish, humble

**degree** *n.* MEASURE: gradation, size, dimension; RANGE: extent, quality, potency, proportion, intensity, scope; DIPLOMA: baccalaureate, doctorate, sheepskin,

**dehydrate** *v.* dry, desiccate, parch, drain

**deify** *v.* exalt, idealize, worship

**deity** *n.* god, divinity

**dejected** *adj.* dispirited, depressed, sad

**delay** *v.* postpone, defer, impede, detain, check, curb, procrastinate, suspend

**delectable** *adj.* delicious, pleasing, tasty

**delegate** *n.* legate, emissary, proxy, deputy, consul, minister, ambassador, agent, representative

**delegate** *v.* authorize, appoint, commission, name, nominate, select, choose, assign, deputize

**deliberate** *adj.* intentional, conscious, willful, considered, planned, calculated, intended, purposeful, premeditated, designed, unhurried

**deliberate** *v.* confer, consider, ponder

**delicacy** *n.* FINENESS: daintiness, flimsiness, softness, lightness; FOOD: tidbit, morsel

**delicate** *adj.* FINE: dainty, fragile, frail; SICKLY: susceptible, feeble, weak

**delicious** *adj.* tasty, savory, appetizing, delectable

**delight** *n.* enjoyment, joy, pleasure, happiness

**delight** *v.* fascinate, amuse, entertain

**delightful** *adj.* charming, amusing, clever

**delinquent** *adj.* LAX: tardy, negligent, derelict; OVERDUE: owed, due, unpaid

**deliver** *v.* BRING FORTH: produce, provide; FREE: liberate, save; TRANSFER: pass, remit, give; DISTRIBUTE: allot, dispense

**delude** *v.* mislead, deceive

**deluge** *v.* flood, overwhelm

**delusion** *n.* phantasm, hallucination, illusion

**demand** *v.* request, charge, direct, command, ask

**demanding** *adj.* challenging, difficult, imperious, fussy, exacting, critical

**demean** *v.* debase, humble

**demented** *adj.* crazy, bemused, unbalanced, insane

**demolish** *v.* destroy, wreck, devastate, obliterate

**demonstrate** *v.* PROVE: show, confirm; ILLUSTRATE: exhibit, manifest, parade, display

**demonstration** *n.* EXHIBITION: showing, presentation, display; RALLY: march, sit–in, protest

**demoralize** *v.* dishearten, weaken, enfeeble, discourage

**demure** *adj.* modest, reserved

**denial** *n.* refusal, repudiation, rejection, refutation

**denounce** *v.* condemn, accuse, blame, revile, reproach, rebuke, scold, reprimand

**dense** *adj.* COMPACT: thick, solid, impenetrable; SLOW–WITTED: stupid, dull, ignorant

**deny** *v.* contradict, disagree, disavow, disclaim, repudiate, controvert, renounce

**depart** *v.* leave, go, quit, withdraw

**departure** *n.* embarkation, evacuation, exodus, exit

**dependable** *adj.* trustworthy, sure, reliable

**depict** *v.* represent, picture,

**depletion** *n.* exhaustion, consumption, deficiency

**deport** *v.* exile, expel, banish

**depreciate** *v.* deteriorate, lessen, worsen, decrease

**depreciation** *n.* harm, shrinkage, loss

**depressed** *adj.* discouraged, disheartened, sad

**deprive** *v.* strip, despoil, divest, seize

**deputy** *n.* assistant, lieutenant, aide, delegate

**derelict** *adj.* abandoned, negligent, delinquent

**derivation** *n.* source, beginning, origin

**derive** *v.* obtain, determine, conclude

**derivative** *adj.* borrowed, learned

**derogatory** *adj.* disparaging, belittling, faultfinding, detracting, critical, sarcastic

**descend** *v.* plunge, sink, dip, plummet, tumble

**descent** *n.* **INCLINE:** declivity, slide, inclination; **RELATIONSHIP:** extraction, lineage, family; **DROP:** sinking, tumble, decline, fall

**describe** *v.* recount, portray, depict, illustrate, define, explain

**description** *n.* portrayal, account, brief, summary, depiction, characterization

**desert** *v.* abandon, defect, leave

**deserter** *n.* runaway, fugitive, defector, traitor

**deserve** *v.* merit, earn, rate

**deserved** *adj.* justified, merited, rightful, fitting, just

**deserving** *adj.* needy; rightful, fitting, worthy

**design** *n.* plan, schematic, rendering, pattern, layout, diagram, drawing, sketch, blueprint, plan

**design** *v.* invent, devise, sketch, plan

**designate** *v.* specify, appoint, indicate, name, choose

**desire** *n.* aspiration, longing, craving, lust, wish, mania, hunger, yearning, hankering, itch, yen, passion

**desire** *v.* want, wish, covet, crave, need

**desist** *v.* cease, abstain

**desolate** *adj.* forsaken, dreary, deserted, uninhabited, abandoned, isolated, disconsolate, forlorn,

**despair** *n.* hopelessness, depression, discouragement, desperation, gloom

**despicable** *adj.* detestable, contemptible, abject, base

**despise** *v.* disdain, scorn, condemn, hate

**despondent** *adj.* dejected, discouraged, depressed

**destiny** *n.* fate, future, fortune, doom

**destitute** *adj.* lacking, impoverished, penniless, poor

**destroy** *v.* ruin, demolish, raze, eradicate, annihilate

**detach** *v.* disconnect, separate, divide

**detached** *adj.* ALOOF: disinterested, apathetic, uninvolved, unconcerned, indifferent; CUT OFF: separated, loosened, divided, disjoined

**detail** *n.* particular, aspect, minutia

**detail** *v.* itemize, catalogue, describe

**detain** *v.* delay, hold, keep, inhibit, restrain

**detect** *v.* distinguish, identify, discover

**deter** *v.* discourage, caution, dissuade, prevent, warn

**deteriorate** *v.* worsen, depreciate, lessen, degenerate

**determine** *v.* DEFINE: circumscribe, delimit, restrict; ASCERTAIN: learn, discover; RESOLVE: settle, conclude, decide

**detest** *v.* dislike, loathe, abhor, despise, hate

**detestable** *adj.* disgusting, abhorrent, despicable

**detract** *v.* diminish, lessen, depreciate, discredit

**devastation** *n.* destruction, waste

**develop** *v.* IMPROVE: enlarge, expand, extend, promote, intensify; GROW: mature, evolve; REVEAL: unfold, unravel, uncover

**deviation** *n.* change, alteration, difference, variation

**device** *n.* APPARATUS: contrivance, mechanism, appliance, contraption, implement, utensil; METHOD: artifice, scheme, design, dodge, trick, ruse, plan, technique

**devious** *adj.* deceptive, crafty, indirect, foxy, insidious, shrewd, dishonest

**devote** *v.* assign, apply, dedicate

**devotion** *n.* affection, allegiance, consecration, faithfulness, loyalty, worship

**devour** *v.* eat, gulp, swallow, gorge

**devout** *adj.* religious, devoted, pious, reverent, faithful, holy

**diabolical** *adj.* fiendish, wicked

**diagnosis** *n.* analysis, determination, investigation, summary

**dialect** *n.* idiom, jargon, cant, vernacular, patois

**dialogue** *n.* conversation, talk, exchange

**diaphanous** *adj.* fine, transparent, thin, airy

**diary** *n.* journal, chronicle, log, record

**diatribe** *n.* tirade, denunciation

**dictator** *n.* ruler, autocrat, despot, tyrant, oppressor

**diction** *n.* enunciation, articulation, vocabulary

**die** *v.* EXPIRE: perish, succumb, croak; DECLINE: fade, ebb, wither, weaken

**diet** *v.* reduce, fast, starve, abstain

**differ** *v.* vary, diverge, contrast, conflict

**difference** *n.*
VARIANCE: deviation, departure, exception; DISAGREEMENT: divergence, diversity, departure, differentiation, contrast

**different** *adj.* UNLIKE: assorted, diverse; UNUSUAL: strange, unconventional

**difficult** *adj.*
LABORIOUS: strenuous, exacting, arduous, demanding, onerous, formidable; INTRICATE: involved, perplexing, puzzling, mystifying, bewildering, complicated

**difficulty** *n.* OBSTACLE: obstruction, impediment, hindrance, barrier; DISTURBANCE: trouble, distress, frustration, anxiety

**diffident** *adj.* shy, insecure

**diffuse** *v.* spread, disperse

**digest** *v.* CONDENSE: summarize, recap; EAT: absorb, consume; UNDERSTAND: learn, study

**dignify** *v.* honor, exalt, elevate, praise

**dignity** *n.* bearing, poise, stateliness, majesty, class, pride

**dilemma** *n.* predicament, quandary, difficulty

**dilettante** *n.* dabbler, trifler

**diligence** *n.* perseverance, industry, vigor, carefulness, intensity, attention, care

**diligent** *adj.* industrious, painstaking

**dilute** *v.* thin, weaken, add, mix, reduce

**diminish** *v.* reduce, lessen, depreciate, decrease

**dingy** *adj.* drab, dirty, grimy, muddy, soiled

**diplomacy** *n.* finesse, tact, artfulness, skill, discretion

**diplomat** *n.* ambassador, consul, minister, legate, emissary, envoy, agent, representative, statesman

**diplomatic** *adj.* tactful, gracious, calculating, conciliatory, subtle, discreet, politic, polite

**dire** *adj.* serious, desperate, dreadful, terrible, frightful

**direct** *adj.* **IMMEDIATE:** prompt, succeeding, resultant; **SINCERE:** frank, straightforward, outspoken, candid; **STRAIGHT:** undeviating, unswerving

**direct** *v.* **POINT OUT:** guide, conduct, show, lead; **COMMAND:** instruct, order, govern, manage, charge; **AIM:** sight, train, level

**direction** *n.* **TENDENCY:** bias, bent, proclivity, inclination; **POSITION:** objective, bearing; **SUPERVISION:** management, superintendence, control, administration

**directly** *adv.* instantly, quickly, immediately

**directory** *n.* reference, list, register, record, roster

**disability** *n.* feebleness, incapacity, injury, weakness

**disable** *v.* incapacitate, cripple, impair

**disadvantage** *n.* obstacle, restraint, handicap, inconvenience, drawback, weakness

**disagree** *v.* **DIFFER:** dissent, object, oppose, quarrel; **EFFECT:** nauseate, bother

**disagreeable** *adj.* obnoxious, offensive, irritable, rude, bothersome, upsetting, disturbing, offensive

**disagreement** *n.* **DISCORD:** contention, strife, conflict, controversy, opposition, hostility, clash, quarrel; **INCONSISTENCY:** discrepancy, dissimilarity, disparity

**disappear** *v.* fade, evaporate, vanish

**disappearance** *n.* departure, desertion, escape, exodus, disintegration, evaporation

**disappoint** *v.* dissatisfy, disillusion, frustrate, miscarry, thwart, foil, baffle

**disapprove** *v.* condemn, chastise, reprove, denounce

**disarray** *n.* confusion, disorder

**disaster** *n.* calamity, mishap, debacle, misadventure, defeat, failure, tragedy, cataclysm, catastrophe

**disburse** *v.* pay, expend, use, contribute, spend

**discard** *v.* reject, expel, dispossess, relinquish

**discerning** *adj.* discriminating, perceptive, penetrating

**discharge** *v.* **UNLOAD:** remove, unpack, empty; **RELEASE:** liberate, free, fire

**discipline** *v.* **TRAIN:** control; **PUNISH:** chastise, correct

**disclose** *v.* reveal, confess, publish

**disclosure** *n.* exposé. confession, admission

**discomfort** *n.* annoyance, uneasiness, trouble, displeasure, embarrassment

**disconcert** *v.* confuse, embarrass

**disconnect** *v.* detach, separate, disengage, cut, divide

**disconsolate** *adj.* dejected, gloomy, inconsolable

**discontinue** *v.* stop, end, close, cease

**discord** *n.* conflict, strife, contention, disagreement

**discount** *v.* **REBATE:** allow, deduct, lower, reduce; **MINIMIZE:** reject, diminish, discredit, decrease

**discourage** *v.* dissuade, repress, scare, dampen, daunt, demoralize, depress

**discourse** *v.* converse, write, speak

**discourteous** *adj.* impolite, rude, boorish, crude

**discourtesy** *n.* impudence, vulgarity, rudeness

**discover** *v.* ascertain, detect, recognize, determine, observe, uncover, find, learn

**discovery** *n.* detection, disclosure, determination

**discredit** *v.* question, disbelieve, distrust, doubt

**discreet** *adj.* prudent, cautious, discerning, reserved, watchful, circumspect, politic, diplomatic

**discrepancy** *n.* variance, inconsistency

**discrete** *adj.* unconnected, distinctive

**discretion** *n.* caution, wariness, prudence, tact

**discriminate** *v.* differentiate, separate, distinguish

**discrimination** *n.* PERCEPTION: acuteness, judgment; PARTIALITY: bias, bigotry, prejudice

**discuss** *v.* talk, argue, debate, dispute, confer, reason

**discussion** *n.* conversation, exchange, contention, dialogue, dispute

**disease** *n.* sickness, malady, ailment, illness, infirmity

**disfavor** *n.* disapproval, displeasure, disappointment

**disfigure** *v.* damage, deface, mar, mutilate

**disgrace** *v.* dishonor, debase, shame, degrade, discredit, humble, stigmatize

**disgraceful** *adj.* dishonorable, disreputable, shocking, offensive, shameful

**disguise** *v.* alter, conceal, cloak, cover, obscure

**disgust** *v.* offend, repel, revolt, nauseate, sicken, shock, upset

**disgusting** *adj.* repugnant, revolting, sickening, offensive

**disheveled** *adj.* untidy, rumpled

**dishonest** *adj.* deceitful, treacherous, deceptive, sneaky, underhanded, unscrupulous, disreputable, contemptible, false

**dishonor** *n.* shame, ignominy, abasement, disgrace

**disillusion** *v.* disenchant, disappoint

**disinclined** *adj.* hesitant, reluctant

**disinfect** *v.* sanitize, sterilize, purify, fumigate, clean

**disintegrate** *v.* crumble, disperse, dissolve

**disinterested** *adj.* impartial, indifferent, unconcerned

**disjointed** *adj.* disconnected, unattached, separated; incoherent, rambling

**dislike** *v.* detest, deplore, abhor, hate, abominate, loathe, despise, scorn

**dislodge** *v.* eject, evict, uproot, oust, remove

**disloyalty** *n.* treason, betrayal, dishonesty

**dismal** *adj.* dreary, bleak, gloomy, melancholy, desolate, morbid, ghastly, gruesome, dusky, cheerless, dingy, murky, bleak, somber

**dismantle** *v.* disassemble, undo, demolish, level, ruin, raze, fell, destroy

**dismay** *n.* terror, dread, anxiety, fear

**dismiss** *v.* reject, repudiate, disperse, expel, abolish, dispossess, exile, expatriate, banish, deport

**dismissal** *n.* expulsion, removal

**disobedience** *n.* insubordination, defiance, insurgence, mutiny, revolt, noncompliance, rebellion

**disobedient** *adj.* insubordinate, refractory, defiant, rebellious, unruly

**disobey** *v.* balk, decline, refuse, disregard, defy

**disorder** *n.* confusion, disarray, rebellion, anarchy, turmoil, chaos

**disorderly** *adj.* UNRULY: intemperate, drunk, rowdy; CONFUSED: jumbled, scattered, messy, untidy, cluttered, unkempt, disorganized

**disorganize** *v.* disperse, scatter, disrupt

**disorient** *v.* confuse, bewilder

**disown** *v.* disinherit, repudiate, deny

**disparage** *v.* discredit, belittle

**disparate** *adj.* dissimilar, diversified

**dispatch** *v.* **SEND:** transmit, forward; **END:** conclude, kill

**dispel** *v.* disperse, dissipate, distribute, scatter

**dispense** *v.* distribute, apportion, assign, allocate

**disperse** *v.* scatter, separate, disband

**displace** *v.* **REMOVE:** transpose, dislodge; **MISLAY:** misplace, disarrange, lose

**display** *n.* exhibition, exhibit, presentation, performance, parade, pageant

**display** *v.* show, exhibit, uncover, present, unveil

**displease** *v.* dissatisfy, annoy, vex, provoke

**displeasure** *n.* disapproval, annoyance, resentment, anger

**disposed** *adj.* prone, inclined, apt, likely

**disposition** *n.* **ARRANGEMENT:** distribution, organization, plan; **TEMPERAMENT:** character, temper, mood

**disproportionate** *adj.* uneven, irregular

**disprove** *v.* refute, invalidate, deny

**disputable** *adj.* doubtful, dubious, questionable

**dispute** *n.* conflict, squabble, disturbance, feud

**dispute** *v.* argue, debate, contradict, quarrel, discuss

**disqualify** *v.* preclude, disentitle, disbar

**disregard** *v.* ignore, neglect

**disreputable** *adj.* offensive, shameful

**disrespect** *n.* discourtesy, insolence, irreverence

**disrupt** *v.* intrude, obstruct, break, interrupt

**disruption** *n.* disturbance, agitation, confusion

**dissatisfaction** *n.* displeasure, disapproval, objection

**disseminate** *v.* scatter, spread, sow, propagate, broadcast, distribute

**dissension** *n.* disagreement, difference, dispute

**dissent** *v.* disagree, contradict, differ

**disservice** *n.* wrong, injury, injustice, insult

**dissident** *adj.* hostile, opposed

**dissipated** *adj.* scattered, dispersed, disseminated, strewn, wasted, squandered, spent, depleted

**dissolution** *n.* dissolving, termination

**dissolve** *v.* liquefy, evaporate, disintegrate: disappear

**distant** *adj.* **RESERVED:** aloof; **AFAR:** abroad, removed

**distasteful** *adj.* unpleasant, disagreeable, repugnant

**distend** *v.* distort, inflate, stretch, enlarge

**distinct** *adj.* **PERCEPTIBLE:** clear, sharp, enunciated, audible lucid, plain, obvious, clear, definite; **DISCRETE:** separate, disunited

**distinction** *n.* **DEFINITION:** separation, difference; **ACHIEVEMENT:** repute, renown, prominence, fame

**distinctive** *adj.* characteristic unique, peculiar, distinguishing,

**distinguish** *v.* **DISCERN:** detect, notice, discover; **HONOR:** celebrate, acknowledge, admire, praise

**distinguished** *n.* **MARKED:** characterized, labeled, identified, unique, conspicuous, separated; **NOTABLE:** celebrated, eminent, illustrious, venerable, renowned, prominent, reputable, famous

**distort** *v.* alter, pervert, misinterpret, misconstrue

**distortion** *n.* **DEFORMITY:** malformation, twist, mutilation, contortion; **MISREPRESENTATION:** perversion, lie

**distract** *v.* detract, amuse, mislead

**distracted** *adj.* distraught, frenzied, troubled

**distraction** *n.* CONFUSION: perplexity, abstraction, complication, confusion; DIVERSION: amusement, pastime, preoccupation, entertainment, game

**distraught** *adj.* troubled, distressed

**distress** *n.* pain, anxiety, worry, sorrow, wretchedness, suffering, ordeal, anguish, grief, trouble

**distress** *v.* irritate, disturb, upset, bother

**distribute** *v.* disburse, dispense, issue, allocate

**distributor** *n.* wholesaler, jobber, merchant

**district** *n.* area, neighborhood, community, vicinity

**distrust** *v.* mistrust, suspect, disbelieve, doubt

**distrustful** *adj.* doubting, fearful, suspicious

**disturb** *v.* trouble, worry, perplex, startle, alarm, arouse, depress, distress, provoke, irritate, harass

**diverge** *v.* radiate, veer, swerve, deviate

**divers** *adj.* several, varied

**diverse** *adj.* dissimilar, assorted, different, distinct

**diversify** *v.* vary, expand, alter, change, increase

**diversion** *n.* entertainment, recreation, amusement, play, sport

**divert** *v.* deflect, redirect, avert, turn; distract, disturb

**dividend** *n.* bonus, profit, share

**divine** *adj.* godlike, sacred, hallowed, consecrated, anointed, sanctified, ordained, revered, venerated

**division** *n.* PARTITION: section, compartment, parcel, branch; RIFT: disagreement, difficulty, dispute

**divulge** *v.* reveal, disclose, impart, confess, expose

**do** *v.* EXECUTE: complete, fulfill, obey, perform, act, work, labor, produce, create, accomplish, succeed, perform; SUFFICE: serve, satisfy

**docile** *adj.* submissive, meek, mild, tractable, pliant, willing, obliging, manageable, tame, obedient

**doctor** *n.* physician, surgeon, intern, veterinarian, chiropractor, homeopath, osteopath, anesthetist, dentist, pediatrician, gynecologist, oculist, obstetrician, psychiatrist, psychoanalyst, orthopedist, neurologist, cardiologist, pathologist, dermatologist, endocrinologist, urologist, hematologist

**doctor** *v.* treat, attend, administer

**doctrine** *n.* policy, conviction, tradition, canon

**document** *n.* record, paper, diary, report

**documentary** *n.* book, movie, report

**dogmatic** *adj.* dictatorial, authoritarian, stubborn, intolerant, opinionated, domineering, tyrannical

**dolt** *n.* simpleton, nitwit, blockhead, fool

**domain** *n.* territory, dominion, field, specialty, area

**domestic** *adj.* indigenous, native, homemade

**domesticate** *v.* control, adapt, tame, breed, teach, train

**domicile** *n.* residence, home

**dominant** *adj.* commanding, authoritative, assertive, aggressive, powerful

**dominate** *v.* control, rule, manage, subjugate, govern

**domineering** *adj.* overbearing, despotic, imperious, oppressive

**dominion** *n.* sovereignty, region, district, state, nation

**donate** *v.* contribute, grant, bestow, bequeath, distribute, give, provide

**donation** *n.* contribution, offering, present, gift

**donor** *n.* benefactor, contributor, patron, philanthropist, giver

**dote** *v.* adore, pet, admire, love

**doubt** *n.* uncertainty, skepticism, mistrust, suspicion, misgiving, apprehension

**doubt** *v.* wonder, question

**doubtful** *adj.* UNCERTAIN: dubious, questioning, unsure, wavering, hesitating, unresolved, suspicious; IMPROBABLE: questionable, unconvincing

**doubtless** *adj.* positively, certainly, unquestionably, surely

**douse** *v.* immerse, wet, submerge, soak

**dowdy** *adj.* shabby, untidy, slovenly, plain

**doze** *v.* sleep, nap, drowse, slumber

**drab** *adj.* dismal, dingy, colorless, dreary, dull

**draft** *n.* SKETCH: layout, plans, blueprint, design; CURRENT: breeze, gust, puff, wind; CONSCRIPTION: induction

**drag** *n.* IMPEDANCE: restraint, hindrance, burden, impediment, barrier; TIRESOME: bother, annoyance, hang–up, nuisance

**drag** *v.* PULL: haul, move, transport, draw; LAG: straggle, dawdle, loiter, pause; SLOW: crawl, delay

**drain** *n.* duct, channel, sewer, conduit, pipe

**drain** *v.* EXHAUST: weary, tire, spend, weaken; EMPTY: exude, trickle, ooze, flow

**drama** *n.* play, production, dramatization, show, melodrama, tragicomedy, opera, operetta, mystery

**dramatic** *adj.* tense, climactic, moving, exciting

**dramatist** *n.* playwright, author, writer

**dramatize** *v.* enact, perform, exaggerate

**drastic** *adj.* extreme, extravagant, exorbitant, radical

**draw** *v.* PULL: drag, attract, lug, tow, haul; PORTRAY: sketch, outline, trace, depict

**drawback** *n.* disadvantage, shortcoming, hindrance

**dread** *n.* awe, horror, terror, fear

**dreadful** *adj.* unpleasant, hideous, fearful, shameful, frightful

**dreary** *adj.* bleak, dismal, dull. damp, raw

**dribble** *v.* trickle, spout, squirt, drop

**drift** *n.* tendency, bent, trend, inclination, impulse, bias, leaning, disposition

**drift** *v.* wander, stray, gravitate, flow

**drink** *v.* swallow, gulp, sip, guzzle, imbibe

**drive** *n.* RIDE: trip, outing, airing, tour, excursion, jaunt, spin, journey; PATH: driveway, approach, boulevard, avenue, road; FORCE: energy, effort, enthusiasm, vigor, impulse

**drive** *v.* urge, impel, propel, compel, coerce, induce, force, press, stimulate, provoke, push

**drop** *n.* SMALL AMOUNT: speck, dash, dab, bit; DECLINE: fall, tumble, reduction, decrease, slump, lowering

**drowsy** *adj.* sleepy, sluggish, languid, indolent, lazy

**drug** *n.* pills, medicine, sedative, potion, essence, salts, powder, tonic, opiate, downers

**drug** *v.* anesthetize, desensitize, deaden

**drunk** *adj.* intoxicated, inebriated, befuddled, tipsy, tanked, soused, pickled, stewed, tight

**dry** *adj.* ARID: parched, desiccated, barren, dehydrated, drained; BORING: uninteresting, tedious, dull; HUMOROUS: sarcastic, cynical, biting, funny

**dry** *v.* evaporate, dehydrate, blot, sponge, scorch

**dubious** *adj.* VAGUE: ambiguous, indefinite, unclear, obscure; DOUBTFUL: indecisive, perplexed, hesitant, uncertain, questionable

**due** *adj.* SCHEDULED: expected; FITTING: deserved; COLLECTABLE: unsatisfied, unpaid, outstanding

**dull** *adj.* COLORLESS: gloomy, somber, drab, dismal, dark, dingy, dusky, plain, gray, flat; UNINTELLIGENT: slow, retarded, witless, stupid; UNINTERESTING: prosaic, hackneyed, monotonous, humdrum, tedious, dreary, dismal, insipid, boring, ordinary, uninspiring, tame, routine, repetitious

**duly** *adv.* properly, rightfully, decorously, justly

**dumb** *adj.* simple-minded, dull, stupid

**dumfound** *v.* astonish, shock

**dungeon** *n.* cell, vault

**duplicity** *n.* artifice, deceit, deception

**durability** *n.* stamina, persistence, endurance

**durable** *adj.* strong, form, enduring, permanent

**duration** *n.* interval, span, term

**duress** *n.* threat, coercion, compulsion, control, pressure, restraint

**dusk** *n.* gloom, twilight, dawn, night

**dutiful** *adj.* obedient, devoted, respectful, conscientious, faithful

**duty** *n.* obligation, liability, burden, responsibility

**dwell** *v.* reside, live, inhabit, stay, lodge, settle, remain, continue, occupy

**dweller** *n.* inhabitant, tenant, occupant, resident

**dwelling** *n.* house, establishment, lodging, home

**dynamic** *adj.* forceful, intense, energetic, compelling, vigorous, electric, effective, influential, charismatic, active, powerful

**dynasty** *n.* succession, sovereignty

**eager** *adj.* impatient, anxious, keen, fervent, zealous

**early** *adj.*, *adv.* primitive; premature, preceding, unexpected

**earn** *v.* DESERVE: win, merit, gain; PAYMENT: obtain, attain, get, procure, realize, acquire, secure

**earnest** *adj.* serious, intense, important, ardent, zealous, warm, enthusiastic

**earthly** *adj.* human, mortal, mundane

**earthy** *adj.* coarse, dull, crude, unrefined, natural

**ease** *n.* COMFORT: rest, peace, prosperity, leisure, calm, tranquillity; EFFORTLESSNESS: snap, breeze, cinch, pushover

**ease** *v.* relieve, alleviate, allay, comfort, soothe, unburden, release, soften, calm, pacify

**easily** *adv.* readily, effortlessly, smoothly

**easy** *adj.* UNTROUBLED: secure, prosperous, leisurely, peaceful, calm, tranquil, contented, carefree, unhurried, relaxing; MANAGEABLE: simple, pushover; LAX: lenient, indulgent, kind

**eat** *v.* DEVOUR: chew, swallow, feast, dine, gorge, feed; REDUCE: erode, corrode, waste, rust, spill

**ebb** *v.* decline, recede, subside, decrease

**ebullient** *adj.* exuberant enthusiastic

**eccentric** *adj.* unconventional, odd, queer, strange, unusual

**eccentricity** *n.* peculiarity, abnormality, idiosyncrasy

**eclipse** *v.* darken, diminish, obscure

**economic** *adj.* financial, commercial

**economical** *adj.*
CAREFUL: thrifty, prudent, frugal, watchful, tight; INEXPENSIVE: cheap, reasonable, fair, moderate; EFFICIENT: practical, methodical

**economist** *n.* statistician, analyst, expert

**economize** *v.* husband, manage, stint, conserve, scrimp

**ecstasy** *n.* joy, rapture, delight, happiness

**ecumenical** *adj.* general, universal,

**edible** *adj.* palatable, good, delicious, satisfying, savory, tasty, nutritious, digestible

**edict** *n.* decree, order

**educate** *v.* teach, train, inform, tutor, instruct

**education** *n.* LEARNING: schooling, study, instruction, guidance, apprenticeship, tutelage, indoctrination; KNOWLEDGE: learning, wisdom, scholarship

**educational** *adj.* enlightening, instructive, enriching, cultural

**educator** *n.* pedagogue, instructor, tutor, teacher

**effect** *n.* conclusion, consequence, outcome, result

**effect** *v.* produce, cause, make, begin

**effective** *adj.* efficient, serviceable, useful, adequate, productive, competent, practical

**effectual** *adj.* adequate, efficient, qualified, effective

**effervescent** *adj.* bubbly, lively, vivacious

**efficiency** *n.* productivity, capability, ability

**efficient** *adj.* competent, fitted, able, capable, qualified, skilled, adept, experienced, practical, productive, economical, effective, expedient, streamlined

**effort** *n.* attempt, undertaking, struggle, try, venture

**effortless** *adj.* simple, offhand, smooth, easy

**effrontery** *n.* boldness, insolence

**egotism** *n.* conceit, vanity, pride, self–love, overconfidence, haughtiness, arrogance

**egotistical** *adj.* conceited, vain, boastful, pompous, arrogant, insolent, affected, self–centered, blustering, proud, pretentious, overbearing

**egregious** *adj.* bad, outrageous

**eject** *v.* discard, reject, oust, evict

**elaborate** *adj.*
DETAILED: intricate, complicated, involved, complex;
ORNAMENTED: gaudy, decorated, showy, fussy, dressy, flowery, flashy, ornate;

**elect** *v.* choose, name, select

**elective** *adj.* optional, voluntary, selective

**elegance** *n.* taste, cultivation, beauty, gracefulness, magnificence, courtliness, charm, polish, sophistication, splendor, style

**elegant** *adj.* ornate, polished, perfected, elaborate, adorned, embellished, artistic, rich

**element** *n.* substance, component, portion, particle, detail, part

**elementary** *adj.* primary, introductory, rudimentary, easy, fundamental, essential, basic

**elevate** *v.* RAISE: lift, hoist, heave, tilt; PROMOTE: advance, appoint, further

**elevated** *adj.* towering, tall, high, raised

**eligibility** *n.* fitness, acceptability, capability, ability

**eligible** *adj.* qualified, suitable, fit, usable

**eliminate** *v.* remove, reject, exclude, disqualify, oust, discard, dismiss, drop

**elongate** *v.* prolong, lengthen, extend, stretch

**eloquence** *n.* fluency, wit, wittiness, expressiveness, diction, articulation, delivery

**eloquent** *adj.* vocal, articulate, outspoken, fluent

**else** *adj.* different, other, more

**elude** *v.* evade, escape, dodge, shun, avoid

**elusive** *adj.* evasive, fleeting, fugitive, intangible, temporary

**embargo** *n.* restriction, prohibition, impediment, restraint

**embarrass** *v.* distress, disconcert, chagrin, confound, trouble, disturb, fluster, shame

**embarrassment** *n.* chagrin, mortification, discomfiture, humiliation, awkwardness

**embezzle** *v.* thieve, forge, pilfer, steal

**embezzlement** *n.* fraud, misappropriation, theft

**embezzler** *n.* fraud, thief, robber, defaulter, criminal

**embrace** *v.* hug, enfold, squeeze, grip

**emerge** *v.* rise, arrive, appear, form, evolve

**emergency** *n.* crisis, predicament, difficulty

**emigrant** *n.* exile, expatriate, colonist, migrant, pilgrim, refugee

**emigrate** *v.* migrate, immigrate, quit, leave

**emigration** *n.* departure, leaving, displacement, exodus, movement, migration, settling

**eminence** *n.* standing, prominence, distinction, fame

**eminent** *adj.* renowned, exalted, celebrated, prominent, dignified, distinguished

**emissary** *n.* intermediary, ambassador, consul, agent

**emotion** *n.* excitement, sentiment, passion

**emotional** *adj.* hysterical, demonstrative, ardent, enthusiastic, passionate, excitable, impulsive, impetuous, temperamental, irrational, sentimental, affectionate, neurotic, high–strung

**emphatic** *adj.* definite, assured, strong, determined, forceful, earnest, positive, dynamic

**employ** *v.* USE: operate, manipulate, apply; ENGAGE: contract, procure, hire

**employer** *n.* owner, manager, proprietor, executive, superintendent, supervisor, businessman

**employment** *n.* job, profession, vocation, business, trade, work

**emulate** *v.* imitate, equal, compete, follow

**encompass** *v.* include, encircle, gird, surround

**encounter** *n.* MEETING: interview, rendezvous, appointment; VIOLENCE: conflict, clash, collision, fight

**encourage** *v.* support, inspire, cheer, praise, fortify, help, aid, reassure, reinforce, back, strengthen

**encouraging** *adj.* bright, good, promising, hopeful

**endeavor** *n.* attempt, effort, enterprise, undertaking

**endeavor** *v.* attempt, aim, try

**endorse** *v.* SUPPORT: approve, sanction, acknowledge; SIGN: countersign, underwrite, subscribe, notarize

**endorsement** *n.* support, sanction, permission

**endurable** *adj.* tolerable, supportable, bearable

**endurance** *n.* sufferance, fortitude, tolerance, perseverance, stamina

**endure** *v.* CONTINUE: sustain, prevail, stay, persist; BEAR UP: suffer, tolerate, allow, permit, withstand

**engross** *v.* absorb, busy, fill, occupy

**enhance** *v.* embellish, magnify, amplify, increase

**enigma** *n.* problem, riddle, parable, puzzle

**enjoy** *v.* relish, luxuriate, delight, like

**enjoyable** *adj.* agreeable, welcome, genial, pleasant

**enjoyment** *n.* satisfaction, gratification, diversion, entertainment, indulgence

**enlighten** *v.* inform, divulge, acquaint, teach, tell

**enormous** *adj.* monstrous, immense, huge, large

**enterprise** *n.* undertaking, endeavor, affair, business

**entertain** *v.* **AMUSE:** cheer, delight, beguile, charm, captivate, stimulate, satisfy, distract, indulge; **HOST:** receive, invite, welcome

**entertainer** *n.* performer, player, artist, actor

**entertaining** *adj.* diverting, amusing, engaging, enchanting, witty, clever, interesting, stimulating, captivating, absorbing

**entertainment** *n.* amusement, enjoyment, diversion

**enthusiasm** *n.* excitement, interest, fervor, ardor, eagerness, zeal

**enthusiast** *n.* **ZEALOT:** fanatic, fan, believer; **FOLLOWER:** partisan, supporter, participant

**enthusiastic** *adj.* interested, excited, exhilarated, eager, ardent, spirited, zestful, fervent

**entrance** *n.* access, entry, passage, approach, admittance, introduction, debut, enrollment

**entrance** *v.* delight, enchant

**envelop** *v.* encompass, contain, hide, surround, wrap

**envelope** *n.* pouch, pocket, wrapper

**enviable** *adj.* good, superior, excellent

**envious** *adj.* covetous, resentful, desiring, wishful, greedy, jealous

**envy** *v.* begrudge, covet, crave

**episode** *n.* event, happening, occurrence, event

**equilibrium** *n.* balance, stability

**equip** *v.* outfit, train, furnish, implement, provide

**equipment** *n.* tools, implements, utensils, apparatus, devices, tackle, machinery, fittings

**equitable** *adj.* fair, impartial, just, moral

**equity** *n.* **FAIRNESS:** impartiality; **ASSETS:** investment, money, property

**equivalent** *adj.* equal, corresponding, commensurate, comparable, similar

**eradicate** *v.* destroy, eliminate, exterminate

**erase** *v.* remove, delete, obliterate, eradicate

**erect** *adj.* vertical, upright, perpendicular, straight

**erect** *v.* construct, fabricate, build

**erection** *n.* building, construction

**erratic** *adj.* **STRANGE:** eccentric, queer, unusual; **WANDERING:** rambling, roving;

**VARIABLE:** deviating, inconsistent, unpredictable, irregular

**erroneous** *adj.* inaccurate, incorrect, untrue, false

**erudite** *adj.* scholarly, learned

**erupt** *v.* eruct, eject, emit, explode

**eruption** *n.* burst, outburst, flow, upheaval, explosion

**escape** *n.* flight, retreat, evasion, avoidance

**escape** *v.* elude, avoid, flee, evade, disappear, vanish

**escort** *n.* guide, attendant, guard, companion

**escort** *v.* accompany, attend, date, guard, guide

**espouse** *v.* marry, advocate, adopt, uphold, support

**essay** *n.* article, dissertation, thesis, tract, treatise, writing

**essence** *n.* pith, core, kernel, gist, nature, basis, substance, nucleus, germ

**essential** *adj.* **BASIC:** fundamental, primary; **NECESSARY:** imperative, required, indispensable

**establish** *v.* **FOUND:** institute, organize, erect, build; **PROVE:** verify, authenticate, confirm; **SECURE:** fix, stabilize, fasten

**establishment** *n.* business, organization, company, corporation, enterprise

**ethical** *adj.* moral, humane, respectable, decent, honest, noble

**ethics** *n.* morality, mores, decency, integrity, honor

**etiquette** *n.* conduct, manners, behavior, convention

**euphoria** *n.* relaxation, health, well–being, happiness

**evade** *v.* avoid, dodge, shun, elude, baffle, shift, conceal, deceive, veil, hide

**evasion** *n.* subterfuge, equivocation, trickery

**evasive** *adj.* vague, fugitive, shifty, sly

**event** *n.* occasion, incident, happening, occurrence, function, situation, affair, experience

**eventful** *adj.* momentous, memorable, important

**eventual** *adj.* inevitable, ultimate, consequent

**eventually** *adv.* ultimately, finally

**evolve** *v.* unfold, develop, emerge, grow

**exact** *adj.* **ACCURATE:** precise, correct, perfect, definite; **CLEAR:** sharp, distinct

**exacting** *adj.* precise, careful, critical, difficult

**exactness** *n.* precision, scrupulousness, accuracy

**exaggerate** *v.* overstate, misrepresent, falsify, magnify, amplify, heighten, distort, stretch, elaborate, color, fabricate

**exaggerated** *adj.* overwrought, extravagant, melodramatic, distorted, pronounced

**exaggeration** *n.* misrepresentation, elaboration

**examination** *n.* TEST: review, questionnaire, quiz, exam, midterm; SCRUTINY: inspection, analysis, study

**examine** *v.* INSPECT: analyze, scrutinize, explore, probe; TEST: question, interrogate

**exasperate** *v.* annoy, irritate

**exceed** *v.* excel, outdo

**exceedingly** *adv.* remarkable, greatly

**excel** *v.* surpass, transcend, exceed

**excellence** *n.* superiority, distinction, perfection

**excellent** *adj.* outstanding, exceptional, first–class, exquisite, choice, select

**excess** *n.* ABUNDANCE: profusion, surplus; OVERINDULGENCE: prodigality, dissipation, intemperance, greed, waste

**excessive** *adj.* immoderate, extravagant, exorbitant, extreme

**excitable** *adj.* sensitive, high–strung, nervous

**excite** *v.* provoke, stimulate, inflame, arouse, stir, provoke, incite

**excitement** *n.* disturbance, tumult, turmoil, stir, agitation, stimulation, commotion, fuss

**exclaim** *v.* shout, call, yell

**exclamation** *n.* yell, clamor, cry

**exclude** *v.* except, reject, ban, bar

**exclusion** *n.* prohibition, repudiation, expulsion, separation, eviction

**execute** *v.* perform, act, do, effect

**exemplify** *v.* illustrate, represent

**exempt** *adj.* privileged, excused, unrestricted, immune

**exemption** *n.* exception, immunity, privilege

**exhaust** *v.* debilitate, tire, weaken, weary; deplete, use

**exhaustion** *n.* weariness, fatigue, depletion

**exhilaration** *n.* elation, excitement

**exhort** *v.* entreat, beg

**exist** *v.* live, survive, be, endure

**existence** *n.* being, actuality, presence, reality

**exorbitant** *adj.* excessive, extravagant, wasteful

**exotic** *adj.* FOREIGN: imported, extrinsic; PECULIAR: strange, different, fascinating, unusual

**expand** *v.* extend, augment, dilate, grow

**expanse** *n.* extent, reach, space, span, spread, scope, range

**expansion** *n.* enlargement, augmentation, extension, increase

**expect** *v.* ANTICIPATE: await, hope; ASSUME: presume, suppose, suspect; REQUIRE: demand, exact

**expectancy** *n.* hope, prospect, likelihood, anticipation

**expectant** *adj.* hopeful, awaiting, anticipating, eager

**expedient** *adj.* convenient, profitable, useful, practical

**expedite** *v.* speed, quicken

**expel** *v.* EJECT: dislodge, evict; DISMISS: suspend, discharge, oust

**expenditure** *n.* outgo, payment, expense

**experience** *n.* background, skill, knowledge, practice, maturity, judgment, know–how

**experience** *v.* undergo, feel, endure

**expert** *adj.* skillful, practiced, proficient, able

**expert** *n.* graduate, master, specialist

**explain** *v.* interpret, elucidate, illustrate, clarify, illuminate, expound, teach, demonstrate, define

**explainable** *adj.* explicable, accountable, intelligible, understandable

**explanation** *n.* account, justification, analysis, commentary, brief, breakdown, proof

**expletive** *n.* exclamation

**explicit** *adj.* clear, express, sure, plain, definite, understandable

**exploit** *n.* deed, venture, achievement, escapade

**exploit** *v.* utilize, employ, use

**exploration** *n.* investigation, research, search

**explore** *v.* examine, search, hunt, seek

**explorer** *n.* adventurer, traveler, pioneer, voyager, mountaineer, seafarer, navigator

**explosion** *n.* detonation, blast, discharge

**explosive** *adj.* stormy, fiery, forceful, raging, violent, uncontrollable, frenzied, savage

**expose** *v.* **UNCOVER:** disclose, reveal, unmask, unfold; **ENDANGER:** imperil

**exposition** *n.* **MAKING CLEAR:** elucidation, delineation, explication, explanation; **EXHIBITION:** exhibit, showing, performance, display

**exposure** *n.* disclosure, betrayal, display, publication, unveiling

**express** *v.* declare, tell, signify, utter

**expression** *n.* appearance, cast, character, looks, grimace, smile, smirk, mug, sneer, pout, grin

**expressive** *adj.* eloquent, demonstrative, dramatic, stirring, articulate, stimulating, spirited, lively

**expulsion** *n.* ejection, suspension, purge, removal

**exquisite** *adj.* fine, scrupulous, precise, dainty

**extemporaneous** *adj.* spontaneous, impromptu

**extend** *v.* enlarge, lengthen, increase, reach, spread, continue

**extension** *n.* section, branch, addition

**extensive** *adj.* wide, broad, great

**extent** *n.* SIZE: span, space, area, expanse, bulk; DEGREE: scope, reach, range, magnitude, intensity

**exterior** *adj.* outer, outlying, outermost, outside

**exterminate** *v.* annihilate, eradicate, destroy, abolish

**extinction** *n.* extermination, destruction

**extinguish** *v.* smother, choke, quench, stifle, douse

**extort** *v.* extract, wrench, force, steal

**extortion** *n.* fraud, blackmail, theft

**extra** *adj.* additional, other, spare, reserve, supplemental, auxiliary, added, more

**extract** *v.* evoke, derive, secure, obtain

**extract** *n.* distillation, infusion, concentration, essence

**extraneous** *adj.* foreign; incidental

**extraordinary** *adj.* unusual, remarkable, curious, amazing

**extravagance** *n.* excess, lavishness, improvidence, waste

**extravagant** *adj.* lavish, prodigal, immoderate, wasteful

**extreme** *adj.* outermost, utmost, immoderate, excessive, outrageous, preposterous, exaggerated

**extremist** *n.* zealot, fanatic, die–hard, radical

**exuberance** *n.* fervor, eagerness, exhilaration, zeal

**exuberant** *adj.* ardent, vivacious, passionate, zealous

**eye** *n.* APPRECIATION: perception, taste, discrimination; CENTER: focus, core, heart, kernel, nub

**eyesore** *n.* distortion, deformity, ugliness

**eyewitness** *n.* onlooker, observer

**fable** *n.* story, allegory, tale, parable

**fabric** *n.* cloth, textile, stuff, material, goods

**fabricate** *v.* PRODUCE: build, construct, erect, make, form, manufacture, devise; LIE: misrepresent, contrive, prevaricate

**fabulous** *adj.* fictitious, remarkable, amazing, immense, unusual

**façade** *n.* face, appearance, look, front

**face** *n.* VISAGE:, countenance, appearance, features, profile; SURFACE: finish, front; PRESTIGE: status, reputation, standing

**face** *v.* CONFRONT: defy, meet, challenge, encounter, endure, suffer, bear; REFINISH: front, cover, redecorate, paint

**facet** *n.* surface, aspect, face, side, plane

**facetious** *adj.* humorous, whimsical, ridiculous, funny

**facile** *adj.* easy, simple, obvious, apparent, fluent

**facilitate** *v.* promote, aid, simplify, help

**facility** *n.* EQUIPMENT: material, tools, plant, buildings; AGENCY: department, bureau, company, office

**facsimile** *n.* copy, duplicate, reproduction, mirror

**fact** *n.* CERTAINTY: truth, actuality, reality, evidence, EVENT: action, deed, happening, occurrence, manifestation, experience, act, episode, incident

**faction** *n.* party, clique, gang, crew, wing, block, lobby, sect, cell

**factious** *adj.* turbulent, contentious, hostile, opposing

**factor** *n.* AGENT: proxy, representative; CONSTITUENT: cause, part, portion, determinant

**factory** *n.* manufactory, plant, shop, industry, mill, foundry, forge

**factual** *adj.* exact, specific, descriptive, accurate

**faculty** *n*. **ABILITY:** aptitude, peculiarity, strength, forte; **TEACHERS:** instructors, mentors, professors, tutors, lecturers, advisers, scholars, fellows

**fad** *n*. fancy, style, craze, fashion, eccentricity, innovation, vogue, fashion

**fade** *v*. **PALE:** bleach, blanch, dim, vanish; **DIMINISH:** hush, quiet, sink, decrease

**fail** *v*. miss, falter, flounder, fizzle, flop, lessen, worsen, sink, decrease

**failure** *n*. **DEFAULT:** fiasco, bankruptcy, miscarriage, breakdown, stoppage, collapse, downfall, flop, washout; **FLOP:** incompetent, underachiever, dropout, dud

**faint** *adj*. **FALTERING:** shaky, dizzy, weak, **VAGUE:** thin, hazy, indistinct, dull; **SUBDUED:** low, soft, quiet, muffled, hushed

**faint** *v*. swoon, drop, collapse, succumb

**fair** *adj*. **JUST:** forthright, impartial, scrupulous, honest, decent, honorable, reasonable, righteous, evenhanded, principled, trustworthy; **AVERAGE:** ordinary, mediocre, commonplace; **PLEASANT:** clear, sunny, bright, calm, placid, tranquil, favorable, balmy, mild

**fair** *n*. exposition, carnival, bazaar, festival, market

**fairly** *adv*. **HONESTLY:** reasonably, honorably, justly; **SOMEWHAT:** moderately, reasonably, adequately

**fairy** *n*. spirit, sprite, elf, enchantress, nymph, pixy

**faith** *n*. **TRUST:** confidence, credence, assurance, acceptance, conviction, sureness, reliance; **FORMAL BELIEF:** creed, doctrine, dogma, tenet, revelation, credo, gospel, canon, theology

**faithful** *adj.* reliable, dependable, incorruptible, scrupulous, firm, sure, unswerving, conscientious, steadfast

**fake** *adj.* pretended, fraudulent, bogus, false

**fake** *n.* counterfeit, copy, imitation, fraud, fabrication, forgery; cheat, charlatan

**fake** *v.* feign, simulate, disguise, pretend

**fall** *v.* DROP: decline, sink, topple, settle, droop, stumble, trip, plunge, descend, totter, recede, ebb, diminish, flop; SUBMIT: yield, surrender, succumb, resign, capitulate

**fallacy** *n.* inconsistency, mistake, ambiguity, paradox, miscalculation, quirk, flaw, heresy, error

**fallibility** *n.* imperfection, frailty

**fallible** *adj.* frail, imperfect, erring, unreliable, questionable, wrong

**fallow** *adj.* dormant, idle, unplowed, unplanted, unproductive, uncultivated

**false** *adj.* UNFAITHFUL: treacherous, disloyal, underhanded, deceitful, unscrupulous, untrustworthy; SPURIOUS: fanciful, untruthful, deceptive, fallacious, misleading, erroneous, inaccurate, fraudulent; COUNTERFEIT: fabricated, bogus, forged, faked, contrived, phony

**falsehood** *n.* deception, distortion, prevarication, story, lie, fabrication

**falsify** *v.* misrepresent, adulterate, counterfeit, deceive, lie, forge

**falter** *v.* waver, fluctuate, hesitate, vacillate, stumble

**fame** *n.* renown, glory, distinction, eminence, esteem, name, note, greatness, rank, position, standing, preeminence, regard, popularity

**familiar** *adj.* everyday, customary, accustomed, common, ordinary, informal, commonplace

**familiarity** *n.* friendliness, acquaintanceship, fellowship, friendship; comprehension, awareness

**familiarize** *v.* acquaint, accustom

**family** *n.* household, relatives, clan, relations, tribe, dynasty, descendants, forbears, heirs, genealogy, descent, parentage, extraction, kinship, lineage

**famine** *n.* starvation, want, misery, hunger

**famished** *a.* starving, hungering, starved, hungry

**famous** *adj.* known, renowned, eminent, foremost, famed, celebrated, noted, prominent, reputable, renowned, notable, notorious

**fan** *n.* supporter, follower, amateur, devotee

**fanatical** *adj.* enthusiastic, obsessed, passionate, devoted, zealous

**fanciful** *adj.* unreal, incredible, whimsical, fantastic

**fancy** *adj.* elaborate, ornamental, intricate, elegant, embellished, rich, adorned, ostentatious, gaudy, showy, baroque, lavish, ornate

**fancy** *n.* **WHIMSY:** imagination, caprice, levity, humor; **WHIM:** notion, impulse, idea; **INCLINATION:** wishes, will, preference, desire

**fantastic** *adj.* fanciful, whimsical, capricious, strange, odd, queer, quaint, peculiar, outlandish, wonderful, exotic, ludicrous, ridiculous, preposterous, grotesque, absurd

**fantasy** *n.* illusion, flight, figment, fiction

**far** *adj.* distant, faraway, remote

**farce** *n.* satire, travesty, burlesque

**fare** *n.* **FOOD:** menu, rations, meals; **FEE:** charge, passage, passage, tariff, expense

**fare** *v.* experience, prosper, happen

**farewell** *n.* good–bye, valediction, parting, departure

**farfetched** *adj.* unbelievable, strained, fantastic

**farm** *v.* cultivate, till, garden, ranch, homestead

**farmer** *n.* planter, grower, stockman, agriculturist, rancher, homesteader, peasant, peon, herdsman, plowman, sharecropper, gardener, horticulturist

**farsighted** *adj.* aware, perceptive, sagacious

**farthest** *adj.* remotest, ultimate, last, furthest

**fascinate** *v.* charm, captivate, entrance, enchant, bewitch, enrapture, delight, please, attract, lure, seduce, entice, intoxicate, tantalize

**fascination** *n.* charm, enchantment, attraction

**fashion** *n.* manner, custom, convention, vogue, mode, usage, observance, style, craze

**fashion** *v.* make, model, shape, form, create, mold, adapt

**fashionable** *adj.* smart, stylish, chic

**fast** *adj.* **RAPID:** swift, fleet, quick, speedy, brisk, accelerated, hasty, nimble; **FIXED:** attached, immovable, firm

**fasten** *v.* lock, fix, tie, lace, close, bind, tighten, attach, secure, anchor, grip, clasp, clamp, pin, nail, tack, bolt, rivet, set, weld, cement, glue

**fat** *adj.* portly, stout, obese, corpulent, fleshy, plump, bulky, heavy

**fatal** *adj.* mortal, lethal, deadly

**fatality** *n.* casualty, death

**fate** *n.* destiny, fortune, luck, doom

**fated** *adj.* lost, destined, elected, doomed

**fateful** *adj.* **FATAL:** deadly, destructive, ruinous, lethal; **MOMENTOUS:** portentous, critical, decisive, crucial

**father** *n.* **PARENT:** sire, progenitor, procreator, forebear, ancestor; **ORIGINATOR:** founder, inventor, promoter, author; **PRIEST:** pastor, ecclesiastic, parson

**fatigue** *n.* weariness, exhaustion, lassitude

**fatten** *v.* feed, stuff, plump, cram, fill

**fault** *n.* **DELINQUENCY:** wrongdoing, transgression, crime, impropriety, misconduct, failing; **ERROR:** defect, blunder, mistake, misdeed; **RESPONSIBILITY:** liability, accountability, blame

**favor** *v.* indulge, prefer, pick, choose, value, prize, esteem

**favorable** *adj.* well–disposed, kind, well–intentioned, propitious, beneficial

**favorite** *adj.* beloved, favored, preferred, adored

**favorite** *n.* darling, pet

**favoritism** *n.* bias, partiality, inequity, inclination

**faze** *v.* discourage, bother, intimidate, worry, disturb

**fear** *n.* dread, fright, dismay, awe, anxiety, foreboding, concern, alarm

**fearful** *adj.* timid, shy, apprehensive, cowardly

**fearless** *adj.* bold, daring, courageous, dashing, brave

**feasible** *adj.* expedient, worthwhile, convenient, practicable, possible, attainable

**feast** *n.* banquet, entertainment, festival, fiesta, barbecue, picnic, dinner

**feast** *v.* eat, entertain

**feat** *n.* deed, act, effort, achievement

**feature** *n.* **ATTRACTION:** highlight, specialty; **CHARACTERISTIC:** quality, peculiarity, property; **ARTICLE:** column, commentary, editorial, story

**federation** *n.* confederacy, affiliation, alliance

**fee** *n.* price, remuneration, salary, charge, honorarium

**feeble** *adj.* weak, faint, fragile, puny

**feeble-minded** *adj.* foolish, retarded, senile, dull

**feed** *n.* fodder, provisions, pasture, forage

**feed** *v.* feast, nourish, dine, fatten, cater, serve

**feel** *v.* **TOUCH:** caress, fondle, paw, grasp; **EXPERIENCE:** sense, perceive; **BELIEVE:** consider, hold, think

**feeling** *n.* **SENSATION:** sensibility, sensitiveness, perception, receptivity, responsiveness, awareness, enjoyment, sensuality, pain, pleasure, reflex; **REACTION:** opinion, thought, outlook, attitude; **SENSITIVITY:** taste, tenderness, discernment, refinement, culture, faculty, judgment

**feign** *v.* pretend, dissemble, imagine, fabricate

**fellow** *n.* **YOUTH:** chap, lad, boy, stripling, apprentice, adolescent, juvenile, youngster, kid; **ASSOCIATE:** member, peer, colleague, friend

**fellowship** *n.* **COMRADESHIP:** conviviality, sociability, intimacy, friendliness, affability, camaraderie; **PAYMENT:** stipend, scholarship, honorarium, subsidy

**felon** *n.* criminal, outlaw, delinquent, convict

**felony** *n.* crime, misconduct, offense, transgression

**feminine** *adj.* soft, delicate, gentle, ladylike, matronly, maidenly, tender, womanly

**fence** *n.* hedge, divider, barrier, backstop, railing, barricade, barrier

**ferment** *v.* effervesce, foam, froth, bubble, seethe, fizz, work, ripen, rise

**ferocious** *adj.* savage, fierce, wild

**ferocity** *n.* fierceness, brutality, barbarity, cruelty

**ferry** *n.* ferryboat, barge, packet

**ferry** *v.* carry, convey

**fertile** *adj.* productive, inventive, fruitful, rich, productive, fat, teeming, yielding, arable, flowering

**fertility** *n.* fruitfulness, virility, productiveness

**fertilization** *n.* impregnation, pollination, breeding, propagation, procreation

**fervent** *adj.* zealous, eager, ardent, enthusiastic

**fervor** *n.* ardor, enthusiasm, zeal

**festival** *n.* celebration, festivity, feast

**festive** *adj.* gay, merry, joyful, happy

**festivity** *n.* revelry, amusement, entertainment

**fetch** *v.* get, retrieve, carry

**fetish** *n.* fixation, craze, mania, obsession

**fetter** *n.* shackle, restraint

**fetus** *n.* embryo, organism, child

**feud** *n.* quarrel, strife, bickering, fight

**feverish** *adj.* burning, hot

**few** *adj.* sparse, scanty, scattering, inconsiderable

**fib** *n.* prevarication, fabrication, misrepresentation, lie

**fiber** *n.* thread, filament, cord, string, strand

**fibrous** *adj.* veined, hairy, coarse, stringy

**fickle** *adj.* inconstant, capricious, whimsical, mercurial, changing

**fiction** *n.* novel, tale, romance, story, fabrication, myth

**fictitious** *adj.* imaginary, made–up, untrue, false

**fidelity** *n.* faithfulness, fealty, loyalty, devotion

**fidget** *v.* stir, twitch, worry, wiggle

**field** *n.* pasture, meadow, acreage, plot, patch, garden, grassland, tract

**fiend** *n.* MONSTER: barbarian, brute, beast, devil; ADDICT: fan, aficionado, monomaniac

**fierce** *n.* ferocious, savage, wild, untamed, brutal, monstrous, vicious, dangerous, violent, threatening

**fiery** *adj.* impetuous, hotheaded

**fight** *n.* CONFLICT: struggle, battle, strife, contention, quarrel, dispute, confrontation, brawl, fracas, altercation, bickering, wrangling, argument, conflict, clash, scuffle, engagement; METTLE: hardihood, boldness, courage

**fight** *v.* conflict, battle, oppose, grapple

**figurative** *adj.* metaphorical, allegorical, illustrative

**figure** *n.* FORM: design, statue, shape, structure; TORSO: body, frame, development, build, posture, attitude, pose, carriage; SUM: total, number; PRICE: value, worth

**figure** *v.* COMPUTE: calculate, reckon, number, count; CONCLUDE: suppose, think, opine, decide

**file** *v.* SMOOTH: abrade, rasp, scrape, finish; ARRANGE: classify, index, categorize, catalogue, register, list

**fill** *v.* pack, stuff, charge, inflate

**filter** *v.* strain, purify, sieve, refine, clarify, separate

**filth** *n.* dirt, contamination, pollution, muck, slop, squalor, grime, garbage, sludge

**filthy** *adj.* dirty, foul, squalid, corrupt

**final** *adj.* last, terminal, concluding, ultimate, decisive

**finance** *n.* business, commerce, economics

**finances** *n.* resources, money, capital, funds, wealth

**financial** *adj.* economic, business, monetary, commercial

**financier** *n.* capitalist, banker, merchant, executive

**find** *v.* discover, detect, notice, perceive, discern, uncover, expose

**finding** *n.* verdict, decision, sentence, judgment

**fine** *adj.* **EXACT:** precise, accurate, definite; **SMALL:** thin, subtle; **LIGHT:** powdery, granular

**fine** *n.* punishment, penalty, damage, forfeit

**fine** *v.* penalize, exact, tax, levy, punish

**finish** *v.* **END:** perfect, achieve; **POLISH:** wax, stain, cover, paint; **COMPLETE:** cease, close, end, stop

**fire** *n.* burning, flame, blaze, embers, sparks, glow, warmth, combustion, conflagration

**fire** *v.* **INFLAME:** kindle, enkindle, ignite, light, burn, rekindle, relight, animate; **DISCHARGE:** shoot, set, off, hurl; **DISMISS:** discharge, eject

**firm** *adj.* **FIXED:** stable, solid, rooted, immovable, fastened, motionless, secured; **HARD:** solid, dense, compact, impenetrable, impervious, rigid, hardened, inflexible, unyielding; **SETTLED:** determined, steadfast, resolute, constant

**firmament** *n.* sky, heavens

**first** *adj.* beginning, original, primary, prime, initial, earliest, introductory

**first-rate** *adj.* prime, choice, excellent, superior, select, exceptional, best

**fishy** *adj.* improbable, dubious, implausible, unlikely

**fit** *adj.* APPROPRIATE: advantageous, suitable, proper, practicable, beneficial, desirable; HEALTHY: trim, competent, robust

**fit** *n.* ADJUSTMENT: adaptation; CONVULSION: attack, rage, spasm, seizure, stroke, paroxysm; TANTRUM: burst, rush, outburst, huff, rage, spell

**fit** *v.* ADAPT: arrange, alter, adjust; CONFORM: qualify, relate, belong, match, correspond

**fitting** *n.* connection, component, constituent

**fixture** *n.* equipment, convenience, appliance, machine, device

**fizzle** *n.* disappointment, fiasco, defeat, failure

**flabby** *adj.* soft, yielding, limp, tender, fat

**flag** *n.* banner, standard, colors, emblem

**flagrant** *adj.* obvious, notorious, disgraceful, infamous, outrageous

**flair** *n.* talent, aptitude, gift, ability

**flamboyant** *adj.* bombastic, ostentatious, ornate

**flame** *n.* blaze, flare, flash, fire

**flame** *v.* burn, blaze, oxidize

**flange** *n.* edge, rim, projection

**flap** *n.* fold, tab, cover, appendage, tag

**flap** *v.* flutter, flash, swing, wave

**flare** *v.* blaze, glow, burn, flash

**flash** *v.* gleam, glimmer, sparkle, glitter, glisten, glare, shine, glow, twinkle, reflect, radiate, flicker

**flashy** *adj.* gaudy, showy, ostentatious, ornate

**flask** *n.* bottle, decanter, jug, canteen

**flat** *adj.* LEVEL: even, smooth, extended, prostrate, horizontal, prone; TASTELESS: unseasoned, insipid, flavorless

**flatter** *v.* adulate, glorify, praise

**flattery** *adj*. adulation, compliments, praise, tribute, fawning, blarney

**flaunt** *v*. display, vaunt, brandish, boast

**flavor** *n*. taste, tang, relish

**flavor** *v*. season, salt, pepper, spice

**flavoring** *n*. essence, extract, seasoning, additive

**flaw** *n*. defect, imperfection, stain, blemish, break, breach

**flaw** *v*. mar, crack

**fleck** *n*. spot, mite, dot, bit

**flee** *v*. run, desert, depart, abscond, escape, retreat

**fleet** *adj*. swift, transient

**flexibility** *n*. pliancy, suppleness, elasticity, litheness

**flexible** *adj*. limber, lithe, supple, elastic, malleable, pliable, tractable

**flicker** *v*. sparkle, twinkle, glitter, flash, shine

**flight** *n*. ESCAPE: fleeing, retreat; STEPS: stairs, staircase, ascent; SOARING: flying, aviation, aeronautics, gliding

**flighty** *adj*. capricious, fickle, whimsical, changing

**flimsy** *adj*. thin; weak; slight, infirm, frail, insubstantial, fragile, decrepit

**flinch** *v*. wince, start, cringe

**fling** *n*. escapade, indulgence, party, celebration

**fling** *v*. hurl, toss, sling, throw

**flippant** *adj*. pert, frivolous, impudent, saucy, rude

**flirt** *n*. coquette, tease, siren

**flirt** *v*. trifle, tease, seduce

**float** *v*. waft, drift

**flock** *n*. congregation, group, pack, litter, herd, gaggle, company, crowd

**flock** *v*. gather, throng, congregate, crowd

**flog** *v*. beat, lash

**flood** *v.* inundate, swamp, overflow, deluge, submerge, immerse

**floor** *n.* DECK: tiles, planking, carpet, rug, linoleum; LEVEL: story, landing, basement, mezzanine, downstairs, upstairs, loft, attic, garret, penthouse

**flop** *v.* FALL: tumble, slump, drop; FAIL: miscarry, founder, bomb

**flounder** *v.* struggle, wallow, blunder

**flourish** *v.* THRIVE: increase, wax, succeed, adorn; BRANDISH: wave

**flout** *v.* sneer, disregard

**flow** *n.* current, tide, movement, progress

**flow** *v.* stream, course, move, run, rush, whirl, surge, spurt, squirt, gush, trickle, spew

**flower** *n.* spray, cluster, shoot, posy, herb, vine, annual, perennial, plant

**flower** *v.* bloom, open, blossom, blow

**flowery** *adj.* elaborate, ornamented, rococo, ornate

**fluctuate** *v.* waver, vacillate, falter, hesitate

**fluctuation**, *n.* variation, inconstancy, change

**fluent** *adj.* eloquent, glib, smooth, verbose, chatty, articulate, persuasive, silver-tongued

**fluid** *adj.* flowing, liquid, watery, molten, liquefied

**fluid** *n.* liquid, liquor, solution

**flunk** *v.* fail, miss, drop

**fluster** *v.* disconcert, confuse

**flutter** *v.* flap, ripple, wiggle, wave

**flutter** *n.* agitation, motion

**fly** *v.* FLEE: escape, retreat, withdraw; SOAR: float, glide, hover, swoop, drift, circle; RUSH: dart, speed

**foam** *n.* froth, fluff, bubbles, lather

**focus** *v.* **ATTRACT:** converge, convene, center; **CLEAR:** adjust, detail, sharpen

**foe** *n.* enemy, opponent, antagonist, adversary

**fog** *n.* mist, haze, cloud, film, steam, wisp, smoke, soup, smog

**foggy** *adj.* dull, misty, gray, hazy

**foible** *n.* failing, weakness

**fold** *v.* **DOUBLE:** crease, crimp, ruffle, pucker, gather, lap, overlap, overlay; **FAIL:** bankrupt, close

**folder** *n.* circular, pamphlet, paper, bulletin, advertisement, brochure, throwaway

**foliage** *n.* leaves, greenery

**folk** *n.* people, race, nation, community, tribe, society, population, clan

**folklore** *n.* custom, superstition, tradition, tales, legend, folkways, myth

**folks** *n.* family, kin, relatives, relations

**follow** *v.* **COME AFTER:** ensue, postdate, succeed; **IMITATE:** conform, copy, mirror, reflect, mimic; **OBSERVE:** heed, regard, watch, comply; **UNDERSTAND:** comprehend, catch, realize; **RESULT:** happen, ensue

**follower** *n.* disciple, pupil, protégé, supporter, backer, devotee, believer, admirer

**following** *adj.* subsequent, succeeding, next, ensuing

**following** *n.* clientele, audience, adherents, supporters, patrons

**foment** *v.* encourage, incite

**fond** *adj.* loving, enamored, attached, affectionate

**food** *n.* victuals, foodstuffs, nutriment, refreshment, edibles, comestibles, provisions, sustenance, rations, board, cuisine, nourishment

**fool** *n.* nitwit, simpleton, dunce, oaf, ninny, nincompoop, dolt, buffoon, blockhead, clown

**fool** *v.* deceive, trick, dupe, mislead

**foolish** *adj.* silly, simple, frivolous

**foothold** *n.* ledge, footing, niche, step

**forbear** *v.* abstain, stop

**forbearance** *n.* patience, clemency

**forbid** *v.* prohibit, debar, restrain, inhibit, preclude, oppose, obstruct, bar, prevent, outlaw, disallow, ban

**forbidding** *adj.* unpleasant, offensive, repulsive, grim

**force** *n.* STRENGTH: energy, power, might; DOMINANCE: competency, energy, willpower, drive, determination, authority; ORGANIZATION: group, band, unit

**force** *v.* compel, coerce, press, drive, make, impel, oblige, require, demand, command, impose, exact

**forceful** *adj.* commanding, dominant, powerful, dynamic, intense

**forebode** *v.* apprehend, foretell

**foreboding** *n.* premonition, dread, presentiment, anticipation, apprehension

**forecast** *n.* prognosis, divination, foresight, prophecy

**forecast** *v.* predict, predetermine, foretell, foresee, anticipate

**forefather** *n.* ancestor, progenitor, forebear, father, parent, sire, forerunner, predecessor, originator, precursor, procreator, patriarch, founder, kinsman

**foregoing** *n.* prior, former, previous, preceding

**foreign** *adj.* alien, remote, exotic, strange, distant, different, alien, imported, borrowed, abroad

**foreigner** *n.* stranger, immigrant, newcomer, alien

**foreman** *n.* overseer, manager, supervisor, superintendent, boss

**foremost** *adj.* original, primary, first

**forerunner** *n.* herald, harbinger, precursor, sign

**foresee** *v.* prophesy, predict, foretell

**foresight** *n.* carefulness, husbandry, prudence

**forestall** *v.* thwart, prevent, preclude, hinder

**foretell** *v.* prophesy, predict, divine, foresee, forebode, augur, portend, foreshadow

**forethought** *n.* provision, planning, foresight

**forever** *adv.* always, everlastingly, perpetually, eternally, endlessly, forevermore

**forewarn** *v.* admonish, alarm, warm

**forfeit** *v.* lose, sacrifice, relinquish, abandon

**forge** *v.* counterfeit, falsify, fabricate, feign, imitate, copy, duplicate, reproduce

**forgery** *n.* imitation, copy, counterfeit, fake

**forget** *v.* neglect, overlook, ignore, slight, disregard, skip, exclude

**forgetful** *adj.* inattentive, neglectful, heedless, careless, distracted

**forgive** *v.* absolve, acquit, pardon, overlook, excuse, exonerate

**forgiveness** *n.* absolution, pardon, acquittal, exoneration, dispensation, reprieve, amnesty, respite

**forgo** *v.* quit, relinquish, waive, abandon

**fork** *v.* branch, divide

**form** *n.* SHAPE: figure, appearance, configuration, arrangement, formation, structure, contour, profile, silhouette; CEREMONY: manner, mode, custom, method; PATTERN: model, die, mold; DOCUMENT: chart, questionnaire, application

**form** *v.* **SHAPE:** mold, model, make, fashion, construct, devise, design, produce, build, create; **INSTRUCT:** rear, breed, teach; **DEVELOP:** accumulate, harden, set, rise, appear, grow, mature, materialize

**formal** *adj.* **REGULAR:** orderly, precise, set; **POLITE:** reserved, conventional, stiff

**formality** *n.* decorum, etiquette, correctness, behavior

**format** *n.* arrangement, construction, form

**formation** *n.* form, structure, arrangement, composition, development, fabrication, generation, creation, genesis, constitution

**former** *adj.* earlier, previous, foregoing, preceding

**formerly** *adj.* before, once, previously, earlier

**formula** *n.* equation, recipe, directions

**formulate** *v.* systematize, express, form

**forsake** *v.* desert, abandon, leave, quit

**fort** *n.* fortress, stronghold, citadel, acropolis, redoubt

**fortification** *n.* stronghold, fort, fortress, defense, barricade, battlement, stockade, bastion, bulwark

**fortify** *v.* strengthen, barricade, entrench, buttress

**fortitude** *n.* strength, firmness, valor, fearlessness, determination

**fortress** *n.* stronghold, fort

**fortune** *n.* **CHANCE:** luck, fate, uncertainty; **WEALTH:** riches, possessions, inheritance, estate

**fortunate** *adj.* lucky, favorable

**forward** *adj.* bold, presumptuous, impertinent, fresh

**fossil** *n.* remains, specimen, skeleton, relic

**foster** *v.* nurse, raise, cherish, nourish, encourage

**foul** *adj.* **FILTHY:** impure, disgusting, nasty, vulgar, coarse, offensive; **UNFAIR:** inequitable, unjust

**found** *v.* institute, establish, endow

**foundation** *n.* **BASIS:** reason, justification, authority; **BASE:** footing, pier, groundwork, bed, substructure, underpinning; **INSTITUTION:** organization, endowment, institute, society, charity

**founder** *n.* originator, patron

**foxy** *adj.* sly, crafty, cunning, artful

**fraction** *n.* fragment, section, portion, part, division

**fractious** *adj.* cross, irritable

**fracture** *n.* rupture, shattering, breach, dislocation, shearing, separating

**fracture** *v.* break, crack

**fragile** *adj.* frail, brittle, delicate, dainty, weak

**fragment** *n.* piece, scrap, remnant, bit

**fragrance** *n.* perfume, aroma, smell

**fragrant** *adj.* aromatic, sweet, perfumed

**frail** *adj.* fragile, feeble, breakable, tender, dainty

**frame** *n.* **SKELETON:** framework, scaffolding, support; **BORDER:** margin, fringe, hem, trim, outline

**frame** *v.* **MAKE:** construct, erect, raise, build; **SURROUND:** encircle, confine, enclose

**franchise** *n.* right, privilege

**frank** *adj.* candid, open, sincere, direct, ingenuous, forthright, outspoken, straightforward, blunt

**frantic** *adj.* excited, distracted, frenetic, frenzied

**fraternity** *n.* society, brotherhood, fellowship

**fraud** *n.* **DECEIT:** trickery, duplicity, guile, deception; **TRICKSTER:** impostor, pretender, charlatan, cheat

**fraudulent** *adj.* dishonest, deceitful, tricky

**freak** *n.* monstrosity, rarity, malformation, oddity, aberration, curiosity

**free** *adj.* **SOVEREIGN:** independent, autonomous, democratic, liberated; **UNIMPEDED:** unobstructed, unconstrained, loose, unhampered; **GRATIS:** gratuitous, complimentary

**free** *v.* release, discharge, rescue, extricate, undo, acquit, dismiss, pardon, redeem, disentangle

**freedom** *n.* **LIBERTY:** independence, sovereignty, autonomy; **EXEMPTION:** privilege, immunity, license, indulgence, latitude

**freeway** *n.* turnpike, highway, road, thoroughfare

**freeze** *v.* **SOLIDIFY:** congeal, harden; **CONTROL:** seal, terminate, immobilize

**freight** *n.* **CARGO:** load, encumbrance, consignment, goods, tonnage

**frenzy** *n.* excitement, rage, craze, furor, insanity

**frequency** *n.* repetition, recurrence, reiteration, regularity

**frequent** *adj.* **OFTEN:** habitual, customary, intermittent, periodic, commonplace; **REGULAR:** repeated, recurrent, incessant, continual

**frequent** *v.* visit, attend

**fresh** *adj.* **NEW:** green, recent, current, late, untried; **UNSPOILED:** uncontaminated, preserved; **COLORFUL:** vivid, bright; **POTABLE:** drinkable, cool, clear, pure, clean, sweet, safe; **REFRESHED:** rested, restored, relaxed, reinvigorated, revived;

**INEXPERIENCED:** untrained, untried, unskilled

**fret** *v.* worry, irritate, agitate, vex, bother

**friction** *n.* **RUBBING:** attrition, abrasion, erosion, grinding; **ANTAGONISM:** trouble, animosity, quarrel, discontent, hatred

**friend** *n.* schoolmate, playmate, roommate, companion, intimate, confidant, comrade, fellow, pal, chum, crony, buddy

**friendly** *adj.* kindly, amiable, neighborly, sociable, civil, affectionate, attentive, agreeable, accommodating, pleasant, cordial, congenial

**fright** *n.* fear, panic, terror, dread, horror

**frighten** *v.* terrify, scare, intimidate, threaten, badger, petrify, terrorize

**frightful** *adj.* **FEARFUL:** awful, dreadful, terrible; **UNPLEASANT:** calamitous, shocking, offensive

**frill** *n.* ruffle, frivolity, ornamentation

**frisky** *adj.* spirited, dashing, playful, active

**frivolous** *adj.* unimportant, slight, trifling, superficial, petty, trivial

**frock** *n.* dress, garment

**frontier** *n.* boundary, wilderness, hinterland

**frosting** *n.* covering, coating, icing

**frosty** *adj.* frigid, freezing, chilly, cold

**froth** *n.* foam, bubbles, fizz, effervescence, lather

**frown** *v.* scowl, grimace, pout, glare, sulk, glower

**frugal** *adj.* thrifty, economical, sparing, saving, parsimonious, careful

**fruitful** *adj.* prolific, productive, fecund, fertile

**fruitless** *adj.* vain, unprofitable, empty, futile

**frustrate** *v.* defeat, thwart, foil, balk, prevent

**frustration** *n.* disappointment, impediment, failure

**fry** *v.* sauté, sear, singe, brown, pan–fry

**fuel** *n.* coal, gas, oil, charcoal, propane, peat, firewood, kindling, gasoline, kerosene

**fugitive** *adj.* fleeting, passing

**fugitive** *n.* outlaw, runaway, exile, outcast

**fulfill** *v.* complete, accomplish, achieve, effect

**full** *adj.* **SATURATED:** crammed, packed, jammed, stuffed, glutted, gorged, loaded; **ABUNDANT:** copious, ample, plentiful, sufficient, adequate, lavish, extravagant, profuse

**fumble** *v.* mishandle, bungle, mismanage, botch

**fun** *n.* amusement, relaxation, diversion, entertainment, pleasure, celebration, holiday, enjoyment

**function** *n.* duty, employment, capacity, use; action, event, party

**function** *v.* perform, run, work, operate

**functional** *adj.* utilitarian, practical

**fund** *n.* money, capital, endowment, gift

**fundamental** *adj.* basic, underlying, primary, rudimentary, elemental, structural, original

**funds** *n.* capital, wealth, cash, collateral, money, assets, currency, savings, revenue, stocks, property, bonds, means, affluence, belongings, resources, securities, profits

**funeral** *n.* interment, burial, entombment, requiem

**funny** *adj.* **COMIC:** laughable, comical, whimsical, amusing, entertaining, diverting, humorous, witty, jocular, droll; **SUSPICIOUS:** curious, unusual, odd

**fur** *n.* pelt, hide, hair, coat, brush

**furbish** *v.* polish, spruce, renovate

**furious** *adj.* raging, enraged, fierce, angry

**furnace** *n.* heater, boiler, kiln, forge

**furnish** *v.* supply, equip, stock, provide

**furor** *n.* tumult, excitement, stir, disturbance

**further** *adj.* additional, more, distant

**further** *v.* promote, advance

**fury** *n.* rage, anger, wrath

**fuse** *v.* meld, blend

**fuss** *n.* quarrel, complaint, bother, disturbance, stir

**fuss** *v.* wrangle, whine, whimper, object, complain

**fussy** *adj.* fastidious, particular, meticulous, careful

**futile** *adj.* useless, vain, fruitless, hopeless, purposeless, ineffective, ineffectual, unproductive, empty, hollow

**future** *adj.* impending, imminent, destined, fated, prospective, expected, approaching, ultimate

**fuzz** *n.* nap, fluff, fur, hair

**gab** *vi.* talk, chatter, gossip, jabber, babble

**gabble** *v.* jabber, cackle

**gadget** *n.* device, contrivance, object, contraption

**gag** *v.* **RETCH:** sicken, choke, vomit; **MUZZLE:** muffle, silence, stifle, throttle

**gaiety** *n.* merriment, jollity, mirth, exhilaration

**gain** *n.* profit, increase, accrual, accumulation

**gain** *v.* **INCREASE:** augment, expand, enlarge, grow; **ADVANCE:** progress, overtake; **ACHIEVE:** attain, realize, reach, succeed

**gait** *n.* walk, step, stride, pace, carriage, movement

**gale** *n.* wind, hurricane, blow, typhoon, storm

**gallant** *adj.* noble, brave, courageous, courteous, intrepid

**gallantry** *n.* heroism, valor, bravery, courage

**gallery** *n.* **ONLOOKERS:** spectators, audience, public; **MUSEUM:** salon, studio, hall, showroom

**gallop** *v.* leap, run, spring, bound, hurdle, swing, stride, lope, amble, trot

**gamble** *v.* bet, wager, plunge, speculate, risk, chance

**gambol** *v.* leap, play

**game** *adj.* spirited, hardy, resolute, brave

**game** *n.* **MEAT:** fish, fowl, quarry, wildlife; **ENTERTAINMENT:** play, sport, recreation;

**gang** *n.* band, group, horde, troop

**gangster** *n.* criminal, gunman, racketeer

**gap** *n.* **BREACH:** cleft, rift, hole; **BREAK:** hiatus, recess, lull, pause; **PASS:** chasm, hollow, ravine, gorge, canyon, gully, gulch

**garbage** *n.* refuse, trash, waste

**garden** *n.* patch, field, plot, bed, terrace, oasis

**garish** *adj.* showy, gaudy, ostentatious, ornate

**garment** *n.* dress, attire, apparel, clothes

**garnish** *v.* adorn, decorate, embellish, beautify, deck

**gaseous** *adj.* vaporous, effervescent, aeriform, light

**gash** *n.* wound, slash, slice, cut

**gasp** *v.* gulp, pant, puff, wheeze, blow, snort

**gate** *n.* entrance, ingress, passage, barrier, doorway

**gather** *v.* **COLLECT:** aggregate, amass, accumulate, assemble, garner; **INFER:** conclude, deduce, assume, learn, understand; **ASSEMBLE:** meet, congregate, flock, convene, collect, reunite, converge, concentrate

**gathering** *n.* assembly, meeting, conclave, caucus, parley, council, conference, congregation, convention, rally, throng, huddle, turnout, meet

**gaudy** *a.* showy, flashy, tawdry, ornate

**gauge** *v.* measure, check, weigh, calibrate, calculate

**gaunt** *adj.* thin, lean, haggard, emaciated, scraggy

**gauze** *n.* fabric, veil, bandage, dressing

**gawk** *v.* stare, ogle, gaze, look

**gay** *adj.* lively, showy, merry, cheerful, vivacious

**gaze** *v.* stare, watch, gape, look

**gazette** *n.* journal, newspaper

**gear** *n.* COG: pinion, sprocket; BELONGINGS: equipment, material, tackle

**gem** *n.* stone, jewel, bauble, ornament

**genealogy** *n.* derivation, lineage, extraction, family

**general** *adj.* COMMON: usual, customary, prevailing; INDEFINITE: uncertain, imprecise; COMPREHENSIVE: extensive, broad, universal, ecumenical, ubiquitous

**generality** *n.* abstraction, principle

**generalize** *v.* theorize, speculate, postulate

**generally** *adj.* commonly, ordinarily, regularly

**generate** *v.* produce, form, make, create

**generosity** *n.* hospitality, benevolence, charity, philanthropy, altruism, unselfishness, kindness

**generous** *adj.* bountiful, lavish, profuse, prodigal, unstinting, magnanimous

**genesis** *n.* generation, creation

**genial** *adj.* cordial, kind, warmhearted, friendly

**genius** *n.* talent, intellect, intelligence, gift, aptitude, astuteness, acumen, capability

**gentility** *n.* decorum, propriety, refinement, behavior

**gentle** *adj.* **SOFT:** tender, smooth; **KIND:** tender, considerate, benign; **TAMED:** domesticated, trained;

**genuine** *adj.* **AUTHENTIC:** actual, original, authenticated; **SINCERE:** unaffected, trustworthy, reliable, staunch, certain, valid, positive, frank

**germ** *n.* microbe, bacterium, virus, parasite, bug

**germinate** *v.* sprout, begin, generate

**gesture** *n.* movement, indication, intimation, sign

**get** *v.* **OBTAIN:** procure, capture, take, grab, attain, gain, secure, collect, purchase, receive, possess, acquire; **BECOME:** grow, develop; **RECEIVE:** take, accept; **BEAT;** vanquish, overpower, defeat; **PREPARE:** make, arrange;

**CONTRACT:** succumb, catch; **UNDERSTAND:** comprehend, perceive, know; **IRRITATE:** annoy, provoke, vex, bother

**ghastly** *adj.* terrifying, hideous, horrible, frightening, frightful, repulsive, disgusting, abhorrent, offensive

**ghost** *n.* spirit, apparition, vision, specter, phantom, spook, devil

**giant** *adj.* monstrous, colossal, enormous, large

**giant** *n.* colossus, behemoth, leviathan

**gibberish** *n.* jargon, chatter, claptrap, nonsense

**gibe** *v.* sneer, mock, taunt

**giddy**, *adj.* high, towering, lofty, steep

**gift** *n.* **PRESENT:** donation, grant, endowment, bequest, legacy, reward, remembrance, bonus, subsidy, contribution; **TALENT:** aptitude, faculty, capacity, capability, ability

**gigantic** *adj.* massive, huge, immense, large

**giggle** *v.* laugh, titter, chuckle, snicker

**gimmick** *n.* device, stratagem, catch, method, trick

**girdle** *n.* belt, cinch, sash, underwear

**girdle** *v.* bind, enclose, encircle, clasp, surround

**girl** *n.* schoolgirl, lass, woman, coed, lassie, damsel, maid, maiden

**girth** *n.* circumference, size

**gist** *n.* substance, essence, basis

**give** *v.* **BESTOW:** donate, grant, confer, impart, present, endow, bequeath, award, contribute, convey; **YIELD:** retreat, collapse, fall, contract, shrink, recede

**glacial** *adj.* icy, frozen, polar, cold

**glad** *adj.* exhilarated, animated, jovial, happy

**glamour** *n.* allurement, charm, attraction, beauty

**glance** *v.* **LOOK:** see, peep, glimpse; **RICOCHET:** skip, rebound, bounce

**glare** *v.* **SHINE:** light, beam, glow, radiate; **STARE:** pierce, glower, scowl, frown

**glaring** *adj.* **SHINING:** blinding, dazzling, blazing, bright; **OBVIOUS:** conspicuous, evident, obtrusive

**glass** *n.* tumbler, goblet, beaker, chalice, cup

**gleam** *v.* glow, flash

**glee** *n.* joy, gaiety, joviality, merriment, mirth

**glib** *adj.* fluent, pat

**glide** *v.* float, drift, waft, skim, fly, flit, soar

**glimmer** *n.* gleam, flash, flicker, light

**glimpse** *n.* view, flash, impression, sight

**glisten** *v.* sparkle, glitter, shimmer, flicker, shine

**glitter** *n.* luster, brilliancy, sparkle, shimmer, gleam

**glitter** *v.* glare, shimmer, sparkle, shine

**globule** *n.* drop, particle

**gloom** *n.* **DARKNESS:** cloudiness; **SADNESS:** depression, dejection, melancholia, despondency, morbidity, pessimism, foreboding, misgiving, mourning

**gloomy** *adj.* dreary, depressing, discouraging, dismal

**glorify** *v.* laud, commend, acclaim, honor, exalt, praise

**glorious** *adj.* splendid, excellent, exalted, celebrated, grand, illustrious, remarkable

**glory** *n.* **SPLENDOR:** grandeur, majesty, brilliance, richness, beauty, fineness; **HONOR:** renown, distinction, reputation, fame

**glory** *v.* triumph, exult, boast

**gloss** *n.* brightness, sheen

**glossy**, *adj.* shining, reflecting, lustrous, bright

**glow** *v.* shine, gleam, redden, radiate, burn

**glower** *v.* stare, scowl

**glue** *n.* adhesive, paste, gum, cement, repair

**glue** *v.* paste, join

**glum** *adj.* sullen, moody, morose, sad

**glut** *v.* **OVEREAT:** stuff, cram, gorge, feast, devour; **OVERSUPPLY:** overwhelm, overstock, fill, flood

**gluttony** *n.* voracity, edacity, intemperance, greed

**gnarled** *adj.* knotted, twisted, contorted, bent

**gnaw** *v.* tear, crunch, champ, masticate, bite, chew

**go** *v.* **LEAVE:** withdraw, depart, vacate, flee, fly, run, escape; **PROCEED:** advance, progress, move; **FUNCTION:** run, perform, operate; **SUIT:** conform, accord, harmonize, agree, fit; **EXTEND:** stretch, cover, reach; **ELAPSE:** transpire, pass; **DIE:** depart, succumb

**goad** *v.* prod, urge, prompt, spur, drive, press, push, impel, force, stimulate, provoke, encourage

**goal** *n.* aim, ambition, objective, intent, end

**go–between** *n.* middleman, referee, mediator, agent

**god** *n.* deity, divinity

**godly** *adj.* righteous, devout, pious, holy

**gone** *adj.* moved, withdrawn, retired, departed, dissolved, decayed, extinct

**good** *adj.* MORAL: upright, honest, respectable, noble, ethical, fair, pure, decent, honorable; KIND: considerate, tolerant, generous; RELIABLE: trustworthy, dependable, loyal; SOUND: safe, solid, stable, reliable; PLEASANT: agreeable, satisfying, enjoyable; HEALTHY: sound, normal, vigorous; OBEDIENT: dutiful, tractable, well–behaved; GENUINE: valid, real, sound;

DELICIOUS: tasty, flavorful, tasteful

**good–for–nothing** *n.* loafer, vagabond, bum, vagrant

**good–looking** *adj.* clean–cut, attractive, impressive, beautiful, handsome

**good–natured** *adj.* cordial, kindly, amiable, friendly

**goodness** *n.* decency, morality, honesty, virtue

**goof** *v.* err, flub, fail

**gorge** *n.* chasm, abyss, crevasse, ravine

**gorge** *v.* glut, surfeit, stuff, eat, fill

**gorgeous** *adj.* beautiful, dazzling, superb, sumptuous, impressive, grand

**gory** *adj.* blood–soaked, bloodstained, offensive

**gossip** *n.* RUMOR: scandal, meddling, hearsay, slander, defamation; TALEBEARER: snoop, meddler, tattler, scandalmonger, muckraker, backbiter

**gossip** *v.* tattle, chat, report, blab, babble, repeat

**govern** *v.* rule, administer, oversee, supervise, dictate, tyrannize

**governmental** *adj.* political, administrative, executive, regulatory, bureaucratic, supervisory

**gown** *n.* dress, garment, garb, clothes, dress

**grab** *v.* seize, clutch, grasp, take

**grace** *n.* **CHARM:** nimbleness, agility, poise, dexterity, symmetry, balance, style, harmony; **MERCY:** forgiveness, love, charity

**graceful** *adj.* **SUPPLE:** agile, lithe, nimble, dexterous, sprightly; **ELEGANT:** neat, trim, dainty, comely, slender, exquisite, statuesque; cultured, seemly, becoming, polite

**gracious** *adj.* **GENIAL:** amiable, courteous, condescending, polite;

**MERCIFUL:** tender, loving, charitable, kind

**grade** *n.* **RANK;** class, category, classification; **SLOPE:** incline, gradient, slant, inclination, pitch, ascent, descent, ramp, climb, elevation, height, hill; **EMBANKMENT:** fill, causeway, dike, dam

**grade** *v.* arrange, rate, assort, rank

**gradual** *adj.* creeping, regular, continuous, regulated, piecemeal, gentle

**grand** *adj.* splendid, stately, dignified, regal, noble, illustrious, august, majestic, overwhelming

**grandeur** *n.* splendor, magnificence, pomp, glory, luxury, stateliness, beauty, ceremony, majesty

**grandstand**, *n.* seats, spectators

**grant** *n.* gift, boon, reward, present, allowance, stipend, donation, endowment, bequest

**grant** *v.* **BESTOW:** impart, allow; **ADMIT:** concede, accede, acquiesce, acknowledge

**graph** *n.* diagram, chart, design, plan

**graphic** *adj.* **PICTORIAL:** illustrated, visual, sketched, pictured; **VIVID:** clear, picturesque, comprehensible, striking, expressive, eloquent, poetic

**grasp** *n.* grip, hold, clutch, cinch

**grasp** *v.* **SEIZE:** clutch, enclose, clasp, grip, hold; **UNDERSTAND:** comprehend, perceive, apprehend, follow

**grassland** *n.* plains, meadow, prairie, field

**grate** *v.* rub, rasp, grind, abrade

**grateful** *adj.* thankful, appreciative, pleased, obliged

**gratify** *v.* please, satisfy

**gratitude** *n.* appreciation, acknowledgment, thanks

**gratuitous** *adj.* free, voluntary

**gratuity** *n.* present, tip, largess

**grave** *adj.* **WEIGHTY:** important, momentous, serious, consequential, critical; **SOMBER:** solemn, serious, sober

**grave** *n.* vault, sepulcher, tomb, crypt, mausoleum, catacomb

**gravity** *n.* importance, seriousness, significance

**gravy** *n.* juices, sauce, dressing

**graze** *v.* **FEED:** browse, nibble, forage, eat, munch, ruminate; **PASS LIGHTLY:** brush, scrape, rub, touch

**greasy** *adj.* creamy, fatty, oily

**great** *adj.* **LARGE:** numerous, big, commanding, vast; **EXCELLENT:** exceptional, surpassing, transcendent; **EMINENT:** grand, majestic, exalted, famous, renowned, celebrated, distinguished, noted

**greedy** *adj.* avid, grasping, rapacious, selfish, miserly, intemperate, mercenary, covetous

**green** *adj.* **VERDANT:** growing, leafy, flourishing, grassy, sprouting, lush; **IMMATURE:** young, unripe, maturing, developing; **INEXPERIENCED:** youthful, callow

**greet** *v.* hail, welcome, address, recognize, embrace, nod, acknowledge, bow

**greeting** *n.* salutation, welcome, regards

**gregarious** *adj.* companionable, friendly

**grief** *n.* sorrow, sadness, melancholy, mourning, misery, anguish, despondency, heartache, gloom

**grievance** *n.* hardship, injury, complaint, objection

**grieve** *v.* lament, bewail, regret, sorrow, mourn

**grill** *v.* broil, roast, sauté, barbecue, cook

**grim** *adj.* **SULLEN:** gloomy, sulky, morose, glum; **STERN:** austere, strict, harsh, severe; **RELENTLESS:** implacable, inexorable, uncompromising

**grimace** *n.* smirk, smile, sneer

**grime** *n.* dirt, soil, smudge, filth

**grin** *n.* smile, simper, smirk, wry

**grin** *v.* smirk, simper, beam, smile

**grind** *v.* crush, powder, mill, granulate, crumble

**grip** *n.* **GRASP:** hold, clutch, clasp, catch, clench, embrace, handshake; **SUITCASE:** valise, satchel, bag

**grip** *v.* grasp, clutch, clasp, seize

**gripe** *n.* complaint, grievance, beef, objection

**gripe** *v.* grumble, mutter, complain

**grit** *n.* pluck, courage; sand, dust

**gritty** *adj.* rough, abrasive, sandy, granular, scratchy

**groan** *n.* moan, sob, grunt, cry

**groan** *v.* moan, murmur, keen, cry

**groceries** *n.* food, edibles, comestibles, foodstuffs

**groggy** *adj.* sleepy, dizzy, reeling, tired

**groom** *v.* tend, rub, down, comb, brush

**groove** *n.* furrow, rut, channel, trench, depression, furrow, gutter, ditch

**grope** *v.* feel, search, fumble, touch, feel

**gross** *adj.* WHOLE: total, entire; FAT: corpulent, obese, huge; OBSCENE: indecent, shameful, lewd, coarse

**grotesque** *adj.* ludicrous, odd, bizarre, malformed, ugly, distorted, deformed

**grotto** *n.* cave, cavern, hollow

**grouch** *n.* complainer, grumbler, growler, sourpuss, sorehead, crank, bellyacher

**grouch** *v.* mutter, grumble, gripe, complain

**grouchy** *adv.* surly, ill–tempered, crusty, irritable

**group** *n.* GATHERING: assemblage, cluster, crowd; COLLECTION: accumulation, assortment, combination; ORGANIZATION: association, club, society

**group** *v.* assemble, file, assort, arrange, classify

**grovel** *v.* crawl, wallow, beg, kneel, crouch, kowtow, cower, snivel

**grow** *v.* INCREASE: expand, swell, wax, thrive, enlarge, multiply, flourish; CHANGE: become, develop, evolve, progress, age, ripen, blossom, mature; CULTIVATE: raise, tend, foster, produce, plant, breed

**growl** *v.* snarl, grumble, bark, grunt, cry

**grown** *adj.* aged, adult, mature

**grub** *v.* dig, root

**grudge** *n.* enmity, spite, rancor, animosity, hatred

**grudge** *v.* envy, begrudge, covet

**gruel** *n.* porridge, cereal

**gruesome** *adj.* horrible, ghastly, grim, grisly, frightful

**gruff** *adj.* bluff, churlish, harsh, grating, hoarse

**grumble** *v.* complain, growl, whine, protest, fuss

**grumpy** *adj.* sullen, grouchy, cantankerous, irritable

**grunt** *v.* snort, groan, mutter, grumble

**guarantee** *n.* surety, promise, bond

**guarantee** *v.* pledge, endorse, warrant, insure

**guaranty** *n.* warranty, contract, certificate

**guard** *n.* sentry, sentinel, watchman

**guard** *v.* protect, watch, patrol, picket, tend

**guarded** *adj.* PROTECTED: safe, secured, defended; CAUTIOUS: circumspect, careful

**guardian** *n.* protector, overseer, trustee, custodian, keeper, defender, supervisor, baby–sitter

**guess** *v.* estimate, presume, infer, speculate, imagine, surmise, theorize, venture, suppose, presume

**guest** *n.* visitor, caller

**guidance** *n.* direction, leadership, supervision

**guide** *n.* leader, pilot, pathfinder, scout, escort, director, conductor, pioneer

**guide** *v.* lead, direct, conduct, escort

**guilt** *n.* responsibility, culpability, blame, error, fault, liability, weakness, failing

**guilty** *adj.* condemned, censured, incriminated, indicted, judged, damned, reproachable, chargeable

**guise** *n.* appearance, disguise

**gulch** *n.* ravine, gully, ditch, gorge

**gulf** *n.* **CHASM:** abyss, abysm, depth, ravine, **BAY:** inlet, sound, cove

**gull**, *v.* deceive, trick, cheat

**gullible** *adj.* innocent, trustful, simple, naïve

**gully** *n.* channel, ditch, chasm, crevasse, ravine

**gurgle** *v.* babble, ripple, murmur

**guru** *n.* teacher, instructor, mentor

**gush** *v.* **FLOW:** pour, well, spew

**gust** *n.* blast, burst, blow, breeze, wind

**gusto**, *n.* enjoyment, zest, zeal, fervor, ardor

**gutter** *n.* channel, gully, sewer, drain, trough

**guttural** *adj.* throaty, gruff, deep, hoarse

**guy** *n.* **MAN:** chap, lad, fellow; **GUIDE:** rope, chain, cable

**guzzle** *v.* swill, quaff, swig, drink

**gymnasium** *n.* arena, coliseum, ring, rink, pit, gym

**gymnast** *n.* acrobat, tumbler, jumper, athlete

**gypsy** *n.* wanderer, tramp, vagrant, traveler

**habiliments** *n.* dress, garments

**habit** *n.* **CUSTOM:** mode, practice, fashion, manner; **DRESS:** costume; **OBSESSION:** addiction, fixation

**habitat** *n.* environment, territory, surroundings

**habitual** *adj.* customary, frequent, periodic, continual, routine, rooted, systematic, recurrent, repeated, accustomed, established, repetitious, stereotyped

**hack** *adj.* routine, trite

**hack** *v.* chop, whack, mangle, cut

**hackneyed** *adj.* commonplace, trite

**hag** *n.* crone, shrew, ogress, hellcat, fishwife, harridan, witch

**haggard** *adj.* gaunt, worn, tired

**haggle** *v.* bargain, wrangle, deal, argue, buy, sell

**hail** *v.* call, greet, salute, cheer, welcome, honor

**halfhearted** *adj.* indecisive, irresolute, indifferent

**halfway** *adj.* partial, midway, incomplete, partially, imperfectly, insufficiently, moderately, middling

**halfway** *adv.* half, partly

**hall** *n.* **PUBLIC ROOM:** chamber, assembly, arena, ballroom, church, clubhouse, salon, lounge, amphitheater, gallery; **ENTRANCE:** foyer, corridor, hallway

**hallmark** *n.* label, endorsement, seal, emblem

**hallow** *v.* bless, consecrate, enshrine, sanctify

**hallucination** *n.* delusion, vision

**hallway** *n.* foyer, entrance, way, corridor, entrance

**halt** *n.* stop, cessation, termination

**halt** *v.* check, terminate, suspend, interrupt, block, stem, deter, stall, curb, restrict, arrest, suppress, intercept, obstruct, hinder, impede, squelch

**halve** *v.* divide, split, bisect

**hamlet** *n.* town, village

**hamper** *v.* hinder, slow, thwart, embarrass

**hand** *n.* **WORKMAN:** helper, worker, laborer; **PENMANSHIP:** calligraphy, script; **APPLAUSE:** ovation, reception, handclapping; **CARDS:** deal, round, game

**handbag** *n.* pocketbook, bag, purse

**handbook** *n.* textbook, directory, guidebook

**handcuff** *v.* restrain, shackle

**handicap** *n.* disadvantage, obstacle, impediment, affliction, hindrance, disorder, injury

**handicap** *v.* encumber, hinder

**handily** *adv.* easily, skillfully, smoothly, cleverly

**handle** *v.* HOLD: touch, finger, check, examine, feel; MANAGE: manipulate, operate, use, work; DEAL: retail, market, sell

**handsome** *adj.* attractive, impressive, stately, robust, well-dressed, slick, beautiful

**hand-to-mouth** *adj.* marginal, minimal, borderline

**handwriting** *n.* penmanship, hand, writing, script, scrawl, scribble, calligraphy, scratching

**handy** *adj.* USEFUL: beneficial, advantageous, gainful, helpful, profitable, usable; CONVENIENT: near, nearby; DEXTEROUS: able

**hang** *v.* SUSPEND: dangle, droop, drape; WAVE: flap, swing; KILL: execute, lynch

**hanging** *adj.* DANGLING: swaying, swinging, overhanging, pendulous, drooping; TENTATIVE: uncertain, pending, indeterminate

**hang-out** *n.* bar, joint, hole, headquarters, room

**hang-up** *n.* problem, predicament, difficulty

**haphazard** *adj.* accidental, random, offhand, casual, slipshod, reckless, irregular, unplanned, aimless

**happen** *v.* befall, occur, ensue, arise, transpire

**happening** *n.* incident, affair, accident, event

**happily** *adv.* joyously, gladly, cheerily, gaily, merrily, brightly, blissfully, cheerfully, gleefully

**happiness** *n.* mirth, merrymaking, cheer, merriment, delight, gladness, hilarity, gaiety, cheerfulness, rejoicing, exhilaration

**happy** *adj.* joyous, merry, mirthful, gay, laughing, contented, genial, cheery, jolly, sparkling, blissful, exhilarated, pleased, gratified, ecstatic, overjoyed, radiant, smiling, elated

**happy–go–lucky** *adj.* easygoing, unconcerned, thoughtless, irresponsible

**harangue** *n.* speech, tirade

**harass** *v.* annoy, attack, tease, vex, irritate, bother

**harbor** *n.* refuge, port, pier, inlet, wharf, dock

**harbor** *v.* **CONSIDER:** entertain, cherish, regard; **PROTECT:** shelter, secure, defend, lodge

**hard** *adj.* **COMPACT:** unyielding, solid, impermeable, tough, dense, firm; **DIFFICULT:** arduous, tricky, trying, tedious, complex, abstract, puzzling, troublesome, laborious;

**CRUEL:** perverse, unrelenting, vengeful; **SEVERE:** harsh, exacting, grim

**harden** *v.* steel, temper, solidify, crystallize, clot, petrify, compact, concentrate, fossilize, toughen

**hardheaded** *adj.* willful, stubborn, headstrong

**hardhearted** *adj.* cold, unfeeling, heartless, cruel

**hardly** *adv.* scarcely, barely, imperceptibly, infrequently, somewhat, rarely, slightly, sparsely

**hardship** *n.* trial, sorrow, worry, difficulty, grief

**hardware** *n.* appliance, fixture, casting, metalware, implement, tool, fitting, utensil, equipment

**hardy** *adj.* tough, resistant, staunch, seasoned, solid, rugged, robust, hearty, hale, vigorous, sturdy, solid, substantial, strong

**hark, harken** *v.* listen, heed, attend, observe

**harm** *n.* **INJURY:** infliction, damage; impairment, **EVIL:** wickedness, abuse, outrage

**harm** *v.* injure, wreck, cripple, hurt

**harmful** *adj.* injurious, detrimental, hurtful, noxious, evil, adverse, sinister, virulent, corroding, toxic, painful, malicious, malignant, unwholesome, corrupting, menacing, damaging, disastrous, catastrophic, destructive, unhealthy

**harmless** *adj.* pure, innocent, powerless, controllable, manageable, safe, trustworthy, sanitary

**harmonious** *adj.* **HARMONIC:** tuneful, musical, melodic; **CONGRUOUS:** agreeable, corresponding, suitable, adapted, similar, like, cooperative, friendly, conforming, balanced, symmetrical

**harp** *v.* carp, nag, repeat, pester, complain

**harridan** *n.* witch, hag, nag

**harrow** *v.* torment, distress

**harry** *v.* plunder, harass

**harsh** *adj.* rough, severe, discordant, jangling, cacophonous, grating, dissonant, creaking, clashing, jarring, clamorous, hoarse, rasping, screeching, earsplitting, tuneless, shrill

**harvest** *n.* crops, yield, fruit, grain, produce, vegetable

**harvest** *v.* glean, gather, accumulate, collect, garner, cut, pluck, pick, cull, hoard, mow

**hasp** *n.* fastener, latch

**hassle** *n.* dispute, squabble

**haste** *n.* speed, dispatch, precipitation, rashness, impetuousness, foolhardiness, recklessness, hastiness, carelessness, heedlessness

**hasten** *v.* **HURRY:** rush, fly, sprint; **EXPEDITE:** accelerate, quicken, push, urge, goad, press

**hasty** *adj.* **HURRIED:** quick, speedy, swift, fast; **CARELESS:** precipitate, foolhardy, careless, rash

**hat** *n.* headgear, headpiece, helmet, chapeau, bonnet, cap, derby, sombrero, topper, bowler, Panama, fedora, beret, turban, hood, cowl, beret

**hate** *n.* dislike, animosity, enmity, hatred

**hate** *v.* **DETEST:** abhor, abominate, loathe, resent, despise, dislike

**hateful** *adj.* odious, detestable, repugnant, offensive

**hatred** *n.* abhorrence, loathing, rancor, repugnance, repulsion, disgust, displeasure, contempt, bitterness, antagonism, animosity, malice, malevolence, spleen, hostility, alienation

**haughty** *adj.* disdainful, arrogant, proud, egotistic

**haul** *n.* **PULL:** tug, lift, wrench; **DISTANCE:** voyage, trip; **SPOILS:** take, find, booty

**haul** *v.* drag, pull, bring, draw

**haunt** *v.* **FREQUENT:** habituate, visit; **OBSESS:** torment, possess, trouble, hound, terrify, plague, vex, worry, frighten, harass, annoy, bother, disturb

**haunting** *adj.* eerie, unforgettable, seductive, frightful

**have** *v.* **OWN:** keep, retain, use, maintain, control, possess, treasure, hold; **BEAR:** beget, produce

**haven** *n.* harbor, port, refuge, shelter

**havoc** *n.* destruction, confusion, devastation, plunder

**hazard** *n.* chance, risk, peril, jeopardy, danger

**hazard** *v.* chance, try, guess, gamble, risk

**haze** *n.* fog, mist, smog, cloudiness

**hazy** *adj.* vague, cloudy, foggy, murky, misty, unclear, overcast, gauzy, vaporous, smoky, dim, indistinct, dusky, obscure, veiled, blurred, faint

**head** *n.* **SKULL:** brainpan, scalp, crown; **LEADER:** chief, commander, officer, ruler; **TOP:** summit, peak, crest; **BEGINNING:** front, start, source, origin; **INTELLIGENCE:** brains, foresight, ingenuity, judgment

**head** *v.* lead, direct, supervise, manage

**headache** *n.* **PAIN:** migraine, neuralgia; **PROBLEM:** vexation, difficulty, trouble

**headway** *n.* progress, advance, increase, promotion

**heal** *v.* cure, restore, renew, regenerate, remedy, rejuvenate, medicate, revive, rehabilitate, resuscitate, salve, help, ameliorate, doctor

**health** *n.* vigor, wholeness, healthfulness, fitness, bloom, hardiness, stamina, energy, strength

**healthy** *adj.* sound, trim, robust, vigorous, well, hearty, athletic, able–bodied, virile, blooming, firm, sturdy, lively, flourishing, fit, rugged

**heap** *n.* pile, mass, stack, quantity

**heap** *v.* pile, add, lump, load, pack

**hear** *v.* **LISTEN:** attend, catch, apprehend, eavesdrop, perceive, overhear; **TRY:** judge, examine, referee

**hearsay** *n.* rumor, scandal, gossip

**heart** *n.* **FEELING:** response, sympathy, sensitivity, emotion; **CENTER:** core, middle, pith; **SPIRIT:** courage, fortitude, gallantry

**heartache** *n.* sorrow, pain, despair, anguish, grief

**heartless** *adj.* cruel, unkind, insensitive, ruthless

**hearty** *adj.* warm, zealous, sincere, cheery, cheerful, jovial, animated, ardent, genial, enthusiastic, genuine, passionate, intense, exuberant, devout, unfeigned, fervent, responsive, friendly

**heat** *n.* **WARMTH:** fever, sultriness; **FERVOR:** ardor, passion, excitement, desire

**heat** *v.* warm, inflame, kindle, thaw, boil, sear, singe, scorch, ignite

**heated** *adj.* **WARMED:** cooked, fried, baked **FERVENT:** fiery, ardent, avid, excited, passionate

**heathen** *adj.* infidel, atheist, barbarian

**heave** *v.* **THROW:** toss; **MOVE:** rock, bob, pitch, lurch, roll, reel, sway, throb, slosh

**heavenly** *adj.* **DIVINE:** celestial, supernal, angelic, holy; **BLISSFUL:** sweet, enjoyable, excellent, pleasant

**heavy** *adj.* **WEIGHTY:** ponderous, huge, stout, dense, substantial, hefty, large; **BURDENSOME:** troublesome, oppressive, vexatious, difficult, disturbing, onerous; **DULL:** listless, slow, apathetic, indifferent; **GLOOMY:** dejected, cloudy, overcast, dismal, dark, sad

**heavy–handed** *adj.* oppressive, harsh, cruel, severe

**heckle** *v.* torment, disturb, pester, ridicule, bother

**hectic** *adj.* frantic, unsettled, boisterous, restless, confused, disordered

**hector** *v.* bully, annoy, tease, vex

**heed** *n.* notice, care

**height** *n.* altitude, elevation, prominence, loftiness, highness, tallness, stature, expanse, extent, length

**heighten** *v.* **INCREASE:** sharpen, strengthen, emphasize; **RAISE:** uplift, elevate, lift

**heinous** *adj.* hateful, atrocious, wicked

**heir** *n.* inheritor, successor, descendent, heiress, beneficiary, inheritor, prince

**heirloom** *n.* legacy, inheritance, bequest, gift, antique

**heist** *n.* robbery, burglary

**helm** *n.* leadership, control

**help** *n.* **ASSISTANCE:** advice, comfort, aid, support, gift, charity, encouragement, subsidy, service, relief, endowment, cooperation, guidance; **EMPLOYEE:** aid, representative, assistant, faculty, staff; **RELIEF:** maintenance, sustenance, nourishment, remedy

**help** *v.* assist, advise, encourage, cooperate, intercede, befriend, accommodate, sustain, benefit, bolster, promote, back, advocate, abet, stimulate, uphold, further, boost, support

**helpful** *adj.* **USEFUL:** valuable, serviceable, profitable, advantageous, favorable, convenient, suitable, practical, usable, applicable, desirable, convenient; **CURATIVE:** healthy, salutary, restorative, healthful; **OBLIGING:** accommodating, considerate, neighborly, kind

**helping** *n.* portion, serving, plateful, share

**helpless** *adj.* **DEPENDENT:** feeble, unable, weak, vulnerable; **INCOMPETENT:** incapable, unfit, inexpert

**hem** *n.* border, skirting, edging, edge, fringe, rim

**henpeck** *v.* nag, bully, suppress, intimidate, bother

**herald** *n.* proclaimer, forerunner

**herd** *n.* flock, group, drove, pack, brood, swarm, lot, bevy, covey, gaggle, nest, brood, flight, school

**herdsman** *n.* shepherd, herder, rancher

**hereditary** *adj.* inherited, genetic, paternal

**heredity** *n.* ancestry, inheritance, genetic

**heresy** *n.* dissent, nonconformity, dissidence, sectarianism, schism, unorthodoxy, secularism

**heretic** *n.* schismatic, apostate, sectarian, cynic

**heritage** *n.* TRADITION: culture, custom, fashion, system; INHERITANCE: legacy, birthright, ancestry, dowry, share, endowment, status, heredity

**hermit** *n.* ascetic, recluse

**hero** *n.* champion, model, martyr, conqueror, god, warrior, saint, knight–errant, star

**heroic** *adj.* valiant, valorous, fearless, brave, noble

**heroism** *n.* fortitude, valor, bravery, courage, strength

**hesitancy** *n.* indecision, wavering, procrastination, delay, pause

**hesitant** *adj.* SLOW: delaying, wavering, dawdling, lazy; DOUBTFUL: skeptical, irresolute, uncertain;

**hesitate** *v.* pause, stop, falter, vacillate, flounder, ponder, delay, weigh, consider, deliberate, linger

**hesitation** *n.* DOUBT: equivocation, skepticism, irresolution, uncertainty; DELAY: wavering, dawdling

**hex** *n.* spell, curse

**hex** *v.* curse, enchant, charm, bewitch

**hiatus** *n.* break, pause

**hidden** *adj.* secluded, private, covert, concealed, occult, masked, screened, veiled, clouded, obscured, disguised, unseen, camouflaged, shrouded, shadowy, clandestine, cloistered, surreptitious

**hide** *n.* skin, pelt, rawhide, fur, leather

**hide** *v.* conceal, shroud, curtain, veil, camouflage, cover, mask, cloak, screen, suppress, withhold, shield, secrete, hoard, closet, obscure, disguise

**hideous** *adj.* frightful, shocking, revolting, hateful, ghastly, grisly, ugly

**hideout** *n.* lair, den, refuge, retreat, shelter

**hierarchy** *n.* government, authority, ministry, regime

**high** *adj.* **TOWERING:** tall, gigantic, big, colossal, tremendous, great, giant, huge, formidable, immense, elevated, lofty, soaring, raised; **EXALTED:** eminent, powerful, distinguished, leading, noble; **EXPENSIVE:** costly, precious, **EXTRAORDINARY:** great, special, unusual; **SHRILL:** piercing, sharp, penetrating; **DRUNK:** intoxicated, tipsy, inebriated

**high-pressure** *adj.* forceful, compelling, powerful

**high-spirited** *adj.* daring, dauntless, reckless, brave

**high-strung** *adj.* nervous, tense, impatient, restless

**highway** *n.* roadway, parkway, freeway, turnpike

**hijack** *v.* rob, steal, privateer, capture, seize

**hike** *n.* walk, tour, trek, trip, backpack, journey

**hike** *v.* **TRAMP:** tour, explore, travel, walk; **RAISE:** lift, advance, increase

**hilarious** *adj.* gay, merry, funny, amusing, lively, witty, entertaining

**hill** *n.* mound, knoll, butte, bluff, promontory, precipice, rising, headland, upland, inclination, slope, ascent, grade, incline, rise, foothill, dune, climb, elevation, hillside, hilltop

**hinder** *v.* stop, impede, obstruct, check, retard, fetter, block, thwart, bar, clog, encumber, burden, inhibit, shackle, interrupt, arrest, curb, oppose, deter, hamper, frustrate, intercept, prohibit, stall, slow, down, smother, disappoint, spoil, gag

**hindrance** *n.* obstacle, barrier, interference

**hinge** *n.* joint, pivot, juncture, articulation, link

**hinge** *v.* hang, turn, depend, connect, couple, join

**hint** *n.* allusion, mention, inkling, implication, reference, observation, notice, tip, clue, omen, scent, notion, taste, suspicion, innuendo, sign, impression, indication, suggestion

**hint** *v.* intimate, inform, imply, infer, acquaint, remind, recall, cue, prompt, insinuate, indicate, wink, advise, suggest

**hip** *n.* **AWARE:** informed, enlightened, knowledgeable, cognizant; **FASHIONABLE:** modern, stylish

**hire** *v.* engage, secure, enlist, appoint, delegate, authorize, retain, commission, empower, select, pick, contract, procure

**historic** *adj.* factual, traditional, chronicled, old

**history** *n.* account, annals, records, archives, chronicle, writings, evidence, record

**hit** *adj.* struck, slugged, smacked, cuffed, smashed, clouted, hurt, tapped, rapped, swatted

**hit** *n.* **STROKE:** blow, slap, rap, punch; **SUCCESS:** favorite, sellout, knockout

**hit** *v.* **STRIKE:** knock, sock, slap, bump, thump, collide, punch, hammer, whack, jab, tap, pelt, cuff, clout, club; **REACH:** find, win

**hitch** *n.* **KNOT:** loop, noose, tie; **DIFFICULTY:** obstacle, hindrance, block

**hitch** *v.* hook, unite, yoke, hook, fasten, join

**hoard** *n.* cache, treasure, store, stockpile

**hoard** *v.* amass, acquire, keep, accumulate, save

**hoary** *adj.* white, old

**hoax** *n.* trick, fabrication, deceit, deception, lie

**hobby** *n.* pursuit, avocation, pastime, diversion, interest, activity, pursuit, sport, amusement, craft

**hobo** *n.* vagrant, vagabond, wanderer, beggar, bum

**hock** *v.* sell, pledge, deposit, pawn

**hod** *n.* trough, scuttle

**hodgepodge** *n.* mixture, jumble, combination, mess

**hoist** *n.* lift, crane, derrick, elevator

**hoist** *v.* raise, lift

**hokum** *n.* nonsense, trickery, chicanery

**hold** *v.* **POSSESS:** keep, retain, have, accept; **SUPPORT:** sustain, brace, buttress, prop; **GRASP:** grip, clutch, embrace, squeeze, hug, seize; **CONFINE:** imprison, enclose, restrain; **RESIST:** persevere, continue, endure; **ADHERE:** cling, fasten, stick

**holdout** *n.* die–hard, objector, resister, resistance, objector, dissenter

**holdover** *n.* remnant, relic, surplus, remainder

**holdup** *n.* robbery, burglary, stick–up, crime, theft

**hole** *n.* **CAVITY:** perforation, puncture, slot, eyelet, split, tear, cleft, opening, fissure, gap, gash, rift, rupture, aperture, breach, eye, crater, gorge, hollow, chasm, crevasse, **BURROW:** den, lair; **DIFFICULTY:** impasse, tangle, mess, crisis, emergency

**holiday** *n.* festival, fiesta, carnival, jubilee, anniversary, celebration

**holiness** *n.* devoutness, humility, saintliness, devotion

**hollow** *adj.* CONCAVE: sunken, depressed, excavated, indented; CAVERNOUS: deep, resonant, booming, rumbling, reverberating, muffled, dull, resounding; UNSOUND: empty, pretentious

**hollow** *n.* cavity, dale, bowl, basin, valley

**hollow** *v.* scoop, excavate, indent, dig, shovel

**holocaust** *n.* loss, fire, destruction, annihilation, catastrophe

**holy** *adj.* devout, pious, righteous, moral, just, good, angelic, godly, reverent, venerable, humble, innocent, saintly, godlike, saintlike, perfect, faultless, chaste, upright, virtuous, dedicated, devoted, spiritual, religious

**homage** *n.* loyalty, worship, respect, adoration, deference, devotion, reverence

**home** *n.* DWELLING: residence, habitation, abode, lodging, quarters, domicile, shelter; ASYLUM: orphanage, sanitarium, hospital

**homecoming** *n.* welcome, celebration, entry, arrival

**homely** *adj.* PLAIN: unattractive, uncomely; UNPRETENTIOUS: plain, snug, simple, cozy, modest

**homespun** *adj.* handcrafted, domestic, homemade

**homestead** *n.* property, house, ranch, estate, home

**homogenize** *v.* blend, combine

**homologous** *adj.* equivalent, associated

**honest** *adj.* TRUTHFUL: trustworthy, unimpeachable, legitimate; FRANK: aboveboard, candid, straightforward; FAIR: just, equitable, impartial

**honesty** *n.* fidelity, scrupulousness, candor, openness, goodness, virtue

**honk** *v.* blare, trumpet, bellow, sound

**honor** *n.* distinction, recognition, attention, reputation, tribute, integrity

**honor** *v.* **RESPECT:** worship, sanctify, venerate, praise; **VALUE:** admire, esteem, compliment; **ACCEPT:** clear, pass, acknowledge

**honorable** *adj.* reputable, creditable, distinguished, noble

**honorary** *adj.* titular, nominal, complimentary

**hood** *n.* **COVERING:** cowl, shawl, bonnet, veil, capuchin, mantle; **CANOPY:** awning, cover; **HOODLUM:** gangster, criminal, crook

**hoodlum** *n.* rowdy, thug, gangster, crook, criminal

**hook** *n.* lock, catch, clasp, fastener

**hook** *v.* **BEND:** curve, angle, crook, arch; **CATCH:** pin, secure, fasten

**hoot** *n.* howl, whoop, boo, cry

**hop** *v.* leap, jump, skip, bounce

**hope** *n.* **FAITH:** expectation, anticipation; **DREAM:** desire, purpose, wish, goal

**hope** *v.* expect, desire, await, suppose, believe, anticipate, trust

**hopeful** *adj.* **OPTIMISTIC:** expectant, trustful, anticipating, trusting, confident; **ENCOURAGING:** promising, reassuring, favorable, propitious, cheering, auspicious, uplifting, heartening, inspiring

**hopeless** *adj.* unfortunate, bad, incurable, vain, irreversible, irreparable, disastrous, tragic, desperate

**horde** *n.* crowd, swarm, pack, throng

**horizon** *n.* range, border, limit, boundary, extent

**horizontal** *adj.* LEVEL: aligned, parallel, flat, straight; EVEN: flush, uniform, regular, smooth

**horrible** *adj.* repulsive, dreadful, disgusting, terrible, frightful, shameful, shocking

**horrid** *adj.* shocking, hideous, disturbing, shameful, offensive, pitiful

**horrify** *v.* shock, terrify

**horror** *n.* fear, terror, awe, fright

**hors d'oeuvre** *n.* appetizer, canapé

**horseman** *n.* cavalryman, knight, dragoon, equestrian, jockey, cowboy, rider

**horticulture** *n.* cultivation, agriculture, farming

**hospitable** *adj.* kind, receptive, courteous, cordial, open, friendly

**hospital** *n.* clinic, infirmary, sanitarium, dispensary

**hospitality** *n.* companionship, fellowship, entertainment, welcome

**hostile** *adj.* unfriendly, antagonistic, hateful, opposed

**hostility** *n.* abhorrence, aversion, bitterness, hatred

**hot** *adj.* BURNING: fiery, flaming, blazing, baking, roasting, scorching, blistering, searing, sizzling, broiling, scalding, parching; AROUSED: furious, ill–tempered, indignant, angry

**hotel** *n.* motel, lodging, inn, hostel, resort, tavern

**hotrod** *n.* car, racer, dragster

**hound** *n.* dog, cur

**hound** *v.* bully, pester, badger, provoke, annoy

**house** *n.* HOME: habitation, dwelling, residence; FAMILY: line, tradition, ancestry; LEGISLATURE: congress, council, parliament

**housekeeper** *n.* caretaker, servant

**hover** *v.* remain, wait, float, linger

**howl** *v.* cry, wail, bawl, lament, yell

**hub** *n.* center, core, middle, focus, heart

**huddle** *v.* crowd, cluster, group, conference

**hue** *n.* color, tint, value, dye

**huff** *n.* anger, annoyance, pique

**huff** *v.* puff, blow, bluster, bully

**huffy** *adj.* offended, piqued, angry, insulted, irritable

**hug** *v.* embrace, hold, squeeze, clasp, press, cling, clutch, envelop, enfold, nestle, cuddle

**huge** *adj.* large, tremendous, enormous, immense

**hulking** *adj.* bulky, massive

**humane** *adj.* merciful, kind, sympathetic, benevolent, understanding, compassionate, kindhearted, forgiving, charitable, tender, lenient, tolerant, altruistic, philanthropic, magnanimous, unselfish, warmhearted

**humanitarian** *adj.* altruist, benfactor, philanthropist

**humble** *adj.* MEEK: submissive, gentle, diffident, retiring, reserved, bashful, shy, timid, deferential, hesitant, mild, withdrawn, fearful, tentative, obedient, passive, tame, restrained, subdued;

UNPRETENTIOUS: unassuming, modest, seemly, becoming, homespun, natural, servile, shabby, insignificant, plain, common, homely, simple

**humble** *v.* humiliate, shame, chasten, mortify, demean, demote, lower, crush, degrade, discredit, squelch, deflate, squash

**humbug** *n.* hoax, fraud, lie, deception, nonsense

**humdrum** *adj.* monotonous, common, uninteresting, dull

**humid** *adj.* moist, damp, stuffy, sticky, muggy, close

**humiliate** *v.* humble, shame, debase, mortify, chasten, dishonor, demean, conquer, vanquish, disgrace, embarrass

**humiliation** *n.* chagrin, mortification, disgrace, embarrassment, shame

**humility** *n.* meekness, timidity, servility, subservience, resignation, shyness

**humor** *n.* **COMEDY:** entertainment, amusement, jesting, raillery; **WITTICISM:** pleasantry, banter, joke, mirth; **DISPOSITION:** gaiety, wittiness, joyfulness, playfulness

**humor** *v.* indulge, pamper, gratify, placate, appease, comfort

**humorous** *adj.* amusing, funny, comical, entertaining

**hunch** *n.* intuition, notion, feeling, premonition, instinct, foreboding, portent, apprehension, misgiving, qualm, suspicion, inkling

**hunger** *n.* longing, yearning, lust, want

**hunger** *v.* crave, desire

**hungry** *adj.* starved, famished, ravenous, desirous, unsatisfied, unfilled, starving, voracious

**hunk** *n.* lump, chunk, mass, clod, slice, morsel

**hunt** *v.* **PURSUE:** follow, stalk, hound, trail, seek, track, chase; **INVESTIGATE:** search, probe, seek

**hurdle** *n.* obstacle, barricade, blockade, barrier

**hurl** *v.* throw, cast, fling, heave

**hurrah** *v.* applaud, cheer, approve

**hurry** *v.* **HASTEN:** scurry, scuttle, dash, sprint, rush, scoot, dart, spring, speed, fly, bustle, race; **URGE:** drive, push, spur, goad

**hurt** *adj.* injured, harmed, wounded, disfigured, suffering, distressed, tortured, unhappy

**hurt** *v.* **INJURE:** cut, bruise, slap, abuse, flog, whip, harm, wound, lacerate, bite, burn, punch, scourge, lash, cane, switch; **HARM:** maltreat, injure, spoil, damage, destroy; **PAIN:** ache, throb, sting

**hurtful** *adj.* aching, injurious, deadly, harmful

**husband** *v.* economize, conserve

**hush** *v.* calm, soothe, quiet, silence, gag, stifle

**husky** *adj.* **HOARSE:** rough, throaty, gruff, growling; **STRONG:** muscular, sinewy, strapping

**hustle** *v.* rush, push, hurry, race, run, speed

**hut** *n.* shanty, lean–to, shack, dugout, hovel

**hygiene** *n.* health, sanitation, cleanliness

**hygienic** *adj.* healthful, sanitary, clean, pure, sterile

**hyperbole** *n.* metaphor, exaggeration

**hypnotic** *adj.* narcotic, soporific, soothing

**hypnotize** *v.* mesmerize, fascinate, captivate, stupefy

**hypocrisy** *n.* pretense, affectation, bigotry, sanctimony, dishonesty, lie

**hypocrite** *n.* pretender, fraud, faker, deceiver, charlatan, trickster

**hypothesis** *n.* theory, supposition, assumption, guess, opinion

**hypothetical** *adj.* **SUPPOSED:** imagined, uncertain, assumed, likely, **POSTULATED:** academic, philosophical, logical

**hysteria, hysterics** *n.* neurosis, emotionalism, delirium, agitation, confusion, excitement, nervousness

**hysterical** *adj.* frantic, raving, delirious, emotional, neurotic, distraught, uncontrollable, frenzied, unrestrained, tempestuous, impassioned, overwrought

**icon** *n.* image, picture

**iconoclast** *n.* dissenter, rebel

**idea** *n.* **CONCEPT:** belief, theory, hypothesis, assumption, conjecture, notion, thought; **FANCY:** imagination, whimsy, whim, fantasy

**ideal** *adj.* **TYPICAL:** model, archetypal; **PERFECT:** best, theoretical, supreme, fitting, exemplary, excellent

**ideal** *n.* concept, paragon, goal, prototype, model

**idealism** *n.* principle, conscience, philosophy, ethics, visionary, conscience

**identical** *adj.* same, alike, twin, indistinguishable

**identification** *n.* **CLASSIFYING:** naming, cataloguing, description, classification; **CREDENTIALS:** passport, testimony, papers, badge

**ideal** *adj.* **TYPICAL:** model, archetypal;

**PERFECT:** best, theoretical, supreme, fitting, exemplary, excellent

**ideal** *n.* concept, paragon, goal, prototype, model

**idealism** *n.* principle, conscience, philosophy, ethics

**identical** *adj.* same, alike, twin, indistinguishable

**identification** *n.* **CLASSIFYING:** naming, cataloguing, description, classification; **CREDENTIALS:** passport, testimony, papers, badge

**identify** *v.* classify, catalog, analyze, describe, name

**identity** *n.* characteristics, identification, individuality, uniqueness, name

**ideology** *n.* philosophy, belief, doctrine, ethics

**idiom** *n.* expression, usage, jargon, argot

**idiot** *n.* simpleton, nincompoop, booby, fool

**idiotic** *adj.* dull, moronic, stupid

**idle** *adj.* unemployed, unoccupied, uncultivated, fallow, motionless, inert, resting

**idle** *v.* loiter, slack, shirk, loaf

**idol** *n.* image, icon, figurine, fetish, totem

**idolatry** *n.* worship, love, infatuation, fervor, zeal

**idolize** *v.* worship, glorify, adore, canonize

**ignite** *v.* fire, light, enkindle, burn

**ignoble** *adj.* mean, dishonorable

**ignominy** *n.* shame, disgrace

**ignorance** *n.* incomprehension, incapacity, inexperience, illiteracy, shallowness, simplicity

**ignorant** *adj.* UNAWARE: superficial, unconscious, shallow, inexperienced, unwitting, obtuse, unintelligent, dense, shallow; UNTRAINED: illiterate, uneducated, misguided, naïve

**ignore** *v.* overlook, disregard, reject, neglect

**ilk** *n.* type, kind

**ill** *adj.* BAD: harmful, evil, noxious, unfavorable; SICK: unwell, unhealthy, ailing

**ill** *n.* evil, depravity, misfortune, mischief, wrong

**illegal** *adj.* unlawful illicit banned outlawed unauthorized unlicensed, illegitimate, prohibited, forbidden, criminal

**illegible** *adj.* unreadable, faint, unintelligible, confused, obscure

**illicit** *adj.* unlawful, prohibited, unauthorized, illegal

**illiteracy** *n.* ignorance, stupidity, idiocy

**illiterate** *adj.* ignorant, uneducated, unenlightened

**illness** *n.* sickness, infirmity, disorder, attack, convalescence, complaint, collapse, breakdown, confinement, weakness, disease, ailment, malady

**illogical** *adj.* irrational, unreasonable, fallacious, absurd, incorrect, inconsistent, unscientific, contradictory, unsound, implausible

**ill–tempered** *adj.* cross, touchy, querulous, irritable

**illuminate** *v.* **CLARIFY:** illustrate, explain, interpret, elucidate; **BRIGHTEN:** lighten, illumine, decorate, light

**illumination** *n.* **LIGHT:** brilliance, lighting, flame; **CLARIFICATION:** instruction, teaching, education, information, knowledge

**illusion** *n.* deception, fancy, hallucination, mirage, apparition, delusion, trick, dream

**illusory** *adj.* deceiving, unreal

**illustrate** *v.* explain; picture, portray, depict

**illustration** *n.* explanation, picture, engraving, vignette, inset, chart, diagram

**illustrative** *adj.* symbolic, representative, pictorial, descriptive, explanatory, graphic

**illustrious** *adj.* distinguished, famous

**image** *n.* **LIKENESS:** idol, representation, effigy, form, drawing, portrait, photograph, replica, picture; **CONCEPT:** conception, perception, thought, idea

**imagery** *n.* metaphor, representation, comparison

**imaginable** *adj.* conceivable, comprehensible, possible, plausible, believable, reasonable, likely

**imaginary** *adj.* fancied, illusory, visionary, hypothetical, theoretical, imagined, hallucinatory, whimsical, fabulous, nonexistent, mythological, legendary, fictitious, unreal

**imagination** *n.* inventiveness, conception, sensitivity, visualization, awareness, insight

**imaginative** *adj.* creative, inventive, artistic, original

**imagine** *v.* conceive, invent, picture, conjure, envision, invent, fabricate, formulate, devise, conceptualize, dream, perceive, create

**imbalance** *n.* unevenness, inequality, irregularity

**imbecilic** *adj.* foolish, silly

**imbibe** *v.* ingest, gorge, guzzle, drink, swallow

**imbroglio** *n.* commotion, entanglement, fracas

**imbue** *v.* permeate, invade, absorb, saturate, teach

**imitate** *v.* MIMIC: impersonate, mirror, simulate, ape, mime, parody; COPY: duplicate, counterfeit, reproduce, falsify; RESEMBLE: simulate, parallel

**imitation** *n.* SIMULATION: duplication, mimicry, impersonation, copy;

COUNTERFEIT: likeness, replica, substitution, forgery

**imitative** *adj.* deceptive, false, forged, sham

**immaculate** *adj.* pure, unsoiled, unsullied, spotless, stainless, bright, clean

**immanent** *adj.* deep-seated, inherent, natural, instinctive

**immaterial** *adj.* unimportant, insignificant

**immature** *adj.* childish, youthful, sophomoric, naïve

**immediate** *adj.* now, next, prompt, following

**immense** *adj.* large, gigantic, tremendous, enormous

**immerse** *v.* plunge, involve, submerge, douse, steep, soak, drench, dunk, souse

**immigrant** *n.* outsider, newcomer, alien

**immigrate** *v.* move, enter

**immigration** *n.* colonization, settlement, migration

**imminent** *adj.* impending, approaching, coming

**immobility** *n.* firm, fixed, motionless

**immodest** *adj.* brazen, shameless, bold, egotistic

**immoral** *adj.* sinful, corrupt, shameless, bad

**immorality** *n.* vice, depravity, dissoluteness, evil

**immortal** *adj.* **DEATHLESS:** undying, imperishable, endless, timeless, everlasting, enduring, eternal; **ILLUSTRIOUS:** celebrated, eminent, glorious, famous

**immovable** *adj.* solid, stable, fixed, firm

**immune** *adj.* exempt, free, unsusceptible, privileged, excused, safe

**immunity** *n.* **EXEMPTION:** privilege, license, freedom; **IMMUNIZATION:** resistance, protection

**immure** *v.* confine, imprison

**impact** *n.* shock, impression, contact, collision

**impair** *v.* lessen, diminish, spoil, blemish, injure, hurt, break, damage

**impart** *v.* **GIVE:** bestow, grant, present, allow; **INFORM:** tell, announce, divulge, admit, reveal

**impartial** *adj.* unbiased, equitable, disinterested, dispassionate, equal, fair

**impartiality** *n.* objectivity, candor, equality, fairness

**impasse** *n.* deadlock, standstill, cessation, pause

**impassioned** *adj.* ardent, fervent, passionate

**impassive** *adj.* emotionless, unemotional, unmoved

**impatience** *n.* agitation, restlessness, anxiety, excitement, nervousness

**impatient** *adj.* anxious, eager, feverish, restless

**impeach** *v.* charge, arraign, denounce, indict, discredit, reprimand, blame, incriminate

**impeccable** *adj.* flawless, perfect

**impede** *v.* hinder, obstruct, slow

**impediment** *n.* obstruction, hindrance, obstacle, difficulty, barrier

**impel** *v.* drive, force, urge

**impend** *v.* approach, threaten

**impenetrable** *adj.* DENSE: impervious, compact, hard, firm, thick, compressed; INCOMPREHENSIBLE: unintelligible, inscrutable, unfathomable, obscure, unexplainable

**impenitent** *adj.* unrepentant, remorseless

**imperative** *adj.* NECESSARY: obligatory, mandatory; AUTHORITATIVE: masterful, commanding, dominant, aggressive, powerful

**imperfect** *adj.* flawed, incomplete, deficient, faulty

**imperfection** *n.* fault, flaw, stain, blemish

**imperious** *adj.* haughty, arrogant

**impersonal** *adj.* detached, disinterested, indifferent

**impersonate** *v.* portray, mimic, represent, imitate

**impersonation** *n.* role, enactment, performance

**impertinent** *adj.* impudent, saucy, insolent, rude

**impervious** *adj.* impassable, impenetrable, watertight, impermeable

**impetuous** *adj.* hasty, impulsive, rash, spontaneous

**impetus** *n.* force, momentum, stimulus, incentive, purpose, reason

**impinge** *v.* encroach, infringe, strike, touch

**impious** *adj.* sinful, profane, blasphemous, bad

**implement** *n.* tool, instrument, appliance, utensil

**implicate** *v.* involve, connect, associate, link, relate

**implication** *n.* indication, inference, guess

**implicit** *adj.* UNDERSTOOD: implied; DEFINITE: certain, absolute, accurate, inevitable

**imply** *v.* indicate, intimate, suggest, hint, implicate, signify, mean, indicate

**impolite** *adj.* discourteous, churlish, rude, sullen

**impolitic** *adj.* imprudent, unwise

**import** *n.* meaning, signification

**importance** *n.* import, consequence, bearing, influence, emphasis, weight, relevance

**important** *adj.* WEIGHTY: significant, momentous, essential, critical, primary, foremost, valuable, crucial, vital, serious, consequential;

EMINENT: illustrious, well–known, influential, famous

**importune** *v.* urge, entreat, press, implore

**impose** *v.* force, presume, burden, compel

**imposing** *adj.* stirring, overwhelming, impressive

**imposition** *n.* burden, pressure, encumbrance, demand, restraint

**impossibility** *n.* hopelessness, difficulty, futility

**impossible** *adj.* inconceivable, vain, unattainable, insurmountable, unworkable, futile, hopeless

**impostor** *n.* fraud, deceiver, pretender, charlatan

**imposture** *n.* ruse, deceit, hoax, sham

**impotent** *adj.* WEAK: powerless, inept, infirm, unable; STERILE: barren, frigid, unproductive

**impound** *v.* appropriate, take, usurp, seize

**impoverish** *v.* bankrupt, exhaust, ruin, destroy

**impoverished** *adj.* bankrupt, broke, poor, insolvent, destitute, ruined

**impractical** *adj.* unrealistic, unworkable, improbable, illogical, absurd, wild, impossible, idealistic

**impregnable** *adj.* invulnerable, unassailable, impenetrable

**impregnate** *v.* **PERMEATE:** fill, pervade, soak, infuse; **BEGET:** conceive, reproduce, fertilize

**impress** *v.* **MARK:** indent, emboss, imprint, dent, stamp; **FASCINATE:** affect, dazzle, stir, fascinate

**impression** *n.* **MARK:** imprint, dent, indentation, depression; **EFFECT:** response, reaction; **NOTION:** theory, conjecture, supposition, opinion

**impressionable** *adj.* perceptive, receptive, affected

**impressive** *adj.* stirring, moving, inspiring, thrilling, intense, dramatic, absorbing, profound, remarkable, extraordinary, notable, momentous

**imprint** *n.* **IDENTIFICATION:** emblem, banner, trademark; **IMPRESSION:** dent, indentation

**imprint** *v.* print, stamp, mark, designate

**imprison** *v.* jail, confine, incarcerate, detain, hold, intern, cage, enclose

**improbable** *adj.* doubtful, unlikely

**improper** *adj.* indecent, incongruous, inadvisable, untimely, inappropriate, unbefitting, unsuitable

**improve** *v.* update, refine, enrich, enhance, augment

**improvement** *n.* betterment, advancement, development, growth, enrichment, renovation, reorganization, amendment, revision, refinement, modernization, enhancement

**impudent** *adj.* bold, insolent, rude

**impulse** *n.* **THROB:** surge, beat, pulsation; **FANCY:** urge, stimulus, whim, caprice, notion, spontaneity, inclination, disposition

**impulsive** *adj.* impetuous, spontaneous

**impure** *adj.* adulterated, diluted, debased, tainted, contaminated, polluted, corrupted, doctored

**impute** *v.* ascribe, assign, charge

**inability** *n.* incompetence, incapacity, shortcoming, failure, weakness, lack, frailty

**inaccessible** *adj.* distant, rare, remote, separated

**inaccuracy** *n.* mistake, exaggeration, deception, error

**inaccurate** *adj.* incorrect, inexact, fallacious, incorrect, mistaken, wrong

**inactive** *adj.* idle, lazy, dormant, still, motionless

**inadequacy** *n.* inferiority, weakness, defect, flaw, drawback, shortcoming, blemish, lack

**inadequate** *adj.* insufficient, lacking, scanty, meager, deficient, imperfect, defective, unsatisfactory

**inane** *adj.* senseless, pointless, foolish, silly

**inanimate** *adj.* lifeless, dull, inert, idle, motionless

**inappropriate** *adj.* improper, unsuitable

**inapt** *adj.* unfit, unsuitable

**inarticulate** *adj.* **MUTE:** reticent, speechless, wordless; **INCOMPREHENSIBLE:** obscure, unintelligible, vague

**inattentive** *adj.* preoccupied, indifferent, negligent, careless, diverted

**inaugurate** *v.* induct, begin, introduce, initiate, begin

**incalculable** *adj.* unpredictable, uncertain

**incantation** *n.* chant, charm, recitation, supplication

**incapable** *adj.* inadequate, incompetent, inexperienced, naïve, poor, unqualified, unsuited

**incapacitate** *v.* disable, disqualify, invalidate

**incarcerate** *v.* confine, imprison

**incarnate** *adj.* bodily, manifest, personified

**incense** *n.* scent, fragrance, essence, perfume

**incense** *v.* inflame, anger, infuriate

**incentive** *n.* motive, spur, inducement, stimulus, impetus, enticement, temptation, inspiration, encouragement, reason

**incessant** *adj.* continual, ceaseless, constant

**inchoate** *adj.* shapeless, formless

**incidence** *n.* range, occurrence, scope

**incident** *n.* occurrence, happening, episode, event

**incidental** *adj.* subsidiary, related, subordinate

**incinerate** *v.* burn, cremate

**incise** *v.* cut, engrave, dissect, chop, split, divide

**incision** *n.* cut, gash, slash, surgery

**incisive** *adj.* cutting, keen, sarcastic, trenchant

**incite** *v.* rouse, stir, stimulate, provoke, spur, goad, persuade, induce, urge, inspire

**inclement** *adj.* stormy, severe; cruel, merciless

**inclination** *n.* TENDENCY: bias, bent, propensity, predilection, penchant, leaning, disposition, preference, drift, trend; SLANT: pitch, slope, incline, angle, ramp, bank, lean, list, grade

**incline** *v.* LEAN: tilt, bow, nod; TEND: prefer, favor

**inclined** *adj.* SLOPING: leaning, slanted, angled; TENDING: likely, prone

**include** *v.* contain, embrace, involve, incorporate, constitute, interject, insert

**inclusive** *adj.* including, incorporating

**incoherent** *adj.* UNCONNECTED: disorganized; INDISTINCT: unintelligible, muddled, muttered, muffled

**income** *n.* revenue, earnings, commission, salary, wages, profit, dividends, proceeds, receipts

**incommensurate** *adj.* disproportionate, inadequate

**incomparable** *adj.* excellent, exceptional, matchless, perfect, superior, unequaled, unique, unusual

**incompatible** *adj.* irreconcilable, incongruous, contrary, clashing, contradictory, inconstant, discordant

**incompetent** *adj.* incapable, unfit, unskilled, bungling, ineffectual, clumsy, awkward, inexperienced

**incomplete** *adj.* imperfect, rough, unfinished

**inconceivable** *adj.* unthinkable, unbelievable

**incongruous** *adj.* inconsistent, contradictory

**inconsequential** *adj.* irrelevant, trivial, unnecessary

**inconsiderate** *adj.* thoughtless, boorish, impolite, discourteous, rude

**inconsistent** *adj.* illogical, contradictory, incoherent

**inconspicuous** *adj.* concealed, hidden, obscure

**inconstant** *adj.* varying, fickle

**inconvenience** *n.* trouble, discomfort, bother

**incorporation** *n.* embodiment, addition

**incorrect** *adj.* false, mistaken, unreliable, wrong

**incorrigible** *adj.* bad, difficult

**increase** *n.* growth, addition, development, spread, enlargement, expansion, escalation

**increase** *v.* extend, enlarge, expand, dilate, broaden, widen, thicken, deepen, build, lengthen, augment, escalate, amplify, supplement

**incredible** *adj.* unbelievable, improbable, ridiculous

**incredulous** *adj.* disbelieving, skeptical

**incriminate** *v.* charge, involve, implicate, blame

**incumbent** *adj.* binding, obligatory

**incurable** *adj.* fatal, serious, hopeless, deadly

**incursion** *n.* inroad, invasion

**indebted** *adj.* obligated, grateful, appreciative

**indecent** *adj.* offensive, immoral, bad, lewd, shameful

**indecency** *n.* vulgarity, impropriety

**indecision** *n.* hesitation, doubt, uncertainty

**indecisive** *adj.* irresolute, unstable

**indefinite** *adj.* vague, uncertain, unsure, unsettled

**indelible** *adj.* ingrained, enduring, strong, permanent

**indemnify** *v.* compensate, protect

**indentation** *n.* imprint, recession, depression, dent

**independence** *n.* freedom, sovereignty, license

**indestructible** *adj.* durable, immortal, permanent

**index** *v.* list, catalog, alphabetize, arrange, tabulate

**indicate** *v.* SIGNIFY: symbolize, betoken, intimate, mean; DESIGNATE: show, name, point

**indication** *n.* symptom, evidence, sign, hint

**indicator** *n.* dial, pointer

**indictment** *n.* accusation, detention, incrimination

**indifferent** *adj.* unconcerned, cool, unemotional, unsympathetic, heartless, unresponsive, unfeeling, nonchalant, impassive, detached, callous, stony, remote, reserved, distant, arrogant, unmoved

**indigent** *adj.* destitute, impoverished, poor

**indignant** *adj.* angry, upset, displeased, piqued

**indignity** *n.* affront, humiliation, injury, insult

**indirect** *adj.* devious, roundabout, tortuous, twisting, devious, sinister, rambling, oblique

**indiscreet** *adj.* imprudent, rash, misguided, tactless

**indiscriminate** *adj.* random, chaotic, aimless

**indispensable** *adj.* necessary, required, essential

**indisposed** *adj.* ILL: ailing, sickly, weak; DISINCLINED: reluctant, unwilling

**indisputable** *adj.* incontrovertible, undeniable, undoubted, unquestionable, certain

**indistinct** *adj.* vague, confused, indefinite, obscure

**individual** *adj.* personal, particular, solitary, distinctive, personalized, sole, private

**indoctrinate** *v.* instruct, implant, influence, teach

**indomitable** *adj.* invincible, unconquerable

**induce** *v.* begin, cause, effect, persuade, instigate, produce

**inducement** *n.* incentive, influence, motive, stimulus

**induct** *v.* admit, recruit, enroll, conscript, draft

**induction** *n.* **REASONING:** rationalization, conjecture, reason; **INITIATION:** ordination, consecration

**indulge** *v.* humor, coddle, entertain, gratify

**indulgence** *n.* **HUMORING:** coddling, pampering, spoiling, placating, gratifying; **REVELRY:** intemperance, greed, waste

**industrious** *adj.* diligent, intent, involved, active, busy

**industry** *n.* perseverance, persistence, application, enterprise, zeal, attention

**inebriate** *v.* exhilarate, intoxicate, stupefy

**ineffective** *adj.* inadequate, incompetent, weak

**inefficient** *adj.* prodigal, wasteful, improvident

**ineligible** *adj.* unqualified, unsuitable, unfit

**inept** *adj.* bungling, clumsy, incompetent, awkward

**inert** *adj.* inactive, sluggish, still, dormant, idle

**inevitable** *adj.* unavoidable, irresistible, fated, sure, inescapable, destined, unalterable, ordained

**inexorable** *adj.* rigid, stubborn, inflexible

**inexperienced** *adj.* unskilled, untried, youthful, new, immature, tender, raw, green

**infallible** *adj.* perfect, accurate, certain

**infamous** *adj.* notorious, wicked, heinous, offensive

**infant** *n.* baby, minor, child, tot

**infantile** *adj.* childlike, juvenile, childish, naïve

**infect** *v.* taint, defile, spoil

**infer** *v.* deduce, conclude, gather, assume

**inferior** *adj.* subordinate, mediocre, common, poor

**inferiority** *n.* deficiency, inadequacy, weakness

**infernal** *adj.* fiendish, devilish

**infest** *v.* **CONTAMINATE:** pollute, infect, corrupt; **INVADE:** crowd, jam, teem, flood, flock, overwhelm

**infidelity** *n.* unfaithfulness, disloyalty, adultery

**infiltrate** *v.* permeate, pervade, penetrate, join

**infinite** *adj.* endless, limitless, countless, incalculable, boundless, immense, endless

**infinitesimal** *adj.* tiny, small

**infirm** *adj.* sickly, decrepit, weak

**infirmary** *n.* clinic, sickroom, hospital

**infirmity** *n.* disease, weakness, frailty, debility

**inflame** *v.* **AROUSE:** incense, disturb, excite; **HURT:** redden, swell; **BURN:** kindle, scorch, ignite

**inflate** *v.* **DISTEND:** expand, swell, bloat, balloon; **EXAGGERATE:** magnify, overestimate, raise

**inflection** *n.* tone, enunciation, intonation, accent

**inflexibility** *n.* toughness, rigidity, stiffness, firmness

**inflexible** *adj.* rigid, unyielding, taut, firm, stiff

**inflict** *v.* impose, administer, deliver, strike, cause

**influence** *n.* power, authority, control, command, esteem, prominence, prestige, reputation

**influence** *v.* affect, impress, compel, urge, shape, convince, persuade, motivate

**influential** *adj.* prominent, substantial, powerful, important, significant

**inform** *v.* tell, betray, instruct, relate, teach

**informal** *adj.* casual, intimate, relaxed, natural, unofficial

**information** *n.* NEWS: report, notice, message; KNOWLEDGE: facts, evidence, details, statistics, data

**infraction** *n.* violation, breach

**infrequent** *adj.* seldom, occasional, scarce, rare

**infringe** *v.* encroach, trespass, transgress, meddle

**infuriate** *v.* aggravate, enrage, provoke, anger

**infuse** *v.* fill, inspire; steep

**ingenious** *adj.* able, clever, cunning, intelligent, gifted, original, resourceful, shrewd, skillful

**ingenuity** *n.* cleverness, imagination, inventiveness, originality, productiveness, resourcefulness

**ingenuous** *adj.* candid, innocent, straightforward

**ingrain** *v.* imbue, fix, instill, teach

**ingratiate** *v.* charm, seduce, disarm

**ingredient** *n.* component, constituent, element

**inhabit** *v.* dwell, occupy, reside, stay

**inhabitant** *n.* occupant, dweller, lodger, roomer, boarder, tenant, resident

**inherent** *adj.* inborn, inbred, inherited, innate, intrinsic, native, natural

**inherit** *v.* acquire, receive, succeed, get

**inheritance** *n.* bequest, legacy, heritage, gift

**inhibit** *v.* check, restrain, repress, frustrate, hinder

**inhibition** *n.* restraint, hindrance, interference, constraint

**inhuman** *adj.* mean, heartless, cruel, fierce, ruthless

**iniquity** *n.* crime, evil, injustice, sin, wickedness, wrong, abomination

**initial** *adj.* beginning, starting, basic, primary, elementary, first, fundamental

**initiate** *n.* beginner, learner, novice

**initiation** *n.* beginning, introduction; indoctrination, induction, orientation

**initiative** *n.* enterprise, responsibility, enthusiasm, ambition

**injure** *v.* harm, damage, wound, abuse, hurt, wrong

**injurious** *adj.* harmful, detrimental, damaging

**injury** *n.* hurt, abrasion, wound, laceration, affliction

**injustice** *n.* infringement, transgression, violation, breach, infraction, wrong

**inkling** *n.* hint, indication, notion, innuendo, suspicion, suggestion

**inmate** *n.* occupant, patient, convict, prisoner

**inn** *n.* tavern, hostel, hotel, motel, resort

**innate** *adj.* inborn, native

**innermost** *adj.* intimate, private, secret

**innocence** *n.* honesty, simplicity, purity, naïveté, chastity, ignorance, virtue

**innocent** *adj.* **PURE:** unblemished, wholesome, upright, virtuous, righteous, angelic; **GUILTLESS:** honest, blameless, faultless; **OPEN:** guileless, frank, childish, naïve, natural, simple; **HARMLESS:** innocuous, inoffensive, safe

**innovation** *n.* change, newness, addition

**innuendo** *n.* hint, insinuation, aside, intimation

**innumerable** *adj.* countless, incalculable, infinite

**inopportune** *adj.* disadvantageous, ill-timed, inappropriate, awkward, untimely

**input** *n.* data, information, knowledge, facts

**input** *v.* add, enter

**inquest** *n.* inquiry, investigation

**inquire** *v.* ask, investigate, probe

**inquiry** *n.* probe, analysis, hearing, examination

**inquisitive** *adj.* curious, questioning, analytical, meddling, prying, snoopy, nosy, interested

**inquisitor** *n.* examiner, questioner

**inroad** *n.* encroachment, invasion

**insane** *adj.* DEMENTED: crazed, frenzied, lunatic, balmy, psychotic, raving, deluded, possessed, obsessed

**insanity** *n.* abnormality, dementia, psychosis, neurosis, phobia, mania

**insatiate** *adj.* ravenous, voracious

**inscribe** *v.* address, carve, dedicate, engrave, write

**inscription** *n.* dedication, engraving, legend

**insecure** *adj.* anxious, vague, uncertain, troubled

**insert** *v.* introduce, place, inject, include

**insidious** *adj.* treacherous, deceitful, corrupting, harmful

**insight** *n.* perspicacity, shrewdness, intelligence, intuition, wisdom, understanding

**insignia** *n.* badge, rank, ensign, symbol, decoration, emblem

**insignificant** *adj.* trivial, unimportant, irrelevant, petty, trifling

**insincere** *adj.* deceitful, pretentious, dishonest, shifty, false, hypocritical, sly

**insinuate** *v.* hint, suggest, imply, purport, mention

**insipid** *adj.* dull, flat, tasteless, uninteresting, bland

**insist** *v.* persist, demand, exhort, urge

**insolent** *adj.* disrespectful, insulting, rude, impertinent, overbearing

**insolvent** *adj.* bankrupt, broke, failed, ruined

**inspect** *v.* examine, probe, scrutinize, scan, audit

**inspiration** *n.* **IDEA:** notion, whim, fancy, impulse, thought; **STIMULUS:** spur, influence, incentive

**inspire** *v.* encourage, enthuse, invigorate, motivate, stimulate

**install** *v.* establish, introduce, inaugurate

**installation** *n.* induction, ordination, inauguration, launching, establishment

**installment** *n.* payment, part

**instance** *n.* example, case, situation, occurrence

**instant** *adj.* momentary, quick, pressing, current

**instantly** *adv.* urgently, directly, immediately

**instigate** *v.* incite, initiate, spur, urge

**instill** *v.* infuse, indoctrinate, implant, teach

**instinct** *n.* impulse, sense, intuition

**instinctive** *adj.* intuitive, spontaneous, natural

**institute** *n.* establishment, foundation, organization

**institute** *v.* establish, found, launch, organize

**institution** *n.* establishment, organization, company, association, business, university

**instruct** *v.* inform, teach, order, direct, educate

**instruction** *n.* guidance, direction, education

**instructor** *n.* professor, tutor, lecturer, teacher

**instrument** *n.* **UTENSIL:** apparatus, implement, device, tool; **CONTRACT:** deed, document

**insubordinate** *adj.* disobedient, mutinous, treacherous, defiant, rebellious

**insufferable** *adj.* difficult, intolerable, unbearable

**insufficient** *adj.* meager, skimpy, inadequate

**insular** *adj.* detached, isolated, narrow, provincial

**insult** *n.* affront, indignity, abuse, impudence, impertinence, insolence, mockery, derision, invective

**insult** *v.* offend, mock, annoy, taunt, ridicule, provoke

**insurance** *n.* security, indemnity, assurance, warrant

**insure** *v.* secure, warrant, protect, guarantee

**insurrection** *n.* uprising, rebellion, insurgence, revolt

**intact** *adj.* entire, whole, together

**intangible** *adj.* indefinite, uncertain, vague

**integral** *adj.* **WHOLE:** entire; **NECESSARY:** essential

**integrate** *v.* blend, combine, mix

**integrity** *n.* morality, honesty, uprightness, honor

**intellect** *n.* understanding, intelligence, mentality

**intellectual** *adj.* smart, creative, intelligent, learned, reasonable, sensible

**intellectual** *n.* highbrow, genius, philosopher, academician, egghead, brain

**intelligence** *n.* **UNDERSTANDING:** discernment, comprehension, judgment; **INTELLECT:** mind, brain, mentality; **INFORMATION:** statistics, facts, news

**intelligent** *adj.* clever, bright, smart, brilliant, keen, perceptive, imaginative, discerning, knowledgeable, understanding, quick, sharp, comprehending

**intelligentsia** *n.* intellectuals, elite, literati, aristocrats

**intelligible** *adj.* understandable, comprehensible, plain, clear, obvious

**intend** *v.* **PROPOSE:** purpose, aspire, aim, plan; **MEAN:** indicate, signify, denote

**intense** *adj.* deep, profound, heightened, impassioned, exaggerated, violent, excessive, keen, piercing, cutting, severe

**intensify** *v.* enhance, heighten, sharpen, emphasize, increase, strengthen

**intensity** *n.* concentration, strength, fervor, power, force, passion, ardor, severity

**intensive** *adj.* accelerated, hard, fast, severe

**intent** *adj.* fixed, absorbed

**intent** *n.* design, plan

**intention** *n.* purpose, aim, end, plan

**intentional** *adj.* deliberate, planned

**inter** *v.* bury, entomb

**intercept** *v.* obstruct, ambush, block, hijack

**intercession** *n.* entreaty, petition, mediation, plea

**interchange** *n.* **BARTER:** trade, exchange, substitution; **INTERSECTION:** cloverleaf, off–ramp

**interest** *n.* **CONCERN:** attention, excitement, curiosity, enthusiasm; **SHARE:** claim, right, stake

**interest** *v.* arouse, involve, fascinate, intrigue, attract, amuse, please, entertain

**interested** *adj.* **AROUSED:** stimulated, curious, responsive, roused, stirred, attracted; **OCCUPIED:** engrossed, obsessed, absorbed, involved

**interesting** *adj.* intriguing, fascinating, engaging, absorbing, captivating

**interfere** *v.* meddle, intervene, interpose, interlope

**interference** *n.* **MEDDLING:** interruption, trespassing, tampering; **OBSTRUCTION:** check, obstacle, restraint

**interior** *adj.* within, inside, inland, inner, internal, inward, central, inside

**interlope** *v.* interfere, intrude, meddle

**intermediate** *adj.* intervening, medium, intermediary, median, central, middle

**intermediary** *n.* mediator, agent

**intermission** *n.* pause, interval, interim

**intermix** *v.* mix, mingle, blend

**intermittent** *adj.* cyclic, recurring, periodic, recurrent, changing, irregular

**intern** *v.* confine, detain, imprison

**internal** *adj.* interior, inner, domestic, inside, inward, intrinsic, innate, inherent

**interpret** *v.* translate, explain, render, delineate, define, describe

**interpretation** *n.* rendition, description, representation, presentation, explanation

**interrogate** *v.* question, ask, examine

**interrogation** *n.* inquiry, investigation, examination

**interrupt** *v.* intervene, interfere, infringe

**intersperse** *v.* scatter, strew

**interval** *n.* time, period, interlude, interim, pause

**intervene** *v.* intercede, mediate, negotiate, reconcile

**intervention** *n.* intercession, interruption, interference, intrusion

**interview** *n.* meeting, audience, conference

**interview** *v.* interrogate, question, examine

**intimacy** *n.* closeness, familiarity, affection

**intimate** *adj.* familiar, close, trusted, secret, special

**intimate** *n.* friend, associate, companion, lover

**intimate** *v.* hint, allude

**intimidate** *v.* frighten, threaten

**intolerable** *adj.* insufferable, unendurable, unbearable, impossible, offensive, painful, undesirable

**intolerant** *adj.* dogmatic, bigoted, prejudiced

**intoxicate** *v.* inebriate, muddle, befuddle

**intransigence** *n.* obstinacy, stubbornness

**intransigent** *adj.* intolerant, uncompromising, stubborn

**intricacy** *n.* elaborateness, complexity, difficulty

**intricate** *adj.* involved, complex, tricky, abstruse, difficult, obscure

**intrigue** *v.* **SCHEME:** plot, devise; **DELIGHT:** please, attract, fascinate, charm, entertain

**intrinsic** *adj.* essential, inborn, inherent

**introduce** *v.* **PRESENT:** submit, advance, offer, propose, acquaint; **INSERT:** add, enter, include

**introduction** *n.* **ADMITTANCE:** initiation, installation, entrance; **PRESENTATION:** debut, acquaintance, start, awakening, baptism; **PREFACE:** preamble, foreword, prologue, overture

**introductory** *adj.* opening, early, starting, beginning, preparatory, primary, original

**introvert** *n.* loner, recluse

**intrude** *v.* encroach, trespass, interfere, meddle

**intuition** *n.* instinct, hunch, feeling, foreknowledge

**intuitive** *adj.* instinctive, natural

**inure** *v.* acclimate, accustom

**inured** *adj.* hardened, cold, unfeeling

**invade** *v.* attack, intrude. infringe, trespass, interfere

**invader** *n.* trespasser, alien, attacker, enemy

**invalidate** *v.* void, revoke, annul, refute, nullify

**invaluable** *adj.* priceless, expensive, dear, valuable

**invariable** *adj.* unchanging, uniform, static, constant

**invective** *adj.* railing, abusive

**inveigh** *v.* protest, declaim, harangue, rant

**inveigle** *v.* coax, entice, flatter

**invent** *v.* create, discover, originate, devise, fashion, form, design, improvise, contrive, build

**invention** *n.* contrivance, contraption, design, innovation

**inventory** *n.* **LIST:** itemization, register, index, record; **INSPECTION:** examination, summary

**inverse** *adj.* reversed, contrary

**invert** *v.* **UPSET:** overturn, tip; **REVERSE:** change, transpose, exchange

**investigate** *v.* inquire, review, examine, analyze, scrutinize, study

**investigation** *n.* inquiry search research examination

**inveterate** *adj.* addicted, well–established, persisting

**invidious** *adj.* envious, malicious, spiteful

**invigorate** *v.* animate, energize, enervate, enliven, excite, exhilarate, freshen, stimulate

**invincible** *adj.* impregnable, invulnerable, powerful, strong, unconquerable

**inviolate** *adj.* hallowed, holy, intact, pure, sacred

**inviting** *adj.* appealing, attractive, encouraging, tempting

**invocation** *n.* prayer, appeal

**invoice** *n.* notice, statement, bill, receipt

**invoke** *v.* implore, solicit, summon

**involuntary** *adj.* unintentional, uncontrolled, instinctive, automatic, habitual

**involve** *v.* associate, commit, connect, comprise, connect, entangle, implicate, include, link

**involved** *adj.* **COMPLICATED:** elaborate, entangled, intricate, sophisticated;

IMPLICATED: con-
nected, emotional,
engrossed, incrimi-
nated

**invulnerable** *adj.* secure, strong, invinci-
ble, indestructible,
formidable, safe

**iota** *n.* jot, particle,
trace, scrap, grain,
bit, speck

**irascible** *adj.* irritable,
temperamental, testy,
touchy, petulant,
cranky

**irate** *adj.* enraged, furious, incensed, agi-
tated, angry

**irk** *v.* vex, annoy, harass, disturb, bother

**irony** *n.* satire, ridicule, mockery, deri-
sion, sarcasm

**irrational** *adj.* illogical,
unreasoning, spe-
cious, fallacious,
wrong, senseless,
silly, ridiculous

**irreconcilable** *adj.* implacable, incompati-
ble

**irrefutable** *adj.* conclusive, evident, in-
disputable, obvious,
undeniable

**irregular** *adj.* UNEVEN:
rough, fitful, random,
occasional, fluctuat-
ing, wavering, inter-
mittent, variable, spo-
radic; QUESTIONABLE:
strange, debatable,
suspicious; UNIQUE:
abnormal, extraordi-
nary, unusual

**irrelevant** *adj.* immaterial, unrelated, ex-
traneous, pointless,
trivial, unnecessary

**irreparable** *adj.* incurable, hopeless, irre-
versible, destroyed,
ruined

**irresistible** *adj.* compelling, overpowering,
overwhelming, pow-
erful

**irresponsible** *adj.* capricious, thoughtless,
flighty, fickle, rash,
unstable, lax, shift-
less, unreliable

**irrevocable** *adj.* permanent, indelible, in-
evitable

**irritable** *adj.* cranky,
testy, touchy, huffy,
peevish, petulant,
surly, moody, churl-
ish, grouchy, grumpy

**irritant** *n.* annoyance, bother, nuisance

**irritate** *v.* **BOTHER:** exasperate, pester, disturb, annoy; **INFLAME:** redden, chafe, sting, burn, hurt, itch

**irritated** *adj.* annoyed, disturbed, upset, bothered

**island** *n.* isle, bar, archipelago

**isolate** *v.* detach, insulate, confine, seclude, divide

**isolation** *n.* solitude, seclusion, segregation, confinement, separation

**issue** *n.* **DISTRIBUTION:** publication; **TOPIC:** subject, concern, argument; **EDITION:** number, copy

**issue** *v.* **EMERGE:** proceed, appear, begin; **RELEASE:** circulate, announce, advertise, declare, publish

**itemize** *v.* list, catalog, enumerate, number, detail

**itinerant** *adj.* traveling, roving, nomadic, wandering

**itinerant** *n.* wanderer, nomad, vagrant, tramp

**jab** *v.* poke, punch, hit, blow

**jacket** *n.* coat, tunic, jerkin, parka, cape

**jackpot** *n.* bonanza, winnings, luck, profit, success

**jaded** *adj.* cold, impassive, indifferent, nonchalant, world–weary

**jail** *n.* penitentiary, cage, cell, dungeon, bastille, stockade, prison, lockup

**jam** *n.* **PRESERVES:** conserve, marmalade, jelly; **TROUBLE:** dilemma, problem, difficulty

**jam** *v.* compress, bind, squeeze, push, pack, press

**jar** *n.* **CONTAINER:** crock, vessel, beaker, cruet, bottle, flagon, flask; **JOLT:** jounce, thud, thump, bump

**jargon** *n.* argot, patois, idiom, vernacular, colloquialism, localism, dialect, slang

**jaunt** *n.* excursion, trip, tour, journey, walk

**jaunty** *adj.* buoyant, chipper, dashing, frisky, rakish

**jealous** *adj.* envious, possessive, resentful

**jeer** *n.* derision, ridicule, taunt

**jeer** *v.* deride, insult, mock, ridicule, taunt

**jell** *v.* set, harden, stiffen, thicken

**jeopardize** *v.* endanger, imperil, expose, venture, risk

**jeopardy** *n.* danger, peril, hazard, chance

**jerk** *n.* **TWITCH:** tic, shake, quiver; **DOLT:** scamp, scoundrel, fool, rascal

**jerk** *v.* **SPASM:** quiver, shiver, shake, twitch; **PULL:** yank, snatch, seize

**jest** *v.* joke, tease, spoof, scoff, deride

**jester** *n.* comedian, buffoon, joker, actor, clown, fool

**jetty** *n.* pier, wharf

**jewel** *n.* prize, bauble, gem, trinket

**jewelry** *n.* bangles, gems, baubles, trinkets, adornment

**jiggle** *v.* shake, twitch, wiggle, jerk

**jingle** *n.* rhyme, verse

**jingle** *v.* tinkle, clink, rattle

**jinx** *n.* hex, spell

**job** *n.* **EMPLOYMENT:** situation, position, calling, vocation, career, pursuit, business, profession, trade; **TASK:** assignment, undertaking, project, chore, errand, duty; **ASSIGNMENT:** output, duty

**jobber** *n.* broker, wholesaler

**jocular** *adj.* comic, frolicsome, funny, witty

**jocund** *adj.* cheerful, happy, joyful, light-hearted

**jog** *v.* **TROT:** canter, lope, nudge, run; **NUDGE:** bump, jar, jostle, shake

**join** *v.* unite, blend, combine, connect, couple, attach, link, fuse, associate

**joint** *adj.* joined, shared, united

**joint** *n.* juncture, union, coupling, hinge, link, seam, connection; **DIVE:** hangout, bar, tavern

**joke** *v.* jest, quip, banter, laugh, play, frolic, wisecrack

**jolly** *adj.* gay, merry, joyful, happy

**jolt** *n.* **BUMP:** jar, bounce, blow, jerk; **SURPRISE:** jar, start, shock, surprise

**jostle** *v.* push, elbow, nudge

**jot** *n.* bit, iota

**jot** *v.* write, note, scribble, record

**journal** *n.* **DIARY:** almanac, chronicle, record; **PERIODICAL:** publication, newspaper, magazine, daily

**journalist** *n.* columnist, commentator, reporter

**journey** *n.* trip, tour, excursion, jaunt, travel

**jovial** *adj.* affable, amiable, merry, happy

**joy** *n.* mirth, delight, playfulness, gaiety, geniality, merriment, levity, jubilation, laughter

**joyful** *adj.* elated, glad, happy, joyous, jubilant

**joyous** *adj.* blithe, glad, gay, happy

**jubilant** *adj.* ecstatic, elated, exuberant, delighted, rapturous, joyous

**jubilee** *n.* anniversary, celebration

**judge** *n.* **MODERATOR:** arbiter, referee, umpire; **CONNOISSEUR:** analyst, critic, expert, specialist

**judge** *v.* hear, decide, adjudicate, rule

**judgment** *n.* **DISCERNMENT:** discrimination, taste; **DECISION:** determination, analysis, pronouncement, conclusion, verdict

**judgmental** *adj.* biased, prejudiced, unfair

**judicial** *adj.* legalistic, administrative, lawful

**judicious** *adj.* prudent, discreet, sound, sensible, practical, reasonable

**jug** *n.* crock, flask, pitcher, container

**juice** *n.* sap, extract, fluid, liquid

**juicy** *adj.* succulent, moist, watery, syrupy

**jumble** *n.* clutter, mess, hodgepodge, confusion

**jump** *v.* **LEAP:** vault, spring, lunge, bound, skip, hurdle; **ACCOST:** attack; **PLUMMET:** plunge, dive, fall

**junction** *n.* **MEETING:** joining, coupling, joint; **CROSSROADS:** crossing, intersection

**juncture** *n.* joining, junction

**jungle** *n.* tangle, wilderness, undergrowth, forest

**junior** *adj.* younger, lower

**junk** *n.* scrap, waste, garbage, filth, trash

**junk** *v.* abandon, discard

**junket** *n.* picnic, excursion, trip

**jurisdiction** *n.* authority, range, province, scope, domain, empire, sovereignty

**jurist** *n.* judge, attorney, adviser, lawyer

**jury** *n.* council, committee, tribunal, panel

**just** *adj.* **PRECISE:** exact, correct, perfect, accurate; **HARDLY:** barely, scarcely; **ONLY:** merely, simply, plainly; **FAIR:** impartial, equal, righteous

**justice** *n.* **FAIRNESS:** right, truth, equity; **LAWFULNESS:** legality, legitimacy, sanction, constitutionality, authority, custom; **ADMINISTRATION:** adjudication, arbitration, hearing, trial, litigation, judgment; **JUDGE:** magistrate, umpire, chancellor

**justification** *n.* excuse, defense, reason, explanation

**justify** *v.* **VINDICATE:** absolve, acquit, clear, excuse, exonerate; **EXPLAIN:** apologize, excuse, defend

**jut** *adj.* extend, bulge, project

**juvenile** *adj.* childish, youthful, adolescent, teenage

**juxtapose** *v.* compare, contrast

**keen** *adj.* **ASTUTE:** clever, intelligent, shrewd; **EAGER:** ardent, intent, zealous; **SHARP:** pointed, edged

**keep** *v.* **HOLD:** retain, possess, have, seize, save; **MAINTAIN:** preserve, retain, conserve; **STORE:** hoard, stash, cache, preserve; **REMAIN:** stay, continue, abide, settle; **CONTINUE:** sustain, endure;

**keepsake** *n.* memento, token, remembrance

**keg** *n.* cask, drum, vat, barrel

**kernel** *n.* seed, grain, core, nut, germ

**kettle** *n.* vessel, cauldron, saucepan, pot

**key** *n.* **OPENER:** latchkey, passkey; **SOLUTION:** clue, code, indicator, answer

**kickback** *n.* **BRIBE:** grease, payback, tribute; **BACKLASH:** backfire, reaction, recoil

**kickoff** *adj.* start, opening, beginning, launching

**kid** *n.* child, son, daughter, tot, boy, girl

**kid** *v.* mock, tease

**kidnap** *v.* abduct, capture, shanghai

**kill** *v.* **SLAY:** slaughter, murder, assassinate, massacre, butcher, finish, execute, liquidate, dispatch; **VETO:** cancel, prohibit, refuse, forbid; **CANCEL:** annul, nullify, counteract

**killer** *n.* murderer, gangster, assassin, cutthroat

**killjoy** *n.* grouch, sourpuss, spoilsport

**kiln** *n.* dryer, oast, oven

**kind** *adj.* accommodating, agreeable, considerate, charitable, compassionate, generous, loving, tender, tactful, kindhearted, sensitive

**kind** *n.* CLASS: classification, species, genus; TYPE: sort, variety, description, designation

**kindhearted** *adj.* amiable, generous, good, humane

**kindle** *v.* fire, excite, light, ignite

**kindly** *adj.* generous, helpful, good, humane, kind

**kindness** *n.* TENDERNESS: consideration, thoughtfulness, humanity, understanding, compassion, graciousness, kindheartedness; SERVICE: benevolence, philanthropy, lift, boost, help

**kindred** *adj.* alike, kin, connected, related, similar

**kingdom** *n.* realm, domain, country, empire, principality, dominions, territory

**kink** *n.* bend, obstacle, hitch

**kinship** *n.* affiliation, relationship, connection, alliance, family

**kit** *n.* EQUIPMENT: material, tools, outfit; PACK: poke, knapsack, satchel, bag, container

**knack** *n.* dexterity, trick, skill, faculty, ability

**knapsack** *n.* sack, bag, pack, kit, rucksack

**knead** *v.* work, shape, twist, press

**kneel** *v.* genuflect, bend, stoop, bow, curtsey

**knickknack** *n.* bric–a–brac, curio, ornament, trifle, bauble, trinket, showpiece, gewgaw

**knife** *n.* blade, dagger, stiletto, lancet, machete, scalpel, dirk

**knit** *v.* unite, join, intermingle, affiliate

**knob** *n.* PROJECTION: bulge, protuberance, bulge, node, bump; HANDLE: doorknob, latch

**knock** *v.* rap, strike, thump, whack, beat, tap, hit

**knoll** *n.* mound, hill, hillock

**knot** *n.* **FASTENING:** bond, cinch, hitch, tie, splice; **CLUSTER:** group, crowd, gang; **SNARL:** snag tangle twist

**know** *v.* **UNDERSTAND:** comprehend, apprehend; **RECOGNIZE:** perceive, discern, acknowledge

**knowing** *adj.* **SHREWD:** acute, clever, intelligent, reasonable, sharp; **DELIBERATE:** conscious, intentional

**knowledge** *n.* information, learning, lore, wisdom, enlightenment, expertise, awareness, insight

**label** *n.* tag, marker, identification, name

**label** *v.* identify, mark, name, specify

**labor** *n.* **TASK:** work, activity, toil, operation, employment, undertaking, job; **EXERTION:** energy, industry, diligence, strain, stress, effort

**labor** *v.* work, toil, strive

**laborious** *adj.* arduous, difficult, exhausting, onerous

**lace** *v.* fasten, tie, adorn, strap, bind, close

**lacerate** *v.* wound, tear, injure, damage

**lacing** *n.* bond, hitch, tie, fastener, knot

**lack** *n.* **ABSENCE:** deficiency, scarcity, insufficiency, inadequacy; **WANT:** need, privation, poverty, distress

**lack** *v.* need, want, require

**lackadaisical** *adj.* halfhearted, indifferent, languid

**lackey** *n.* **MENIAL:** servant; **FLUNKY:** toady, underling

**laconic** *adj.* concise, curt, succinct, terse

**lad** *n.* fellow, youth, stripling, boy, child

**ladle** *n.* spoon, skimmer, scoop

**lady** *n.* woman, female, matron, gentlewoman

**ladylike** *adj.* cultured, well–bred, polite, refined

**lag** *v.* tarry, straggle, falter, delay

**laggard** *n.* loiterer, idler

**lair** *n.* den, cave, home, pen

**lame** *adj.* halt, impaired, handicapped, limping

**lament** *v.* grieve, deplore

**lamentation** *n.* dirge, mourning, tears, wailing

**lampoon** *v.* satirize, burlesque

**lance** *v.* foil, point, spear

**land** *n.* **PROPERTY:** estate, tract, ranch, farm, lot; **COUNTRY:** province, region, nation

**landing** *n.* **ARRIVING:** docking, anchoring, arrival; **DOCK:** marina, pier, wharf

**landlord** *n.* innkeeper, landowner, lessor, owner

**landscape** *n.* countryside, scenery, panorama, view

**lane** *n.* way, alley, passage, path, road

**language** *n.* expression, tongue, word, sign, signal, gesture, vocabulary, diction, dialect, idiom, patois, vernacular, speech, jargon

**languid** *adj.* spiritless, sluggish

**languish** *v.* weaken, decline

**lank** *adj.* angular, bony, gaunt. lean, slender, spare

**lanky** *adj.* lean, rangy

**lantern** *n.* light, torch, lamp

**lap** *n.* **EXTENSION:** fold, flap, projection; **RACECOURSE:** circuit, round, course, distance

**lapidary** *n.* jeweler, engraver

**lapse** *v.* pass, void, slip, deteriorate, decline, weaken

**larceny** *n.* theft, burglary, thievery, robbery, crime

**large** *adj.* huge, wide, grand, great, considerable, substantial, vast, massive, immense, spacious

**largely** *adv.* **MOSTLY:** mainly, chiefly, principally; **EXTENSIVELY:** abundantly, comprehensively, widely

**lariat** *n.* lasso, riata, tether, line, rope

**lascivious** *adj.* bawdy, carnal, immoral, lewd, licentious, lurid, sensual, sexual

**lash** *n.* whip, stroke

**lash** *v.* strike, flog, thrash, scourge, beat, hit

**lass** *n.* girl, woman, lady, damsel, maiden

**lassitude** *adj.* weariness, listlessness

**lasso** *n.* rope, lariat, tether, noose

**lasso** *v.* rope, catch

**last** *adj.* **FINAL:** ultimate, concluding, ending, terminal, decisive, crowning, climactic, closing; **RECENT:** latest, newest, freshest

**last** *v.* **ENDURE:** continue, maintain, persist, remain, stay, survive, sustain; **SUFFICE:** do, satisfy, serve

**lasting** *adj.* enduring, abiding, constant, permanent

**latch** *n.* catch, hasp, hook, bar, fastener, lock

**latch** *v.* fasten, lock, cinch, close

**late** *adj.* **OVERDUE:** tardy, lagging, delayed; **DEFUNCT:** deceased, dead, departed; **RECENT:** new, fresh

**latent** *adj.* potential, undeveloped, dormant

**lather** *n.* foam, froth, suds, bubbles

**lather** *v.* foam, froth, soap

**latitude** *n.* freedom, degree, measure, extent, scope

**latter** *adj.* after, following, late, last, recent

**lattice** *n.* arbor, framework, trellis

**laud** *v.* glorify, honor, praise

**laugh** *v.* chuckle, guffaw, snicker, titter, chortle, cackle, giggle, roar

**launch** *v.* initiate, originate, start, begin

**launder** *v.* cleanse, wash, clean

**lavatory** *n.* basin, privy, bathroom, washroom, toilet

**lave** *v.* clean, wash

**lavish** *adj.* profuse, extravagant, generous, unstinted, unsparing, plentiful, improvident, excessive

**lawful** *adj.* LEGAL: legitimate, decreed, permitted, constitutional; LEGISLATED: enacted, official, enforced, protected, legitimized, established

**lawless** *adj.* WILD: untamed, uncivilized, uncontrolled, barbarous, savage, disordered; UNRESTRAINED: riotous, insubordinate, disobedient, unruly, revolutionary, mutinous

**lawsuit** *n.* action, suit, case, prosecution, claim, trial

**lawyer** *n.* attorney, solicitor, jurist, defender, prosecuting, counsel, solicitor, barrister, advocate

**lax** *adj.* slack, loose, remiss, soft, careless, indifferent

**laxity, laxness** *n.* slackness, negligence, indifference, neglect

**layer** *n.* stratum, thickness, fold, lap, floor, story, tier

**layman** *n.* nonprofessional, novice, dilettante, amateur, recruit

**layout** *n.* arrangement, design, organization, plan, proposal, draft, schematic

**lazy** *adj.* indolent, idle, sluggish, apathetic, loafing, flagging, slothful, lethargic

**lead** *n.* GUIDANCE: leadership, direction; CLUE: evidence, trace, hint, proof, sign; ROLE: part, character

**lead** *v.* CONDUCT: steer, pilot, show, guide; DIRECT: manage, supervise

**leaden** *adj.* heavy, burdensome, oppressive, weighty

**leader** *n.* GUIDE: conductor, pilot;

**DIRECTOR:** manager, officer, captain, master, ruler, boss, brains

**leading** *adj.* foremost, chief, dominating, best

**leaflet** *n.* brochure, handbill, circular, pamphlet

**league** *n.* union, alliance, group, unit, organization

**leak** *n.* HOLE: puncture, chink, crevice; WASTE: loss, leakage, seepage, expenditure, decrease; NEWS: exposé, slip

**leak** *v.* ESCAPE: drip, ooze, drool, flow

**lean** *v.* INCLINE: slant, sag, list, tip, veer, droop, pitch, tilt; TEND: favor, prefer

**lean** *adj.* THIN: lank, meager, slim, skinny; FIBROUS: muscular, sinewy

**leaning** *n.* inclination, preference, tendency

**lean-to** *n.* shelter, shanty, hut, hovel

**leap** *v.* jump, bound, spring, vault, bounce

**learn** *v.* acquire, read, master, ascertain, determine, unearth, hear, memorize, study

**learned** *adj.* scholarly, erudite, cultured, accomplished, well-informed, professorial, educated

**learning** *n.* lore, training, knowledge, education

**lease** *v.* let, rent, charter

**least** *adj.* SMALLEST: tiniest; TRIVIAL: piddling, unimportant; MINIMAL: bottom, lowest

**leave** *n.* PARTING: departure, farewell; PERMISSION: consent, dispensation, indulgence, authorization, consent; LIBERTY: furlough, vacation

**leave** *v.* ABANDON: forsake, desert; DEPART: withdraw, part, defect, flee, embark, emigrate, scram, split, vacate, go; BEQUEATH: transmit, will, give, dower; OMIT: drop, forget, neglect

**leaving** *n.* departure, exodus

**lecher** *n.* debaucher, rake

**lecture** *n.* **REPROOF:** dressing–down, rebuke, reprimand; **INSTRUCTION:** address, discourse, lesson, oration, speech, talk

**lecture** *v.* **INSTRUCT:** address, instruct, talk, teach; **REPROVE:** rebuke, reprimand

**ledge** *n.* shelf, mantle, bar, step, ridge, rim

**ledger** *n.* accounts, books, records, journal

**leech** *n.* **PARASITE:** tapeworm, hookworm, bloodsucker; **DEPENDENT:** hanger–on, sponger, weakling

**leer** *n.* glance, grin, look, smirk

**leery** *adj.* distrustful, doubting, suspicious, wary

**leeway** *n.* space, margin, latitude, extent

**left** *adj.* **REMAINING:** staying, continuing, over, extra; **RADICAL:** left–wing, liberal, progressive, revolutionary; **DEPARTED:** gone, absent, lacking

**legacy** *n.* bequest, inheritance

**legal** *adj.* lawful, constitutional, permissible, allowable, legalized, sanctioned, legitimate, authorized

**legality** *n.* legitimacy, lawfulness, authority, law

**legalize** *v.* authorize, sanction, approve

**legate** *n.* ambassador, envoy, deputy, representative, delegate

**legation** *n.* delegation, embassy

**legend** *n.* story, myth, saga, fable; inscription

**legendary** *adj.* fabulous, mythical, fanciful, allegorical

**legerdemain** *n.* deception, trickery

**legible** *adj.* readable, distinct, plain, sharp, clear

**legion** *n.* multitude, horde, throng, crowd

**legislate** *v.* enact, pass, constitute

**legislation** *n.* bill, enactment, act, law

**legislature** *n.* lawmakers, congress, parliament, senate, house, representatives

**legitimate** *adj.* LICIT: statutory, authorized, lawful, legal, honorable; LOGICAL: reasonable, probable, consistent, understandable; AUTHENTIC: real, verifiable, valid, reliable, genuine

**leisure** *n.* relaxation, recreation, holiday, vacation

**leisurely** *adj.* unhurried, lazily, calmly, listlessly

**lend** *v.* loan, advance, furnish, entrust, accommodate

**length** *n.* DISTANCE: measure, span, range, longitude, magnitude, dimension; DURATION: period, interval

**lengthen** *v.* extend, stretch, protract, increase;

**lengthy** *adj.* tedious, long, dull, protracted, prolonged

**lenient** *adj.* mild, merciful, tolerant, kind, sympathetic

**lesion** *n.* abrasion, injury, tumor, wound

**less** *adj.* fewer, smaller, reduced, declined, inferior, secondary, subordinate, diminished, shortened

**lessen** *v.* diminish, dwindle, decline, decrease; reduce

**lesser** *adj.* inferior, minor, secondary, subordinate

**lesson** *n.* learning, precept, assignment

**let** *v.* PERMIT: approve, authorize, consent, tolerate, allow; LEASE: rent, hire, sublet

**letdown** *n.* frustration, setback, disillusionment, disappointment

**lethal** *adj.* deadly, fatal, mortal, malignant, harmful

**lethargic** *adj.* apathetic, listless, sluggish

**lethargy** *n.* stupor, dullness, drowsiness

**letter** *n.* MESSAGE: memo, note, epistle,

memorandum, mis-
sive, line, mail;
**SYMBOL:** character,
type

**letter** *v.* inscribe, write

**letup** *n.* reduction,
slowdown, pause, in-
terval, respite

**levee** *n.* embankment,
dike

**level** *adj.* **SMOOTH:**
planed, even, flat;
**REGULAR:** uniform,
flush, straight, trim,
precise, exact,
matched, unbroken,
aligned, continuous

**level** *v.* **STRAIGHTEN:**
flatten, surface, bull-
doze, smooth;
**DEMOLISH:** destroy,
ruin, wreck, raze

**lever** *n.* bar, fulcrum,
pry, crowbar

**leverage** *n.* power,
purchase; lift, hold,
support

**leviathan** *n.* monster,
beast

**levity** *n.* flippancy, frivolity

**levy** *n.* collection, seizure, toll, duty, cus-
tom, tax

**levy** *v.* collect, assess

**lewd** *adj.* **RIBALD:**
smutty, indecent,
sensual; **LUSTFUL:**
wanton, lascivious, li-
centious, lecherous,
dissolute, debauched,
corrupt, depraved,
vulgar

**lexicon** *n.* dictionary,
vocabulary, glossary

**liability** *n.* obligation,
responsibility, debt,
indebtedness, respon-
sibility

**liable** *adj.* **APT:** inclined, likely, tending;
**RESPONSIBLE:** ac-
countable, answer-
able, exposed, obliged

**liaison** *n.* **LINK:** agent,
connection, emissary,
proxy; **AFFAIR:** in-
trigue, romance, tryst

**liar** *n.* prevaricator, deceiver, perjurer, falsi-
fier, fibber

**libel** *v.* defame, slander, smear, vilify

**libelous** *adj.* defama-
tory, derogatory,
slanderous

**liberal** *adj.*
**PROGRESSIVE:** broad-
minded, noncon-
formist, permissive,

radical, tolerant; **GENEROUS:** indulgent, lavish, magnanimous

**liberate** *v.* free, loose, release, lberate, extricate, disentangle

**liberation** *n.* rescue, freedom, deliverance, release

**libertine** *n.* lecher, pervert, rake, roué

**liberty** *n.* **DELIVERANCE:** emancipation, enfranchisement, rescue, freedom; **LEAVE:** relaxation, rest, leisure, recreation; **PRIVILEGE:** permission, decision, selection; **RIGHTS:** freedom, independence

**libretto** *n.* lyric, words

**license** *n.* **CONSENT:** authorization, permission, sanction; **DOCUMENT:** permit, certificate, registration; **FREEDOM:** looseness, excess, immoderation, latitude

**license** *v.* grant, authorize, permit, allow, sanction

**licit** *adj.* authorized, lawful, sanctioned

**lick** *v.* beat, thrash, whip, defeat, overcome, vanquish, conquer, frustrate

**lid** *n.* cover, cap, top, roof, hood

**lie** *n.* falsehood, untruth, misrepresentation, prevarication, falsification, fabrication, distortion

**lie** *v.* **FIB:** falsify, prevaricate, deceive, misinform, exaggerate, distort, concoct, misrepresent, dissemble, delude; **PROSTRATE:** recline, retire, rest, sleep; **ABIDE:** remain, exist

**lieu** *n.* place, stead

**life** *n.* **BEING:** entity, presence, consciousness, vitality; **BIOGRAPHY:** story, memoir; **DURATION:** lifetime, span, career, generation, season, cycle; **SPIRIT:** animation, excitement, zeal

**lifeless** *adj.* **INERT:** inanimate, departed, dead; **LACKING SPIRIT:** lackluster, listless, heavy, dull, slow

**lifetime** *n.* existence, endurance, continuance

**lift** *v.* **ELEVATE:** raise, hoist; **STEAL:** filch, pilfer, swipe; **RESCIND:** repeal, reverse, revoke, cancel

**light** *adj.* **ILLUMINATED:** radiant, luminous, bright; **SUPERFICIAL:** slight, frivolous, trivial, unimportant; **VIVID:** colorful, rich, clear; **LIVELY:** spirited, animated, active; **ETHEREAL:** airy, fluffy, downy, dainty, thin, sheer, insubstantial, graceful

**light** *v.* **ILLUMINATE:** illumine, lighten, brighten; **IGNITE:** inflame, spark, kindle, burn; **REST:** stop, arrive

**lighten** *v.* unburden, lessen, uplift, alleviate, reduce, shift, change, unload

**light–headed** *adj.* **GIDDY:** inane, fickle, frivolous, silly; **FAINT:** tired, delirious, dizzy, weak

**light–hearted** *adj.* gay, joyous, cheerful, happy

**lightly** *adj.* delicately, airily, daintily, gently, subtly, softly, tenderly

**like** *adj.* similar, resembling, close, matching, related, analogous, corresponding, comparable

**like** *v.* **ENJOY:** relish, savor, fancy; **ADMIRE:** esteem, approve; **PREFER:** choose, desire, fancy

**likelihood** *n.* possibility, probability

**likely** *adj.* probable, conceivable, rational, plausible, apt, tending, prone, liable

**likeness** *n.* **SIMILARITY:** resemblance, correspondence; **REPRESENTATION:** image, effigy, portrait, picture

**liking** *n.* desire, fondness, devotion, affection, love

**limb** *n.* **BRANCH:** arm, bough, offshoot; **APPENDAGE:** arm, leg, wing, fin, flipper

**limber** *adj.* flexible, pliant, supple, nimble

**limit** *n.* boundary, frontier, border, extent, extremity

**limit** *v.* confine, bound, curb, restrict

**limitation** *n.* **RESTRICTION:** restraint, control; **CONDITION:** qualification, stricture, inhibition, constraint; **SHORTCOMING:** inadequacy, deficiency, flaw, weakness, failing, frailty

**limp** *adj.* weak, pliant, flaccid, flabby, pliable, slack, loose, flimsy

**limp** *n.* hitch, hobble

**limp** *v.* halt, stumble, shuffle, stagger, totter, falter

**line** *n.* **BORDER:** limit, boundary, edge, boundary; **ROW:** rank, file, order, arrangement, sequence, column, groove, thread; **JOB:** profession, career, vocation; **ROPE:** cord, filament; **DESCENT:** pedigree, lineage, family, heredity; **WARES:** goods, merchandise, produce, material; **TALK:** speech, patter

**line** *v.* **ARRANGE:** align, order, dress, array, fix, place; **BORDER:** edge, bound, fringe; **PROTECT:** face, back, bind, trim, pad; **TRACE:** delineate, outline, draw

**linear** *adj.* successive, direct, straight

**linger** *v.* remain, loiter, tarry, lag, delay, dawdle, wait

**linguist** *n.* lexicographer, translator, grammarian

**liniment** *n.* ointment, lotion, balm, medicine

**lining** *n.* interlining, filling, quilting, stuffing, padding

**link** *n.* **LOOP:** ring, coupling; **CONNECTION:** seam, weld, intersection, fastening, splice, articulation, joint

**link** *v.* connect, associate, combine, join

**lint** *n.* fluff, raveling, fiber, dust

**liquid** *adj.* **WATERY:** molten, moist, aqueous, liquefied, dissolved, wet, melted, thawed; **FLOWING:** running, splashing, thin, viscous, fluid

**liquidate** *v.* **CHANGE:** sell, exchange, convert; **DESTROY:** eliminate, kill, cancel

**list** *n.* roll, record, agenda, slate, inventory, account, tally, roster, muster, menu, docket

**list** *v.* **ARRANGE:** catalogue, register, tally, inventory, index; **LEAN:** pitch, slant, incline

**listen** *v.* hear, heed, attend, overhear

**listless** *adj.* languid, sluggish, indolent, indifferent

**litany** *n.* form, ritual

**literacy** *n.* scholarship, education, knowledge

**literal** *adj.* precise, exact, verbatim, accurate

**literally** *adj.* actually, exactly, strictly, verbatim

**literary** *adj.* scholarly, learned, bookish, literate

**literate** *adj.* lettered, learned, scholarly, educated

**lithograph** *n.* print, copy

**lithograph** *v.* engrave, print

**litter** *n.* **DEBRIS:** mess, jumble, hodgepodge, trash, clutter; **BROOD:** piglets, puppies, kittens, offspring

**litter** *v.* scatter, confuse, jumble

**little** *adj.* **SMALL:** diminutive, tiny, wee, slight, miniature, puny; **INADEQUATE:** inconsiderable, insufficient; **TRIFLING:** shallow, petty, superficial, frivolous, paltry, trivial; **BASE:** weak, shallow, mean, petty

**livable** *adj.* **HABITABLE:** inhabitable, comfortable; **BEARABLE:** acceptable, adequate, tolerable

**live** *adj.* **ACTIVE:** energetic, vital, vivid;

**AWARE:** conscious, existing

**live** *v.* **EXIST:** subsist, survive, breathe, be; **RELISH:** savor, experience; **DWELL:** inhabit, abide; **CONTINUE:** remain, survive, endure, last

**livelihood** *n.* job, career, trade, vocation, occupation, means, subsistence

**lively** *adj.* active, animated, brisk, energetic, spirited, vigorous, vivacious

**living** *adj.* **ALIVE:** active, live, existing, breathing, being; **VIGOROUS:** awake, brisk, alert, active

**living** *n.* means, sustenance, maintenance, subsistence, work, vocation, business

**load** *n.* **BURDEN:** cargo, lading, shipment, capacity, payload, bundle; **RESPONSIBILITY:** charge, obligation, trust, duty

**loaf** *v.* loiter, idle, lounge, relax, shirk, dream

**loafer** *n.* malingerer, slacker, goldbrick, deadbeat

**loan** *v.* lend, provide, advance

**loath** *adj.* disinclined, unwilling

**loathe** *v.* detest, dislike

**lobby** *n.* **ENTRYWAY:** antechamber, foyer, hall, vestibule; **INFLUENCE:** pressure

**lobby** *v.* influence, promote

**local** *adj.* **LIMITED:** confined, restricted, bounded; **INDIGENOUS:** native, territorial, provincial, regional

**locale** *n.* vicinity, territory, district, area, region

**locality** *n.* district, section, sector, region, location, site, neighborhood, block, vicinity

**locate** *v.* **DISCOVER:** find, establish, determine, place; **SETTLE:** inhabit, dwell

**lock** *n.* **HOOK:** catch, latch, bolt, bar, hasp, bond; **TRESS:** tuft, ringlet, curl

**lock** *v.* fasten, bolt, bar

**locker** *n.* cabinet, wardrobe, cupboard, closet

**locket** *n.* case, pendant, jewelry

**lodge** *n.* **RETREAT:** inn, hostel, chalet, hotel, motel, resort, cabin, cottage; **SOCIETY:** club, fraternity

**lodge** *v.* **SHELTER:** board, harbor, quarter; **PLACE:** fix, leave, deposit, embed

**lodging** *n.* accommodation, refuge, shelter, residence, home, hotel, motel, resort

**lofty** *adj.* **HIGH:** elevated, tall, towering, raised; **EXALTED:** arrogant, commanding, haughty, proud

**log** *n.* **WOOD:** limb, timber, stick **JOURNAL:** account, register, ledger, diary, record

**logic** *n.* reasoning, deduction, induction, thought

**logical** *adj.* coherent, consistent, probable, sound, congruent, reasonable

**logistics** *n.* procurement, distribution, management

**loiter** *v.* linger, dawdle, idle, loll, tarry, wait

**lone** *adj.* solitary, deserted, alone

**lonely** *adj.* abandoned, homesick, forlorn, deserted, solitary, secluded

**lonesome** *adj.* forlorn, homesick, lonely

**long** *adj.* **ELONGATED:** extended, lengthy, outstretched; **PROLONGED:** protracted, meandering, lengthy, sustained; **TEDIOUS:** dull

**long** *v.* desire, yearn, wish, want

**longing** *n.* craving, yearning, pining, desire, wish

**long–lived** *adj.* perpetual, enduring, permanent

**look** *n.* **SIGHT:** glance, survey, glimpse, peek, peep, leer, stare; **APPEARANCE:** presence, mien, expression, looks, manner, aspect

**look** *v.* **EYE:** view, gaze, behold, contemplate, scrutinize, regard, inspect, observe, examine, watch; **SEEM:** resemble, appear

**lookout** *n.* **VIEW:** panorama, scene, observatory, station; **WATCHMAN:** watcher, sentinel, scout

**loom** *v.* **APPEAR:** rise, emerge; **MENACE:** threaten, hulk, hover, approach

**loop** *v.* curve, encircle, connect, bend

**loophole** *n.* escape, omission, avoidance

**loose** *adj.* **SLACK:** free, careless; **LICENTIOUS:** wanton, unrestrained, dissolute; **UNBOUND:** unattached, disconnected, baggy, free; **VAGUE:** random, obscure

**loose** *v.* **FREE:** release, liberate; **RELAX:** slack ease

**loosen** *v.* extricate, untie, undo, disentangle, free

**loot** *n.* plunder, spoils, take, booty

**loot** *v.* plunder, steal, thieve, rifle, rob

**lop** *v.* cut, trip, prune, chop

**lope** *v.* jog, run, trot

**lopsided** *adj.* uneven, unbalanced, tipped, irregular

**lordly** *adj.* grand, dignified, honorable, noble

**lore** *n.* enlightenment, wisdom, learning, knowledge

**loss** *n.* **RUIN:** destruction, calamity, disaster; **DEPRIVATION:** bereavement, destitution

**lost** *adj.* **MISPLACED:** mislaid, obscured, vanished, strayed; **BEWILDERED:** perplexed, puzzled; **DESTROYED:** demolished, wasted, ruined

**lot** *n.* **FATE:** destiny, fortune, chance; **PORTION:** cluster, array, bunch, group; **LAND:** tract, parcel, division, patch, field; **LOAD:** consignment; **ABUNDANCE:** plenty, loads, oodles

**lotion** *n.* cream, balm, salve, unguent, cosmetic

**loud** *adj.* CLAMOROUS: noisy, vociferous, boisterous, cacophonous, raucous, harsh; BRASH: offensive, vulgar, loud–mouthed, rude; GARISH: gaudy, flashy, tawdry, ornate

**lounge** *n.* SOFA: couch, divan; ROOM: bar, lobby, parlor, salon

**lounge** *v.* recline, ease, idle, repose, loaf, rest

**lovable** *adj.* winning, winsome, friendly

**love** *n.* DEVOTION: attachment, infatuation, rapture, ardor; ESTEEM: respect, regard, admiration

**love** *v.* adore, idolize, prize, treasure, cherish

**lovely** *adj.* beautiful, attractive, comely, fair, handsome, engaging, enchanting, captivating, pleasing

**lover** *n.* suitor, sweetheart, admirer, escort, paramour, fiancé, boyfriend, girlfriend

**loving** *adj.* devoted, thoughtful, passionate, amorous, affectionate, caring, considerate

**low** *adj.* SQUAT: flat, prostrate, crouched, sunken; FAINT: muffled, hushed, quiet; SAD: dejected, moody, blue; ECONOMICAL: moderate, inexpensive, cheap; VULGAR: base, mean, coarse

**lower** *adj.* inferior, beneath, under

**lower** *v.* diminish, fall, sink, depress, decrease, drop

**lowering** *adj.* threatening, dark, gloomy, menacing

**lowly** *adj.* unpretentious, meek, humble, unassuming

**loyal** *adj.* faithful, true, dependable, firm, faithful

**loyalty** *n.* fidelity, allegiance, faithfulness, constancy, attachment, support, devotion

**lucid** *adj.* CLEAR: obvious, unmistakable;

**SHINING:** bright, luminous; **SANE:** rational, normal

**luck** n. **FORTUNE:** prosperity, wealth, windfall, blessing; **CHANCE:** fate, opportunity, break, accident

**lucky** adj. **BLESSED:** wealthy, favored, successful, prosperous, fortunate; **AUSPICIOUS:** providential, propitious, magic

**lucrative** adj. profitable, fruitful, productive, gainful

**ludicrous** adj. absurd, ridiculous, laughable, farcical, incongruous

**lug** v. carry, tug, lift, draw

**luggage** n. baggage, trunks, bags, valises

**lukewarm** adj. cool, tepid, chilly

**lull** n. pause, hiatus, stillness, hush, silence

**lull** v. soothe, quiet, calm

**lumber** v. slog, plod

**luminescence** n. fluorescence, fire, radiance, light

**luminous** adj. lighted, glowing, radiant, bright

**lump** n. mass, clump, block, chunk, hunk

**lunacy** n. **INSANITY:** madness, dementia, mania; **FOOLISHNESS:** silliness

**lunatic** adj. **INSANE:** demented, deranged, psychotic; **FOOLISH:** irrational, idiotic, daft, stupid

**lunge** v. thrust, surge, bound, jump

**lurch** v. roll, stagger, weave, sway, totter

**lure** n. bait, decoy, trick

**lure** v. entice, enchant, bewitch, allure, attract, tempt

**lurid** adj. ghastly, gruesome, sensational

**lurk** v. skulk, slink, prowl, wait, crouch, conceal, hide

**luscious** adj. toothsome, palatable, delicious

**lush** adj. **GREEN:** verdant, dense, grassy; **DELICIOUS:** rich, juicy, succulent;

**ELABORATE:** extravagant, luxurious, ornamental, ornate

**lust** *n.* desire, appetite, passion, sensuality

**luster** *n.* brightness, radiance, glow, brilliance, light

**lusty** *adj.* hearty, boisterous, robust, vigorous

**luxuriant** *adj.* exuberant, overabundant

**luxuriate** *v.* indulge, bask, revel

**luxurious** *adj.* comfortable, affluent, expensive, rich

**luxury** *n.* indulgence, idleness, leisure, lavishness, extravagance, excess

**lying** *adj.* **FRAUDULENT:** deceitful, double–dealing, dishonest; **FALSIFYING:** prevaricating, misrepresenting; **UNRELIABLE:** unsound, tricky, treacherous, false

**lynch** *v.* punish, hang, murder

**lyrical** *adj.* melodious, sweet, rhythmical, poetic

**machination** *n.* conspiracy, plot

**machine** *n.* contrivance, device, implement

**machinist** *n.* operator, engineer, workman

**macrocosm** *n.* universe, world

**mad** *adj.* **INSANE:** demented, deranged, psychotic; **ANGRY:** provoked, enraged, exasperated

**madden** *v.* craze, infuriate, enrage, anger, annoy, irritate

**maddening** *adj.* annoying, infuriating, disturbing

**made** *adj.* fashioned, built, formed, manufactured

**made–up** *adj.* invented, concocted, devised, fictitious

**madhouse** *n.* bedlam, confusion

**madman** *n.* lunatic, maniac, screwball, oddball

**magazine** *n.* periodical, journal, publication

**magic** *adj.* enchanting, mystic, enchanting

**magic** *n.* occultism, legerdemain, wizardry, sorcery, divination, witchcraft, voodooism, soothsaying

**magical** *adj.* occult, enchanting, mystic, mysterious

**magician** *n.* conjurer, sorcerer, wizard, shaman

**magnanimous** *adj.* charitable, noble, unselfish, forgiving, generous

**magnate** *n.* tycoon, mogul

**magnetic** *adj.* alluring, appealing, attractive, irresistible, captivating, charming, fascinating

**magnetism** *n.* attraction, allure, charm, appeal

**magnetize** *v.* fascinate, attract

**magnificence** *n.* grandeur, majesty, stateliness, glory, radiance, luxuriousness, greatness, lavishness, brilliance, pomp, splendor, richness

**magnificent** *adj.* splendid, grand, exalted, majestic

**magnify** *v.* amplify, expand, increase, enlarge

**magnitude** *n.* SIZE: extent, quantity; IMPORTANCE: greatness, consequence, significance

**maid** *n.* GIRL: maiden, woman; SERVANT: nursemaid, housemaid, chambermaid

**mail** *v.* post, send, drop

**maim** *v.* disfigure, mutilate, disable, damage, hurt

**main** *adj.* principal, chief, leading, dominant, foremost

**main** *n.* conduit, channel, duct, pipe

**mainly** *adv.* chiefly, largely, predominantly, principally

**maintain** *v.* UPHOLD: support, sustain, affirm, defend; ASSERT: state, attest, declare, say; PRESERVE: keep, conserve, reserve, save, manage

**majestic** *adj.* stately, dignified, exalted, grand, noble

**majesty** *n.* grandeur, nobility, splendor, magnificence

**major** *adj.* important, significant, principal, main

**make** *v.* MANUFACTURE: construct, fabricate, assemble, fashion, produce, build, form; CREATE: originate, generate, devise, conceive, invent; FORCE: constrain, compel, coerce; WAGE: conduct, engage, act; PREPARE: ready, arrange, adjust, cook; OBTAIN: earn, gain; ATTAIN: reach, arrive

**makeshift** *adj.* temporary, expedient, stopgap

**make–up** *n.* COSMETICS: mascara, liner, rouge, powder; COMPENSATION: payment, conciliation, atonement; COMPOSITION: structure, formation, arrangement

**maladroit** *adj.* awkward, clumsy, inept, bungling

**malady** *n.* affliction, ailment, disease, sickness

**malformation** *n.* deformity, distortion

**malfunction** *n.* breakdown, slip, failure

**malice** *n.* hatred, spite, animosity, resentment

**malicious** *adj.* hateful, spiteful, bad

**malign** *v.* vilify, defame, slander

**malignant** *adj.* lethal, poisonous, deadly, harmful, destructive, deleterious, corrupt, dangerous

**malinger** *v.* lounge, loll, loaf, loiter

**mall** *n.* market, shop

**malnutrition** *n.* starvation, hunger

**malodorous** *adj.* stinking, fetid

**malpractice** *n.* negligence, neglect, carelessness

**mammoth** *adj.* huge, large

**manacle** *v.* chain, handcuff, shackle

**manage** *v.* **DIRECT:** control, lead, oversee, mastermind, engineer, handle, supervise; **CONTRIVE:** accomplish, achieve, effect; **ENDURE:** survive, withstand

**manageable** *adj.* docile, compliant, tractable, obedient, submissive, yielding

**manager** *n.* supervisor, administrator, director, superintendent, executive

**managerial** *adj.* executive, administrative

**mandate** *v.* decree, require

**mandatory** *adj.* imperative, compulsory, obligatory

**mane** *n.* hair, ruff, fur

**maneuver** *v.* plot, scheme, contrive, design, conspire

**manger** *n.* trough, tub

**manhandle** *v.* damage, maul, mistreat, abuse, beat

**mania** *n.* craze, lunacy, madness, desire, obsession

**maniac** *n.* madman, lunatic

**manifest** *adj.* apparent, clear, evident, obvious

**manifest** *v.* exhibit, express, show, reveal, prove, demonstrate

**manifestation** *n.* evidence, indication, sign

**manipulate** *v.* control, shape, mold, form manage

**mankind** *n.* humanity, society, man

**mannequin** *n.* model, dummy, display

**manner** *n.* **CONDUCT:** deportment, demeanor, behavior; **CUSTOM:** habit, use, way, practice

**mannerism** *n.* peculiarity, idiosyncrasy, quirk

**mannerly** *adj.* polished, considerate, charming

**mansion** *n.* house, villa, hall, estate, home

**mantel** *n.* shelf, ledge

**mantle** *n.* cloak, blanket

**manual** *n.* handbook, guidebook, reference, instructions

**manufacture** *v.* make, fabricate, produce, build, fashion, construct

**manuscript** *n.* book, paper, document, composition

**many** *adj.* numerous, multiple, innumerable, several

**map** *n.* chart, graph, drawing, portrayal, draft, plan

**mar** *v.* damage, spoil, deface, harm, disfigure, scratch

**maraud** *v.* raid, attack, plunder, pillage

**march** *v.* parade, proceed, tramp, advance

**margin** *n.* edge, border, lip, shore, boundary

**marina** *n.* dock, mooring, landing, harbor

**marine** *adj.* nautical, maritime, oceanic

**maritime** *adj.* nautical, marine, seafaring, aquatic

**mark** *n.* stamp, imprint, impression, emblem, label

**mark** *v.* **BRAND:** imprint, label, identify, earmark; **SIGNIFY:** denote mean characterize, qualify

**marker** *n.* ticket, trademark, seal, brand, stamp, pencil, pen, boundary, inscription, label

**market** *v.* sell, trade, exchange, barter

**marquee** *n.* awning, canopy

**marry** *v.* **WED:** espouse; **JOIN:** unite, combine

**marsh** *n.* swamp, morass, bog, quagmire

**marshal** *v.* arrange, gather, lead

**martial** *adj.* warlike, combative, aggressive

**martyr** *n.* saint, victim, sufferer, offering, scapegoat

**marvel** *v.* wonder, awe, stare

**marvelous** *adj.* fabulous, astonishing, spectacular

**mash** *v.* crush, bruise, squash, pulverize

**mask** *v.* disguise, cloak, conceal, veil, hide

**mass** *n.* **MATTER:** piece, portion, wad, hunk, lump; **HEAP:** volume quantity; **SIZE:** magnitude, extent

**massacre** *v.* slaughter, kill, exterminate, annihilate

**massage** *v.* rub, knead, stimulate, caress

**massive** *adj.* weighty, bulky, huge, cumbersome, large

**master** *n.* lord, teacher, mentor, maestro

**master** *v.* **CONQUER:** subdue, overcome, humble; **LEARN:** understand, comprehend

**masterful** *adj.* commanding, excellent

**mastery** *n.* **CONTROL:** dominance, sovereignty, superiority; **SKILL:** capacity, proficiency, ability

**match** *n.* **EQUAL:** peer, equivalent, counterpart, approximation; **CONTEST:** race, rivalry, competition

**match** *v.* equalize, liken, coordinate, even, balance

**material** *adj.* **REAL:** physical, tangible; **MEANINGFUL:** essential, substantial

**materialize** *v.* form, become, actualize

**maternal** *adj.* motherly, protective

**mathematics** *n.* arithmetic, geometry, algebra, computation, trigonometry, calculus, logarithms

**matrimony** *n.* marriage, wedlock, union

**matrix** *n.* mold, die

**matron** *n.* dame, dowager, lady, wife, mother, woman

**matter** *n.* **SUBSTANCE:** material, constituents, object, thing, element; **SUBJECT:** interest, focus, theme; **AFFAIR:** undertaking, circumstance, concern

**mature** *adj.* developed, ripe, grown, cultured

**maturity** *n.* competence, development, cultivation; adulthood, majority

**maudlin** *adj.* tearful, sentimental

**maxim** *n.* saying, proverb, aphorism, adage, epithet

**maximum** *adj.* greatest, supreme, highest, best

**maybe** *adv.* perhaps, possibly, conceivable

**mayhem** *n.* crime, violence

**maze** *n.* labyrinth, tangle, convolution, intricacy

**meadow** *n.* grass, pasture, field

**meager** *adj.* lean, scanty, spare, wanting

**meal** *n.* **FOOD:** repast, feast, chow, spread, banquet tea; **GRAIN:** fodder, provender, forage, feed

**mean** *adj.* **HUMBLE:** servile, pitiful, shabby; **VICIOUS:** contemptible, despicable, degenerate, knavish, unscrupulous; **BASE:** low, vulgar, common

**mean** *v.* **SIGNIFY:** denote, symbolize, imply, suggest, designate, intimate;

**INTEND:** propose, expect

**meander** *v.* wander, wind, roam, ramble

**meaning** *n.* sense, import, definition, implication, intent, connotation, context, significance

**meaningful** *adj.* significant, essential, important

**means** *n.* **WEALTH:** resources, substance, property; **INSTRUMENTALITY:** machinery, method, system, agency

**measure** *n.* **EXTENT:** degree, dimension, capacity, weight, volume, distance, quantity, area, mass; **STANDARD:** rule, test, norm, criterion

**measured** *adj.* steady, systematic, deliberate, regular

**mechanical** *adj.* **AUTOMATED:** programmed, automatic; **PERFUNCTORY:** stereotyped, unchanging, monotonous

**mechanism** *n.* machine, device, process, tool

**medal** *n.* badge, award, decoration, commemoration

**meddle** *v.* interfere, interlope, intervene, encroach

**meddlesome** *adj.* intrusive, snoopy, prying, nosy

**mediate** *v.* arbitrate, negotiate, intercede, reconcile

**medication** *n.* remedy, pill, vaccination

**mediocre** *adj.* middling, average, common, ordinary

**meditation** *n.* contemplation, reflection, thought

**medium** *n.* **MEANS:** mechanism, tool, agency, device; **SPIRITUALIST:** seer, oracle, prophet

**medley** *n.* mixture, conglomeration, variety, melange, assortment

**meek** *adj.* humble, unassuming, passive, docile

**meet** *v.* **ENCOUNTER:** engage, battle, match, face; **TOUCH:** coincide, join, intersect; **CONVENE:** assemble, gather, converge, congregate; **SATISFY:** fulfill, suffice

**melancholy** *adj.* gloomy, depressed, dispirited, sad

**mellow** *v.* ripen, mature, age

**melodramatic** *adj.* artificial, sensational, exaggerated

**melody** *n.* song, tune, air, lyric, strain

**melt** *v.* **DISSOLVE:** liquefy, thaw, soften, **DWINDLE:** vanish, go, pass; **RELENT:** forgive, yield

**member** *n.* **LIMB:** organ, arm, leg; **ASSOCIATE:** constituent, affiliate; **PART:** segment, fragment, division

**memento** *n.* keepsake, reminder, souvenir

**memoir** *n.* autobiography, account

**memorabilia** *n.* memento, souvenir

**memorable** *adj.* unforgettable, notable, significant, monumental, eventful, exceptional, singular

**memorial** *n.* monument, tablet, tombstone, mausoleum, statue; celebration, ceremony

**memorize** *v.* retain, learn, remember

**memory** *n.* recollection, retrospection, reminiscence

**menace** *v.* threaten, intimidate, portend

**mend** *v.* repair, patch, fix, aid, remedy, cure, correct

**menial** *n.* servant, domestic, maid, lackey

**mental** *adj.* thoughtful, rational, intellectual, subconscious, telepathic, psychic

**mentality** *n.* intellect, comprehension, reasoning

**mention** *v.* remark, comment, infer, intimate, suggest

**merchandise** *n.* goods, wares, commodities, stock

**merchandise** *v.* advertise, sell

**merchant** *n.* trader, shopkeeper, dealer, jobber

**merciful** *adj.* lenient, softhearted, tolerant, compassionate, humane, kind

**mercurial** *adj.* changeable, volatile

**mere** *adj.* minor, insignificant, little

**merge** *v.* combine, fuse, join, blend, mix, unite

**merit** *n.* worth, excellence, honor, character, virtue

**merit** *v.* earn, warrant, justify, deserve

**merriment** *n.* mirth, joy, gaiety, happiness, humor

**mesh** *v.* engage, coincide, suit, agree, fit

**mess** *n.* confusion, disorder, jumble, clutter

**message** *n.* communication, tidings, information

**messenger** *n.* courier, envoy, minister, herald, runner, emissary, angel, prophet

**metamorphosis** *n.* change, transformation

**metaphorical** *adj.* figurative, symbolical, allegorical

**method** *n.* procedure, process, technique, system

**meticulous** *adj.* mindful, cautious

**metropolitan** *adj.* cosmopolitan, modern, urban

**mettlesome** *adj.* spirited, active

**middle** *adj.* median, mean, midway, equidistant, central, halfway, intermediate

**middleman** *n.* wholesaler, jobber

**miff** *v.* offend, annoy

**might** *n.* power, ability, strength, force, sway

**mighty** *adj.* powerful, great, imposing, impressive

**migrate** *v.* move, emigrate, leave

**migration** *n.* voyage, departure, journey, movement

**mild** *adj.* moderate, gentle, temperate

**militant** *adj.* aggressive, warlike, belligerent

**millinery** *n.* hats, bonnets

**mimic** *v.* **IMITATE:** copy, simulate, impersonate; **MOCK:** burlesque, caricature, ridicule

**mind** *n.* **MENTALITY:** perception, judgment, wisdom, intellect; **INTENTION:** inclination, determination

**mind** *v.* **OBEY:** heed, behave, attend, regard; **OBJECT:** complain, deplore, dislike

**mindless** *adj.* **CARELESS:** inattentive, oblivious, neglectful, indifferent; **FOOLISH:** senseless, rash

**miniature** *adj.* small, tiny, little, minute

**minimize** *v.* reduce, lessen, depreciate, decrease

**minister** *n.* clergyman, ambassador

**minister** *v.* attend, tend, help

**ministration** *n.* assistance, comfort, relief

**minor** *adj.* inferior, secondary, lesser, trivial

**minor** *n.* adolescent, child, infant, youth

**minute** *adj.* SMALL: tiny, microscopic; TRIVIAL: paltry, immaterial; EXACT: particular, detailed

**minutiae** *n.* trivia, particulars, details

**miracle** *n.* marvel, revelation, wonder, phenomenon

**miraculous** *adj.* supernatural, wonderful, marvelous, phenomenal, mysterious

**mirage** *n.* illusion, phantasm, hallucination, fantasy

**mirth** *n.* gaiety, laughter, frolic, jollity, fun

**misbehave** *v.* sin, trespass, err

**miscalculate** *v.* blunder, miscount, err, mistake

**miscellaneous** *adj.* DIVERSE: unmatched, unlike; MIXED: muddled, scattered, confused, disordered

**mischievous** *adj.* playful, roguish, naughty

**misconduct** *n.* misbehavior, wrongdoing, mischief

**miser** *n.* niggard, skinflint, money–grubber

**miserable** *adj.* distressed, wretched, troubled

**misery** *n.* PAIN: distress, suffering, agony; TROUBLE: grief, anxiety; DESPAIR: depression, sadness

**misfortune** *n.* calamity, adversity, unpleasantness

**misgiving** *n.* mistrust, doubt, uncertainty

**misguided** *adj.* misled, deceived, confused

**misjudge** *v.* miscalculate, overestimate, underestimate

**mislead** *v.* delude, trick, beguile, dupe, misrepresent

**mismatched** *adj.* incompatible, discordant, unfit

**misrepresent** *v.* distort, falsify, deceive, lie, mislead

**miss** *n.* FAILURE: slip blunder mishap mistake deviation WOMAN: lass maid female girl

**mission** *n.* purpose, charge, commission

**missionary** *n.* apostle, evangelist, messenger

**mist** *n.* vapor, cloud, rain, haze, fog

**mistake** *n.* BLUNDER: error, slip, omission; MISUNDERSTANDING: confusion, misinterpretation

**mistake** *v.* err, blunder, misjudge, botch, bungle

**mistreat** *v.* harm, injure, wrong, abuse

**mistrust** *v.* suspect, distrust, doubt

**misunderstanding** *n.* MISAPPREHENSION: misinterpretation; DISAGREEMENT: quarrel, dispute

**mix** *v.* BLEND: combine, mingle, stir, unite; CONFUSE: jumble, tangle; ASSOCIATE: fraternize

**mixture** *n.* combination, blend, compound, amalgam, medley, potpourri, incorporation, hodgepodge

**mix–up** *n.* chaos, commotion, confusion, disorder

**moan** *v.* groan, wail, whine

**mob** *n.* throng, crowd, rabble, multitude, horde

**mob** *v.* attack, crowd, swarm, press, overwhelm

**mobile** *adj.* movable, loose, free

**mock** *adj.* imitation, counterfeit, sham, fake, fraudulent

**mock** *v.* deride, taunt, mimic, caricature, imitate

**mockery** *n.* disparagement, ridicule

**mode** *n.* manner, fashion

**model** *n.* EXAMPLE: prototype, ideal; PATTERN: design, standard; POSER: sitter, mannequin, nude

**model** *v.* FORM: shape, fashion; SIT: pose; DEMONSTRATE: show, wear, display

**moderate** *adj.* **MODEST:** temperate, calm, reserved; **INEXPENSIVE:** cheap, economical; **TOLERANT:** restrained, cautious; **PLEASANT:** temperate, mild

**moderate** *v.* abate, decline, decrease, diminish, calm

**moderation** *n.* restraint, temperance, balance

**modern** *adj.* **STYLISH:** chic, smart, fashionable; **CONTEMPORARY:** new, current, renovated, improved

**modest** *adj.* **HUMBLE:** unassuming, meek, diffident;
**UNPRETENTIOUS:** plain, seemly, tasteful, unadorned, unaffected; **MODERATE:** reasonable, inexpensive, economical; **PROPER:** pure, chaste, seemly, decent; **LOWLY:** simple, unaffected

**modify** *v.* change, vary, alter

**moist** *adj.* wet, humid, dank, moistened, damp

**mold** *n.* **FORM:** matrix, shape, frame, pattern, die, cast; **GROWTH:** rust, parasite, fungus, lichen, decay

**molest** *v.* disturb, bother, annoy, irritate, badger

**mollify** *v.* assuage, pacify

**molten** *adj.* melted, liquefied

**moment** *n.* **TIME:** instant, jiffy, twinkling; **IMPORTANCE:** significance, note, consequence

**momentary** *adj.* fleeting, passing, transient, cursory

**momentum** *n.* impetus, impulse, force, drive, energy

**monetary** *adj.* pecuniary, financial, fiscal

**money** *n.* currency, cash, notes, specie, funds

**monologue** *n.* speech, talk, discourse, address

**monopolize** *v.* dominate, engross, corner

**monopoly** *n.* trust, syndicate, cartel

**monotonous** *adj.* tiresome, tedious, wearying, dull

**monster** *n.* **BRUTE:** criminal, rascal, savage; **MONSTROSITY:** chimera, werewolf; **FREAK:** abnormality

**monstrous** *adj.* **HUGE:** stupendous, prodigious, enormous, large; **UNNATURAL:** abnormal, unusual

**monument** *n.* memorial, shrine, statue, monolith

**monumental** *adj.* lofty, impressive, majestic, grand

**mood** *n.* state, condition, temper, humor, disposition

**moody** *adj.* downcast, pensive, unhappy, sad

**moot** *adj.* disputable, disputed, arguable, controversial

**mope** *v.* fret, pine, sorrow, brood, sulk

**moral** *adj.* virtuous, proper, scrupulous, honorable, aboveboard, principled, chaste, noble

**morale** *n.* assurance, resolve, spirit, confidence

**morality** *n.* righteousness, uprightness, virtue

**morals** *n.* ethics, ideals, standards, mores, principles

**moratorium** *n.* delay, halt, suspension

**morbid** *adj.* **DISEASED:** sickly, unhealthy, ailing; **PATHOLOGICAL:** gloomy, melancholic, depressed

**morning** *n.* dawn, morn, daybreak, cockcrow, sun–up

**morose** *adj.* surly, downcast, gloomy

**morsel** *n.* piece, bite, chunk, bit, part

**mortal** *adj.* **FATAL:** malignant, lethal, deadly; **TEMPORAL:** human, transient, perishable, temporary

**mostly** *adv.* **FREQUENTLY:** often, regularly; **LARGELY:** chiefly, essentially, principally

**motel** *n.* hotel, cabin, inn, resort

**motherly** *adj.* maternal, devoted, protective, loving

**motif** *n.* theme, melody

**motion** *n.* MOVEMENT: change, act, action, passage; PROPOSAL: suggestion, proposition, plan

**motivate** *v.* inspire, stimulate, incite, spur, goad

**motive** *n.* cause, purpose, idea, reason

**motto** *n.* maxim, adage, saw, aphorism, sentiment, slogan, catchword, axiom, proverb, saying

**mound** *n.* pile, heap, knoll, hill

**mount** *v.* RISE: ascend; CLIMB: scale, clamber

**mountainous** *adj.* steep, lofty, craggy, rugged

**mourn** *v.* grieve, sorrow, bemoan, languish, pine

**mournful** *adj.* sorrowful, unhappy, sad, saddened, sorry

**movable** *adj.* portable, mobile, detachable, free

**move** *v.* EXCITE: arouse, stir, stimulate; PROPEL: impel, actuate; PROPOSE: introduce, submit; ADVANCE: go, walk, run, travel, progress, proceed, traverse

**movement** *n.* CHANGE: migration, evolution, transition, progression; TREND: drift, tendency, inclination

**mow** *v.* cut, scythe, reap, harvest

**mud** *n.* muck, mire, slush, silt, ooze

**muddle** *v.* confuse, disarrange, mix, jumble, snarl, befuddle, entangle

**muddy** *adj.* MURKY: dull, cloudy, obscure, indistinct; SWAMPY: slushy, soggy, sodden, boggy

**muffle** *v.* deaden, mute, stifle, decrease, soften

**muffler** *n.* scarf, neckpiece, choker

**mug** *n.* vessel, stein, flagon, cup

**muggy** *adj.* damp, humid, moist

**multitude** *n.* throng, mob, crowd, gathering, people

**mumble** *v.* mutter, utter, murmur

**munch** *v.* chew, masticate, crunch, bite, eat

**mundane** *adj.* normal, ordinary, common, mediocre, everyday

**municipality** *n.* community, district, village, town

**murder** *n.* homicide, carnage, slaying, butchery

**murder** *v.* kill, slay, assassinate, butcher

**murky** *adj.* gloomy, dark, dim, dusky, dingy, dirty

**muscular** *adj.* brawny, powerful, husky, strong

**museum** *n.* collection, archives, treasury, depository

**music** *n.* melody, harmony, tune, air, strain

**musical** *adj.* tuneful, sweet, pleasing, lyrical

**musty** *adj.* moldy, sour, stale, crumbling

**mutation** *n.* change, modification, deviation

**mute** *adj.* speechless, silent, bewildered, unspoken

**mutilate** *v.* maim, damage, injure, deface, disfigure

**mutiny** *n.* insurrection, revolt, resistance, revolution

**mutter** *v.* mumble, murmur, grumble, complain

**mutual** *adj.* reciprocal, common, joint, shared

**muzzle** *v.* gag, muffle, silence, suppress, hush, quiet

**myriad** *n.* variable, innumerable, multiple

**mysterious** *adj.* PUZZLING: enigmatic, strange, unnatural; SECRET: veiled, obscure, hidden, ambiguous

**mystical** *adj.* occult, spiritual, mysterious, secret

**mystify** *v.* puzzle, perplex, hoodwink, deceive

**myth** *n.* legend, fable, lore, saga, parable, tale, story

**mythological** *adj.* whimsical, fantastic, imaginary

**nab** *v.* grab, take, snatch, seize

**nag** *v.* scold, vex, annoy, pester, bother

**naïve** *adj.* unaffected, artless, innocent, unsophisticated, gullible, credulous, trusting, inexperienced

**naïveté** *n.* inexperience, innocence

**naked** *adj.* uncovered, unclad, bare, exposed

**name** *n.* REPUTATION: renown, fame; TITLE: designation, appellation; STAR: hero, lion, celebrity

**name** *v.* appoint, nominate, select, delegate, designate

**nameless** *adj.* undistinguished, obscure, unknown

**namely** *adv.* specifically, particularly

**nap** *n.* REST: sleep, siesta, doze; PILE: shag, texture

**narrate** *v.* tell, recite, describe, reveal, report

**narrow** *adj.* CRAMPED: close, confined; DOGMATIC: intolerant, prejudiced; CLOSE: precarious, dangerous

**nasty** *adj.* OFFENSIVE: foul, gross, vulgar; INDECENT: immodest, smutty, lewd; UNKIND: sarcastic, mean

**nation** *n.* PEOPLE: populace, community, society; STATE: realm, country, domain

**nationalism** *n.* chauvinism, jingoism, loyalty

**native** *adj.* NATURAL: innate, inborn, hereditary; INDIGENOUS: aboriginal, primeval, domestic, local

**natty** *adj.* trim, spruce

**natural** *adj.* INTRINSIC: original, fundamental, inherited, native; TYPICAL: characteristic, usual, customary; UNSTUDIED: ingenuous, artless, spontaneous; REAL: actual, tangible, physical

**naughty** *adj.* bad, mischievous, wayward, roguish

**nausea** *n.* sickness, queasiness, vomiting, illness

**nauseate** *v.* sicken, repulse, bother, disgust, disturb

**nauseous** *adj.* ill, queasy, squeamish

**navigable** *adj.* passable, open, safe

**near, nearby** *adj., adv.* **BORDERING:** adjacent, adjoining, neighboring; **EXPECTED:** approaching, coming

**neat** *adj.* **TIDY:** trim, prim, spruce, dapper, orderly, precise; **CLEVER:** dexterous, skillful, agile

**nebulous** *adj.* vague, cloudy, hazy

**necessary** *adj.* essential, important, requisite, required, imperative, compulsory, mandatory

**necessitate** *v.* compel, constrain, oblige, force

**necessity** *n.* requirement, need, requisite

**nectar** *n.* drink, juice, fluid

**need** *n.* **POVERTY:** indigence, penury; **LACK:** shortage, inadequacy; **REQUIREMENT:** necessity, requirement

**needy** *adj.* destitute, indigent, penniless, poor

**nefarious** *adj.* vile, wicked

**negate** *v.* repeal, retract, neutralize, cancel, nullify

**negative** *n.* **REFUSAL:** contradiction, disavowal, refutation, denial; **PICTURE:** film, image, plate

**neglect** *v.* **SLIGHT:** disregard, disdain, affront, ignore, spurn; **EVADE:** defer, procrastinate, postpone

**negligent** *adj.* careless, indifferent, inattentive

**negotiate** *v.* bargain, mediate, conciliate, arbitrate

**negotiation** *n.* compromise, intervention, mediation

**neighborhood** *n.* vicinity, locality

**neophyte** n. convert, novice, apprentice

**nerve** n. **COURAGE:** resolution, mettle, boldness; **IMPUDENCE:** temerity, audacity, effrontery, rudeness

**nervous** adj. **EXCITABLE:** impatient, restless, uneasy, unstable; **EXCITED:** fidgety, jittery, agitated, bothered

**nestle** v. snuggle, cuddle, huddle

**neurosis** n. compulsion, nervousness, obsession

**neurotic** adj. disturbed, unstable, troubled

**neutral** adj. **UNBIASED:** impartial; **DULL:** drab, vague

**new** adj. **RECENT:** current, late; **MODERN:** contemporary, fashionable; **NOVEL:** unique, original, unusual; **INEXPERIENCED:** unseasoned, unskilled, incompetent

**newcomer** n. outsider, alien, stranger

**news** n. information, tidings, report, account

**next** adj., adv. **FOLLOWING:** succeeding, subsequent; **ADJACENT:** beside, adjoining, neighboring, touching

**nibble** v. nip, gnaw, snack, bite, eat

**nice** adj. pleasant, likable, agreeable, amiable, pleasing

**niche** n. cubbyhole, recess, cranny, corner,

**nick** v. indent, notch, slit, cut, dent

**night** n. evening, nightfall, twilight, bedtime

**nimble** adj. **AGILE:** light, quick, spry, active, graceful; **ALERT:** bright, clever, intelligent

**noble** adj. **EXALTED:** courtly, lordly, dignified, distinguished; **MERITORIOUS:** virtuous, refined, chivalrous; **TITLED:** aristocratic, patrician; **GRAND:** stately, impressive, imposing

**nobody** *n.* nonentity, upstart, cipher

**nod** *v.* **SIGNAL:** bow, acknowledge; **NAP:** drowse, sleep

**noise** *n.* sound, clamor, racket, fracas, din, uproar

**noisome** *adj.* unhealthy, disgusting, offensive, rank

**noisy** *adj.* clamorous, vociferous, boisterous, loud

**nomad** *n.* wanderer, migrant, vagabond, traveler

**nominate** *v.* name, appoint, propose, designate

**nonchalant** *adj.* **CASUAL:** unconcerned, impassive, detached, indifferent; **CARELESS:** negligent, trifling

**nonconformist** *n.* radical, rebel, eccentric, maverick

**nonprofit** *adj.* charitable, altruistic, humane

**nonsense** *n.* **INANITY:** trash, senselessness, buncombe; **FUN:** jest, absurdity

**nonviolent** *adj.* passive, calm, quiet

**nook** *n.* niche, cubbyhole, cranny, hole

**noose** *n.* loop, hitch, lasso, rope

**normal** *adj.* **USUAL:** ordinary, typical, common **REGULAR:** routine, orderly, methodical; **SANE:** lucid, rational, reasonable; **HEALTHY:** whole, sound

**nostalgia** *n.* longing, homesickness, wistfulness

**nosy** *adj.* snoopy, curious, inquisitive, interested

**notable** *adj.* remarkable, distinguished, striking, important, celebrated

**notch** *n.* nick, indent, cut, dent, groove

**note** *n.* memo, reminder, memorandum

**note** *v.* **NOTICE:** perceive, see; **RECORD:** transcribe

**noted** *adj.* well–known, celebrated, notorious, famous

**notice** *n.* warning, notification, announcement

**noticeable** *adj.* appreciable, conspicuous, obvious

**notion** *n.* whim, fancy, idea, assumption

**notorious** *adj.* infamous, known, disreputable

**notwithstanding** *adv.* despite, although, but

**nourish** *v.* feed, encourage, sustain

**nourishing** *adj.* healthy, nutritious

**novel** *adj.* new, strange, odd, unique, unusual

**novelist** *n.* writer, narrator, author

**novelty** *n.* fad, innovation, creation

**novice** *n.* beginner, neophyte, amateur

**now** *adv.* momentarily, promptly, instantly

**noxious** *adj.* injurious, harmful

**nuance** *n.* subtlety, distinction, difference

**nucleus** *n.* essence, core, kernel, center, hub, focus

**nudge** *v.* poke, bump, tap, push, touch

**nugget** *n.* lump, ingot, chunk, rock

**nuisance** *n.* **BOTHER:** annoyance, vexation, trouble; **CRIME:** breach, infraction, affront

**null** *adj.* void, invalid, vain, unsanctioned

**numb** *adj.* deadened, unfeeling, senseless

**numb** *v.* deaden, stupefy, paralyze, stun, dull

**numerous** *adj.* many, copious, diverse, infinite

**nuptials** *n.* wedding, marriage, matrimony

**nurse** *v.* tend, minister, aid, treat

**nurture** *v.* nourish, feed, sustain, cherish, support

**nutriment** *n.* food, nourishment, provisions, victuals

**nutritious** *adj.* nourishing, wholesome, healthful

**nuzzle** *v.* caress, cuddle, snuggle, nestle

**oasis** *n.* refuge, retreat

**oath** *n.* **PROMISE:** vow, pledge; **PROFANITY:** curse, swearword, blasphemy

**obdurate** *n.* stubborn, hardhearted

**obedient** *adj.* **DUTIFUL:** loyal, devoted, deferential, faithful; **DOCILE:** submissive, compliant

**obese** *adj.* fat, corpulent, plump, stout

**obey** *v.* yield, conform, submit, serve comply

**object** *n.* **THING:** article, gadget; **GOAL:** aim, objective

**object** *v.* disapprove, protest, complain, dispute

**objective** *adj.* impartial, impersonal

**objective** *n.* goal, aim, target, mission, destination

**obligate** *v.* bind, restrict, constrain, force

**obligatory** *adj.* required, essential, binding, necessary

**oblige** *v.* **ACCOMMODATE:** assist, aid, contribute, help; **REQUIRE:** constrain, bind, force, compel, coerce

**obliging** *adj.* amiable, accommodating, kind, helpful

**oblivion** *n.* obscurity, void, nothing, emptiness

**oblivious** *adj.* distracted, preoccupied, absorbed

**obnoxious** *adj.* offensive, annoying, disagreeable, displeasing, repulsive

**obscene** *adj.* indecent, lewd, wanton, lascivious

**obscure** *adj.* vague, indistinct, unclear, hazy, arcane

**obscure** *v.* **DIM:** cloud, screen; **CONCEAL:** cover, veil

**observable** *adj.* perceptible, noticeable, discernible

**observance** *n.* **CUSTOM:** ritual, practice, rite; **AWARENESS:** observation, notice

**observant** *adj.* alert, discerning, perceptive, bright

**observe** *v.* **WATCH:** scrutinize, see, notice; **COMMEMORATE:** dedicate, solemnize; **COMMENT:** remark, note, mention; **OBEY:** comply, discharge, follow

**obsessed** *adj.* haunted, beset, controlled, troubled

**obsession** *n.* fixation, fascination, passion, mania, preoccupation, craze

**obsessive** *adj.* compulsive, preoccupied

**obsolete** *adj.* antiquated, archaic, out–of–date

**obstacle** *n.* hindrance, restriction, obstruction, restraint

**obstinate** *adj.* stubborn, headstrong, opinionated

**obstreperous** *adj.* noisy, unruly

**obstruct** *v.* block, interfere, bar, hinder, prevent

**obtain** *v.* get, take, acquire, seize, procure

**obtuse** *adj.* blunt, ignorant, dull

**obvious** *adj.* apparent, perceptible, open, clear, intelligible, comprehensible, understandable

**occasion** *n.* event, occurrence, incident, happening

**occasional** *adj.* sporadic, random, infrequent

**occult** *adj.* hidden, mysterious, supernatural, secret

**occupancy** *n.* possession, occupation

**occupation** *n.* vocation, employment, job, profession

**occupy** *v.* **SEIZE:** conquer, invade; **FILL:**, pervade, permeate; **ENGAGE:** absorb, engross, involve, fascinate

**occur** *v.* happen, transpire, befall

**oceanic** *adj.* marine, aquatic, maritime, nautical

**odd** *adj.* **UNUSUAL:** unique, strange; **SINGLE:** sole, unpaired, unmatched, lone

**odious** *adj.* hateful, offensive, repulsive, despicable, repellent

**odor** *n.* smell, perfume, fragrance, bouquet

**offal** *n.* refuse, rubbish

**offend** *v.* displease, annoy, affront, outrage, bother

**offense** *n.* **MISDEED:** transgression, sin; **RESENTMENT:** pique, indignation, anger; **ATTACK:** assault, aggression

**offensive** *adj.* **AGGRESSIVE:** assaulting, attacking, invading; **REVOLTING:** disgusting, repulsive, detestable

**offer** *v.* present, proffer, tender, propose, submit

**offering** *n.* contribution, donation, present, gift

**offhand** *adj.* impromptu, informal, improvised

**officer** *n.* executive, manager, director, president

**official** *adj.* **FORMAL:** proper, accepted; **AUTHORIZED:** sanctioned, endorsed; **RELIABLE:** authentic, genuine

**official** *n.* **UMPIRE:** referee, judge, linesman; **ADMINISTRATOR:** comptroller, director, executive;

**offspring** *n.* child, progeny, issue, descendant, heir

**ointment** *n.* salve, unguent, lotion, cream, balm

**old** *adj.* **AGED:** venerable, seasoned, enfeebled; **WORN:** thin, faded; **ANCIENT:** archaic, prehistoric, antique

**ombudsman** *n.* investigator, mediator

**omen** *n.* warning, portent, augury, indication, sign

**ominous** *adj.* threatening, dismal, forbidding, menacing, portentious

**omission** *n.* exclusion, lack, need, want

**omit** *v.* exclude, ignore, slight, overlook, disregard

**omnipotent** *adj.* all–powerful, almighty

**omnipresent** *adj.* universal, pervasive

**once** *adj.*, *adv.* formerly, previously

**oncoming** *adj.* impending, imminent, approaching

**only** *adj.* **SOLELY:** exclusively, entirely, totally; **MERELY:** simply, barely, hardly; **SOLE:** single, isolated, unique

**onset** *n.* beginning, opening, start, origin

**ooze** *v.* leak, seep, exude, flow

**opaque** *adj.* dim, dusky, darkened, murky, gloomy

**open** *adj.* **CLEAR:** divulged, revealed, unobstructed; **UNRESTRICTED:** free, public; **UNGUARDED:** accessible; **UNDECIDED:** debatable, questionable; **FRANK:** plain, candid, straightforward

**open** *v.* **BEGIN:** inaugurate, initiate; **UNLOCK:** undo, unbolt; **BREACH:** penetrate, pierce; **EXPOSE:** reveal

**openly** *adv.* **FRANKLY:** candidly, honestly; **SHAMELESSLY:** immodestly, flagrantly, wantonly

**operate** *v.* **FUNCTION:** work, serve, run, percolate; **MANAGE:** manipulate, conduct, administer

**operation** *n.* **ACTION:** act, deed, undertaking, work; **METHOD:** process, formula, procedure

**operative** *adj.* effective, functioning

**opinion** *n.* belief, view, sentiment, conception

**opinionated** *adj.* obstinate, bigoted, stubborn, unyielding, prejudiced

**opponent** *n.* rival, competitor, adversary, antagonist

**opportunity** *n.* chance, circumstance

**oppose** *v.* **CONTRADICT:** dispute, defy, confront, resist; **FIGHT:** compete, encounter, assail, storm, clash

**opposite** *n.* opposition, antithesis, counterpart

**opposition** *n.* **DISLIKE:** antagonism, defiance, abhorrence, antipathy; **CONFLICT;** hostility, resistance;

**oppress** *v.* harass, maltreat, abuse, bother

**oppression** *n.* tyranny, domination, persecution

**opprobrium** *n.* disgrace, shame

**optimal** *adj.* favorable, desirable, optimum

**optimism** *n.* faith, cheerfulness, confidence, enthusiasm, expectation, certainty

**option** *n.* choice, selection, alternative

**optional** *adj.* discretionary, elective, voluntary

**opulence** *n.* riches, wealth

**oracle** *n.* prophet, seer, sage, fortuneteller

**oral** *adj.* spoken, vocal, verbal, uttered, voiced

**orbit** *v.* revolve, encircle, encompass

**ordain** *v.* **ESTABLISH:** install, appoint; **DESTINE:** foreordain, intend; **CONSECRATE:** invest, bless

**ordeal** *n.* trial, test, distress, difficulty

**order** *n.* **ARRANGEMENT:** plan, method, system; **ORGANIZATION:** fraternity, club, society; **COMMAND:** stipulation, mandate, injunction; **CLASS:** kind, hierarchy; **SEQUENCE:** progression, succession, series

**order** *v.* **ARRANGE:** classify, organize; **COMMAND:** direct, instruct, require; **BUY:** secure, reserve, request

**orderly** *adj.* **NEAT:** tidy, arranged; **METHODICAL:** systematic, thorough, precise, careful

**orderly** *n.* aide, assistant

**ordinance** *n.* law, direction, mandate

**ordinarily** *adv.* usually, generally, habitually

**ordinary** *adj.* USUAL: normal, common; AVERAGE: mediocre, accepted, typical, characteristic

**ordination** *n.* investment, investiture, induction

**organization** *n.* SYSTEM: arrangement, classification; ASSOCIATION: federation, institute, alliance

**organize** *v.* ARRANGE: systematize, coordinate, classify; ESTABLISH: build, found, plan, formulate

**orientation** *n.* familiarization, introduction

**origin** *n.* birth, start, foundation, source, beginning, inception, genesis

**original** *adj.* FIRST: fundamental, primary; CREATIVE: imaginative, inventive; GENUINE: authentic, real, actual

**originate** *v.* introduce, found, start, begin

**ornament** *n.* decoration, embellishment, adornment, beautification

**ornate** *adj.* showy, gaudy, adorned, embellished

**orphan** *n.* foundling, waif, stray

**ostensible** *adj.* professed, apparent

**other** *adj.* separate, distinct, opposite, extra

**oust** *v.* eject, expel, discharge, evict, dislodge

**out** *n.* escape, excuse, explanation

**outbreak** *n.* ERUPTION: explosion, outburst, commotion, tumult; VIOLENCE: mutiny, revolution

**outburst** *n.* discharge, eruption, outbreak

**outcast** *n.* exile, fugitive, pariah, refugee

**outcome** *n.* upshot, consequence, result

**outcry** *n.* complaint, clamor, objection

**outdated** *adj.* outmoded, antiquated, old

**outdo** *v.* surpass, best, beat, exceed

**outfit** *v.* supply, equip, provide

**outflank** *v.* surround, outmaneuver, defeat

**outgrowth** *adj.* end, result, outcome, effect, result

**outing** *n.* excursion, airing, drive, vacation

**outlandish** *adj.* STRANGE: unusual, quaint, foreign; BARBARIC: rude

**outlast** *v.* outlive, outwear, endure, survive

**outlaw** *v.* forbid, ban, banish, condemn

**outline** *n.* CONTOUR: boundary, frame; PLAN: framework, draft; SILHOUETTE: profile, shape, formation

**outlook** *n.* VIEWPOINT: scope, vision; PROSPECT: likelihood, possibility, opportunity, probability

**outlying** *adj.* exterior, frontier, distant

**outnumbered** *v.* exceeded, bested, overcome, beaten

**outrage** *v.* offend, wrong, affront, insult, abuse

**outrageous** *adj.* shameless, disgraceful, scandalous, flagrant, contemptible, ignoble, atrocious

**outright** *adj.* unmitigated, unconditional, obvious

**outside** *adj.* outermost, external, outer

**outsider** *n.* foreigner, stranger, refugee, alien

**outskirts** *n.* suburbs, limits, boundary, edge

**outspoken** *adj.* blunt, candid, artless, frank

**outstanding** *adj.* distinguished, conspicuous, notable

**outwit** *v.* trick, bewilder, confuse, deceive

**ovation** *n.* outburst, applause

**over** *adj.* ABOVE: overhead, higher; AGAIN: afresh; BEYOND: past, farther; DONE: accomplished, finished

**overbearing** *adj.* domineering, tyrannical, dictatorial

**overcast** *adj.* cloudy, gloomy, dark

**overcome** *v.* conquer, overwhelm, best, vanquish

**overconfident** *n.* reckless, impudent, heedless, rash

**overdo** *v.* **MAGNIFY:** amplify, overreach, exaggerate, enhance; **WEARY:** tire, fatigue, exhaust, overtax

**overdue** *adj.* late, delayed, belated, tardy

**overestimate** *v.* overvalue, overrate, exaggerate

**overflow** *v.* **SPILL OVER:** waste, cascade, spout, gush, surge; **FLOOD:** inundate

**overhaul** *v.* recondition, modernize, fix, renew, repair

**overpower** *v.* overwhelm, master, subjugate, defeat

**overrate** *v.* overvalue, magnify, exaggerate

**overrule** *v.* invalidate, override, cancel, revoke, reject

**overrun** *v.* **DEFEAT:** overwhelm, invade, occupy; **INFEST:** ravage, invade, overwhelm

**oversee** *v.* superintend, supervise, manage

**oversight** *n.* failure, overlooking, mistake, error

**overt** *adj.* apparent, open

**overtake** *v.* catch, exceed, surpass, reach

**overthrow** *v.* upset, overcome, overrun, overpower

**overture** *n.* **PRELUDE:** prologue, introduction, preface; **SUGGESTION:** advance, tender, negotiations;

**overturn** *v.* subvert, ruin, reverse, overthrow, upset

**overwhelm** *v.* **DEFEAT:** overcome, overthrow, conquer; **ASTONISH:** bewilder, confound, confuse, surprise

**overwrought** *adj.* excited, overexcited

**owed** *adj.* owing, due, indebted, unpaid

**own** *v.* **ACKNOWLEDGE:** grant, admit, declare;

**POSSESS:** hold, have, enjoy, retain, keep

**owner** *n.* proprietor, landlord, landlady

**ownership** *n.* possession, claim, deed, title, control

**pace** *n.* step, gait, movement, speed

**pacify** *v.* calm, soothe, conciliate, appease, placate

**package** *n.* bundle, parcel, packet, box, carton

**pact** *n.* contract, agreement, bargain, treaty

**pad** *n.* **TABLET:** stationery, notebook; **STUFFING:** cushion, wadding, waste, filling

**pad** *v.* **STUFF:** pack, fill, **INCREASE:** inflate, increase

**padding** *n.* stuffing, wadding, waste, filling

**paddle** *v.* spank, thrash, rap, punish

**padlock** *n.* lock, latch, fastener, catch

**pagan** *adj.* heathen, unchristian, idolatrous

**pagan** *n.* heathen, gentile, unbeliever, infidel

**page** *n.* leaf, sheet, folio, side, surface, recto, verso

**page** *v.* call, summon

**pageant** *n.* parade, celebration, pomp

**pail** *n.* vessel, bucket, pot, receptacle, jug, container

**pain** *n.* **SUFFERING:** anguish, distress, misery, wretchedness, torment; **HURT:** ache, spasm, cramp, agony, sting, burn; **GRIEF:** despondency, worry, anxiety, depression, sadness

**pain** *v.* distress, hurt, grieve, trouble

**painful** *adj.* **SORE:** raw, throbbing, burning, hurtful, piercing, smarting, sensitive, tender

**paint** *v.* **PORTRAY:** sketch, picture, depict; **COAT:** brush, swab, daub, cover, spread

**pair** *n.* set, two, brace, couple

**pair** *v.* join, couple, combine, match, balance

**palace** *n.* manor, mansion, castle

**pale** *adj.* wan, pallid, sickly, anemic, cadaverous, haggard, deathlike, ghostly

**palpitate** *v.* tremble, quiver, pulsate

**paltry** *adj.* worthless, small, insignificant, trifling

**pamper** *v.* overindulge, spoil, indulge, pet, humor, gratify, coddle, please

**pamphlet** *n.* booklet, leaflet, brochure, bulletin, circular, handbill, broadside, announcement

**pan** *n.* vessel, kettle, pail, bucket, container

**pandemonium** *n.* noise, disorder, uproar, anarchy, riot, confusion

**pane** *n.* panel, window, glass

**panel** *n.* ornament, tablet, inset, decoration

**pang** *n.* pain, throb, sting, bite

**panhandle** *v.* solicit, ask, bum, beg

**panic** *n.* dread, alarm, fright, fear

**panorama** *n.* view, spectacle, scenery, prospect

**pant** *v.* gasp, desire, wheeze, throb, palpitate

**pantomime** *n.* sign, charade, mime

**pantry** *n.* storage, provisions, storeroom, larder, cupboard, closet, room

**pants** *n.* trousers, breeches, slacks, jeans, overalls, cords, shorts, corduroys, pantaloons, chaps, bloomers, rompers

**paper** *n.* DOCUMENT: record, abstract, affidavit, bill, certificate, contract, credentials, deed, diploma; NEWSPAPER: journal, daily; ESSAY: article, theme

**par** *n.* equality, standard, level, norm, model

**parable** *n.* fable, allegory, moral, story, tale

**parade** *n.* **PROCESSION:** spectacle, ceremony, demonstration, review, pageant, ritual

**parade** *v.* march, demonstrate, display, exhibit

**paradox** *n.* mystery, enigma, ambiguity, puzzle

**paragon** *n.* model, example, ideal, perfection, best

**parallel** *n.* match, correspond, correlate, equal

**paraphernalia** *n.* trappings, equipment, gear

**parasite** *n.* dependent, sponger, hanger–on, toady

**parcel** *n.* package, bundle, packet, carton

**parch** *v.* scorch, dry, shrivel, desiccate, dehydrate

**pardon** *v.* exonerate, clear, absolve, reprieve, acquit, liberate, discharge, free, release, forgive, condone, overlook, exculpate, excuse

**pare** *v.* cut, diminish, shave, skin

**parentage** *n.* birth, descent, parenthood

**parental** *adj.* paternal, maternal, familial, genetic

**park** *n.* plaza, square, lawn, green, promenade, tract, grounds, woodland, meadow

**parochial** *adj.* limited, restricted, narrow, provincial, insular, sectional, local, regional

**parody** *v.* mimic, copy, caricature, imitate, joke

**parole** *v.* release, discharge, pardon, liberate, free

**parson** *n.* clergyman, cleric, preacher, minister

**part** *n.* **PORTION:** piece, fragment, fraction, section, sector, segment, particle, component, share; **ROLE:** character, hero, heroine, constituent

**part** v. DIVIDE: separate, sever; DEPART: withdraw

**partial** adj. INCOMPLETE: unfinished; PREJUDICED: unfair, influenced, biased, inclined

**partiality** n. fondness, inclination, preference

**participate** v. compete, play, strive, engage

**particle** n. jot, scrap, atom, molecule, fragment, piece, shred, bit, part

**particular** adj. SPECIFIC: distinct, singular, appropriate, special; ACCURATE: precise, minute, exact

**particularly** adj. expressly, especially

**partisan** n. adherent, supporter, disciple, follower

**partition** n. DIVISION: apportionment, distribution, BARRIER: separation, wall, obstruction

**partly** adj. partially, somewhat

**partner** n. associate, co-worker, ally

**partnership** n. alliance, union, brotherhood, society

**party** n. AFFAIR: social, reception, gathering, function; PERSON: someone, somebody; GROUP: company, crowd, assembly; ORGANIZATION: bloc, faction

**pass** v. ELAPSE: transpire; TRANSFER: relinquish, give; ENACT: legislate, establish; EXCEED: excel, transcend; PROCEED: progress, advance; THROW: toss, fling

**passable** adj. open, navigable, accessible

**passage** n. JOURNEY: voyage, crossing, trek; PASSAGEWAY: entrance, hall; READING: excerpt, section, portion, paragraph, quote

**passenger** n. traveler, commuter

**passion** n. feeling, craving, desire, emotion

**passionate** adj. excitable, tempestuous, impassioned, fervent, moving, inspiring, dramatic, stirring, eloquent, spirited, intense

**passive** *adj.* complacent, inert, lifeless, idle

**passport** *n.* pass, permit, visa, identification

**password** *n.* countersign, watchword, identification

**past** *adj.* former, preceding, foregoing, earlier

**past** *n.* antiquity, history

**paste** *n.* adhesive, cement, glue, mucilage

**paste** *v.* fasten, affix, patch, stick

**pastime** *n.* amusement, recreation, sport, hobby

**pastor** *n.* priest, rector, clergyman, minister

**pastry** *n.* dessert, delicacy

**pasture** *n.* grass, grazing, meadow, field

**pat** *v.* tap, touch, stroke, pet, rub

**patch** *n.* piece, bit, scrap, spot

**patch** *v.* repair, darn, mend

**path** *n.* trail, way, track, byway

**pathetic** *adj.* sad, touching, affecting, moving, pitiful

**pathos** *n.* pity, sorrow, grief

**patience** *n.* forbearance, fortitude, endurance, perseverance, persistence

**patient** *adj.* submissive, forbearing, unruffled, imperturbable, passive, persevering, calm

**patio** *n.* porch, courtyard, square, yard

**patriarch** *n.* ruler, master, ancestor, chief

**patriot** *n.* statesman, nationalist, loyalist, chauvinist

**patrol** *v.* watch, walk, inspect, guard

**patron** *n.* protector, sponsor, benefactor, backer

**patronize** *v.* condescend, stoop, snub

**pattern** *n.* model, original, guide, copy

**pause** *n.* delay, respite, suspension, hiatus, interim, lapse, cessation, interval

**pause** *v.* STOP: halt, cease, interrupt, suspend; REFLECT: deliberate

**pawn** *v.* deposit, pledge, hock, sell

**pay** *n.* PROCEEDS: return, recompense, indemnity, reparation, settlement, reimbursement; WAGES: compensation, salary, remuneration, earnings

**pay** *v.* COMPENSATE: recompense, remunerate, repay, reimburse; RETURN: yield, profit, pay, dividends

**payment** *n.* REIMBURSEMENT: restitution, refund, reparation; INSTALLMENT: portion, part

**peace** *n.* ARMISTICE: pacification, conciliation, agreement; CALM: tranquillity, harmony, silence, stillness; COMPOSURE: contentment

**peaceful** *adj.* quiet, tranquil, serene, calm

**peak** *n.* summit, top, crown, zenith, height

**peasant** *n.* laborer, farmer, worker, workman

**peculiar** *adj.* UNUSUAL: wonderful, singular, outlandish, strange; UNIQUE: characteristic, eccentric

**peddle** *v.* hawk, vend, trade, sell

**pedestal** *n.* base, stand, foundation, support

**pedestrian** *adj.* common, ordinary

**peek** *n.* sight, glimpse, glance, look

**peek** *v.* glance, peep, glimpse

**peel** *n.* skin, rind, husk, bark, shell

**peel** *v.* strip, skin, pare, flay, uncover

**peep** *v.* CHIRP: cheep; PEEK: glimpse, glance

**peer** *n.* equal, match, rival, companion

**peer** *v.* gaze, inspect, scrutinize

**peeve** *v.* irritate, annoy, anger, bother

**peevish** *adj.* cross, fretful, angry

**pen** *n.* cage, coop, sty, enclosure

**pen** *v.* ENCLOSE: confine; WRITE: compose

**penalize** *v.* chasten, castigate, punish

**penalty** *n.* punishment, fine, discipline

**penance** *n.* repentance, atonement, reparation

**penchant** *n.* inclination, taste, bias

**pencil** *v.* write, sketch, mark,

**pendant** *n.* locket, lavaliere, decoration, jewelry

**pending** *adj.* continuing, awaiting, ominous

**penetrable** *adj.* permeable, open, accessible, porous

**penetrate** *v.* pierce, perforate, puncture

**penetrating** *adj.* keen, astute, shrewd, sharp, intelligent, perceptive

**penitentiary** *n.* prison, reformatory, pen, jail

**pension** *n.* annuity, payment, allowance, retirement

**perceive** *v.* OBSERVE: note, look, notice; UNDERSTAND: comprehend, sense, grasp

**perceptible** *adj.* discernible, recognizable, obvious

**perception** *n.* judgment, understanding, apprehension, discernment, insight

**perceptive** *adj.* alert, incisive, keen, observant

**perch** *v.* roost, land, rest, sit

**peremptory** *adj.* decisive, final, imperious, dictatorial

**perfect** *adj.* COMPLETE: absolute, whole; FAULTLESS: impeccable, immaculate, untainted, ideal, sublime, excellent; EXACT: precise, sharp, distinct, accurate

**perfect** *v.* finish, fulfill, realize, achieve, complete

**perfectly** *adj.* flawlessly, faultlessly, ideally

**perforate** *v.* bore, pierce, drill, slit, stab, penetrate

**perforation** *n.* break, aperture, slit, hole

**perform** *v.* **PRESENT:** enact, show, exhibit, display, dramatize, execute; **ACCOMPLISH:** do, achieve, fulfill, discharge, complete, effect, finish, realize;

**performance** *n.* exhibition, appearance, offering, representation, revue, play, concert, drama

**perfume** *n.* scent, fragrance, aroma, odor, essence

**perhaps** *adj.* maybe, possibly, conceivably, reasonably

**perilous** *adj.* precarious, unsafe, dangerous

**perimeter** *n.* boundary, margin, outline, border, edge

**period** *n.* **EPOCH:** era, age; **END:** limit, conclusion

**periodical** *adj.* rhythmic, regular, recurrent

**periodical** *n.* publication, magazine, newspaper

**periphery** *n.* circumference, perimeter, border

**perish** *v.* die, pass, depart

**perjure** *v.* prevaricate, falsify, lie

**permanence** *n.* continuity, durability, stability

**permanent** *adj.* fixed, enduring, abiding, continuing, lasting, imperishable, persevering, constant

**permeate** *v.* penetrate, pervade, saturate, fill

**permissible** *adj.* allowable, sanctioned, permitted

**permission** *n.* liberty, consent, license, authorization, approval, sanction, endorsement, affirmation

**permit** *n.* permission, warrant, license, grant

**permit** *v.* consent, sanction, tolerate, let, allow

**perpetrate** *v.* perform, commit, act, do

**perpetual** *adj.* **UNENDING:** continual, unceasing, constant, endless; **REPETITIOUS:** repeating, recurrent

**perplex** *v.* puzzle, confound, bewilder, confuse

**perplexed** *adj.* troubled, uncertain, bewildered

**persecute** *v.* oppress, harass, victimize, abuse

**persecution** *n.* torture, torment, teasing, provoking

**perseverance** *n.* grit, resolution, pluck, determination

**persevere** *v.* persist, remain, pursue, endure

**persist** *v.* persevere, pursue, strive, continue, endure

**person** *n.* individual, being, character, personage

**personable** *adj.* agreeable, friendly, pleasant, charming, sociable, amiable

**personage** *n.* someone, individual, person

**personal** *adj.* **PRIVATE:** secret, confidential; **INDIVIDUAL:** peculiar, particular, individual, special

**personality** *n.* **CHARACTER:** disposition, nature, temper, individuality; **CELEBRITY:** star, luminary

**personify** *v.* represent, symbolize, exemplify

**personnel** *n.* employees, workers, group, staff

**perspective** *n.* view, vista, aspect, attitude, outlook

**persuade** *v.* influence, induce, convince, cajole

**persuasion** *n.* **BELIEF:** creed, tenet, religion, faith, conviction; **INFLUENCE:** inducing, enticement

**persuasive** *adj.* convincing, influential, winning, enticing, compelling, potent, powerful, forceful, plausible

**pertain** *v.* belong, relate, refer, concern

**pertinent** *adj.* relevant, pertaining, related

**perturb** *v.* disturb, pester, worry, irritate, bother

**pervade** *v.* penetrate, spread, suffuse, permeate

**perverse** *adj.* deviant, wayward, delinquent, bad

**perversion** *n.* DISTORTION: deception, lie; CORRUPTION: depravity, wickedness, vice

**pervert** *v.* corrupt, ruin, vitiate, divert

**pessimism** *n.* unhappiness, gloom, sadness

**pessimistic** *adj.* DISCOURAGING: worrisome, troubling, dismal; CYNICAL: hopeless, gloomy, sad

**pester** *v.* annoy, harass, provoke, bother

**pestilence** *n.* disease, epidemic, sickness, illness

**pet** *n.* darling, lover, favorite, idol, adored

**pet** *v.* caress, fondle, cuddle, touch embrace

**petition** *n.* request, prayer, supplication, appeal

**petrified** *adj.* stone, hardened, mineralized, firm

**petty** *adj.* small, contemptible, insignificant, frivolous, trivial, unimportant

**phantasm** *n.* vision, illusion, specter, apparition, ghost

**phenomenal** *adj.* extraordinary, unique, remarkable

**philanthropic** *adj.* benevolent, humanitarian, kind

**philosophic** *adj.* thoughtful, reflective, cogitative, rational, profound, erudite, deep, learned

**philosophy** *n.* STUDY: wisdom, theory, explanation; PRINCIPLE: truth, axiom, conception, basis; BELIEF: outlook, view, position, opinion, viewpoint

**phlegmatic** *adj.* calm, sluggish, indifferent

**phobia** *n.* avoidance, aversion, hatred, resentment

**phony** *adj.* affected, imitation, artificial, false

**photograph** *n.* print, portrait, likeness, snapshot

**photographic** *adj.* accurate, detailed, exact, graphic

**physical** *adj.* material, corporeal, visible, tangible, palpable, substantial, real

**physician** *n.* healer, practitioner, surgeon, doctor

**physique** *n.* structure, build, constitution, body

**pick** *v.* CHOOSE: select, separate; GATHER: pluck, pull

**picket** *n.* STAKE: pole, post; WATCHMAN: guard, sentry

**picket** *v.* strike, blockade, boycott, protest

**picture** *n.* REPRESENTATION: photograph, image, portrait; DESCRIPTION: depiction, portrayal

**picture** *v.* DEPICT: sketch, portray, draw, paint, represent, describe; IMAGINE: create, conceive

**picturesque** *adj.* charming, pictorial, scenic, graphic, striking, quaint

**piece** *n.* part, portion, share, section

**pierce** *v.* penetrate, stab

**piety** *n.* reverence, devotion, veneration

**pigment** *n.* coloring, paint, dye, color

**pile** *n.* heap, collection, mass, quantity

**pile** *v.* amass, stack, gather, accumulate, store

**pilgrim** *n.* traveler, wayfarer, wanderer, sojourner

**pill** *n.* tablet, capsule, pellet, medicine, drug

**pillage** *v.* plunder, loot, rob, destroy, steal

**pillar** *n.* COLUMN: pedestal, mast, shaft, post; SUPPORT: mainstay, prop

**pillow** *n.* cushion, pad, support, headrest

**pilot** *v.* guide, conduct, manage, lead

**pin** *v.* close, clasp, bind, fasten

**pinnacle** *n.* apex, zenith, crest, summit, climax

**pious** *adj.* reverent, devout, divine, holy, religious

**pipe** *n.* tube, conduit, culvert, duct

**piracy** *n.* robbery, theft, pillage, holdup

**pirate** *n.* plunderer, marauder, privateer, buccaneer

**pit** *n.* hole, abyss, cavity, depression

**pitch** *n.* SLOPE: slant, incline, angle, grade; THROW: toss, hurl, cast; FREQUENCY: tone, sound

**pitfall** *n.* snare, mesh, deadfall, trap

**pith** *n.* center, essence, heart, core

**pitiful** *adj.* sorry, mean, despicable, miserable, distressed, pathetic, pitiable, depressing

**pity** *n.* compassion, charity, tenderness, kindliness, benevolence, clemency, humanity, sympathy

**pity** *v.* COMMISERATE: sympathize, console, grieve, weep, comfort; FORGIVE: pardon, reprieve, spare

**pivot** *v.* turn, whirl, swivel, rotate

**place** *n.* POSITION: point, spot; LOCALITY: locus, site, area, region; RANK: status, position

**place** *v.* PUT: locate, deposit; ARRANGE: fix, order

**placement** *n.* situation, position, arrangement

**plague** *n.* pestilence, illness, epidemic

**plague** *v.* afflict, vex, disturb, trouble, irk, bother

**plain** *adj.* OBVIOUS: open, manifest, clear, understandable; SIMPLE: unadorned, unpretentious, modest; ORDINARY: everyday, commonplace;

**BLUNT:** outspoken, candid, impolite, rude

**plan** *n.* **DRAFT:** diagram, design, schematic, drawing; **SCHEME:** project, idea, undertaking, plot, conspiracy, strategy; **ARRANGEMENT:** layout, disposition, order,

**plan** *v.* **SCHEME:** plot, devise, contrive, intrigue, conspire, calculate; **OUTLINE:** draft, sketch, map; **INTEND:** propose, think, expect, contemplate

**plane** *n.* level, horizontal, flat

**plane** *v.* smooth, finish, level, flatten

**planned** *adj.* projected, budgeted, programmed

**plantation** *n.* farm, acreage, estate, ranch

**plateau** *n.* tableland, mesa, elevation, hill

**platform** *n.* **STAGE:** dais, rostrum, stand, terrace; **PROGRAM:** principles, policies

**plausible** *adj.* convincing, probable, credible, likely

**play** *n.* **AMUSEMENT:** enjoyment, diversion; **RECREATION:** games, sports; **THEATER:** drama, musical

**play** *v.* revel, carouse, gambol, cavort, participate

**player** *n.* athlete, contestant, actor, performer

**playful** *adj.* joking, whimsical, comical, funny

**playmate** *n.* comrade, neighbor, companion, friend

**playwright** *n.* writer, author, tragedian

**plea** *n.* appeal, request, supplication, pleading

**plead** *v.* **BEG:** implore, beseech, solicit, ask; **ARGUE:** present, allege, cite, declare

**pleasant** *adj.* affable, agreeable, obliging, charming, gracious, amiable, polite, civil, cordial, sociable

**please** *v.* gratify, delight, satisfy

**pleasing** *adj.* charming, agreeable, delightful, pleasant

**pleasure** *n.* enjoyment, delight, happiness, amusement, preference, desire

**pledge** *n.* security, surety, guarantee, agreement

**pledge** *v.* promise, swear, vow, vouch

**plentiful** *adj.* bountiful, prolific, profuse, lavish, extravagant, copious, abundant, abounding

**plenty** *n.* abundance, lavishness, deluge, torrent, bounty, profusion, flood

**pliable, pliant** *adj.* flexible, limber, supple, plastic

**plight** *n.* condition, dilemma, state

**plod** *v.* trudge, hike, walk

**plot** *v.* **INTRIGUE:** frame, contrive, scheme, conspire; **PLAN:** sketch, outline, draft

**plump** *adj.* obese, stout, fleshy, fat

**plunder** *v.* seize, burn, steal, raid, ravage

**plunge** *v.* cast, fall, rush, dive, jump

**plus** *adj.* increase, additionally, surplus, extra

**poach** *v.* steal, filch, pilfer, smuggle

**pocket** *n.* **CAVITY:** hollow; **POUCH:** poke, sac

**pocket** *v.* take, conceal, hide, enclose, steal

**poetic** *adj.* lyrical, romantic, imaginative

**poetry** *n.* verse, rhythm, rhyme, poesy

**poignant** *adj.* penetrating, moving, touching

**point** *n.* **POSITION:** location, locality; **PURPOSE:** aim, object, intent; **MEANING:** force, drift, import

**point** *v.* **INDICATE:** show, name, denote; **DIRECT:** guide, steer, influence, lead

**pointer** *n.* **INDICATOR:** dial, gauge; **HINT:** clue, tip

**pointless** *adj.* **DULL:** prosaic, trivial, unnecessary; **INEFFECTIVE:** useless, impotent, incompetent, weak

**poise** *n.* carriage, bearing, grace, composure, dignity

**poisonous** *adj.* noxious, venomous, toxic, harmful

**poke** *v.* jab, punch, crowd, push

**policy** *n.* principle, doctrine, scheme, design

**polish** *v.* smooth, burnish, finish, shine

**polite** *adj.* polished, mannerly, amiable, gracious, cordial, diplomatic, civil, sociable, respectful

**politeness** *n.* refinement, culture, civility, courtesy

**poll** *v.* sample, canvass, question, register, enroll, list

**pollute** *v.* soil, defile, stain, contaminate, corrupt

**pollution** *n.* dirt, grime, smog, sewage, garbage, waste, exhaust, pesticides, smoke

**poltergeist** *n.* ghost, spirit, apparition, specter, spook

**pomp** *n.* pageantry, magnificence, splendor

**pompous** *adj.* pretentious, haughty, arrogant, proud

**ponder** *v.* meditate, think, deliberate, consider

**ponderous** *adj.* heavy, weighty, dull, lifeless

**pool** *n.* WATER: puddle; STAKES: ante, pot, kitty

**pool** *v.* merge, unite, consolidate, combine, blend, join

**poor** *adj.* INSOLVENT: indigent, penniless, destitute, needy, starved, beggared, broke, WEAK: puny, feeble, infirm; INFERIOR: mediocre, trashy, shoddy, deficient, cheap, flimsy

**pop** *n.* SODA: beverage, seltzer, cola; NOISE: report, burst, shot, crack, detonation

**poppycock** *n.* drivel, nonsense, gibberish

**populace** *n.* people, multitudes, masses, people

**popular** *adj.* liked, favorite, beloved, celebrated, admired, famous, widespread

**popularity** *n.* acceptance, notoriety, prevalence

**populated** *adj.* inhabited, occupied, peopled, urban

**population** *n.* inhabitants, citizenry, populace, society

**porous** *adj.* absorbent, pervious, permeable

**port** *n.* harbor, haven, refuge, anchorage, dock

**portable** *adj.* movable, transportable, transferable

**portal** *n.* entrance, archway, gateway

**portend** *v.* foretell, predict, herald

**porter** *n.* doorkeeper, custodian, caretaker

**portfolio** *n.* **CASE:** briefcase, folder; **ASSETS:** holdings, stocks, bonds

**portion** *n.* **PART:** scrap, fragment, piece; **ALLOTMENT:** share, quota

**portrait** *n.* likeness, painting, picture

**portray** *v.* draw, describe, depict, characterize

**portrayal** *n.* description, replica, likeness

**pose** *n.* position, attitude, pretense, affectation

**pose** *v.* **MODEL:** sit; **PRETEND:** profess, act, feign

**posh** *adj.* rich, smart, comfortable

**position** *n.* **LOCATION:** whereabouts, bearings; **OPINION:** view, belief; **PROFESSION:** job, office, occupation; **STATION:** status, rank; **POSTURE:** carriage, bearing

**positive** *adj.* decisive, emphatic, assertive, resolute, certain, confident, sure

**possess** *v.* have, hold, own, occupy, control

**possessions** *n.* belongings, effects, estate, property

**possessor** *n.* owner, holder, proprietor, occupant

**possibility** *n.* plausibility, feasibility, chance, hazard, hope, prospect

**possible** *adj.* likely, conceivable, imaginable

**possibly** *adv.* likely, maybe, perhaps, potentially

**post** *n.* column, pillar, pedestal, upright, mast

**poster** *n.* advertisement, sign, card, note

**posterior** *adj.* SUBSEQUENT: coming, after, succeeding, next, following, later; BEHIND: back

**posterity** *n.* eternity, descendants, children, offspring

**postpone** *v.* defer, table, delay, suspend, retard, withhold, shelve, adjourn, pause

**postscript** *n.* appendix, addition, supplement

**posture** *n.* STANCE: pose, carriage, aspect, presence; ATTITUDE: feeling, sentiment, disposition

**pot** *n.* KITTY: jackpot, ante; CONTAINER: vessel, kettle, pan, crock, receptacle, urn, bowl

**potable** *adj.* clean, fresh, unpolluted

**potency** *n.* STRENGTH: power, energy, vigor; AUTHORITY: influence, control, dominion, command

**potential** *adj.* possible, latent, implied, likely

**pouch** *n.* bag, sack, receptacle, container

**pounce** *v.* seize, spring, attack, bound, jump

**pound** *v.* beat, crush, pulverize, strike, hit

**pour** *v.* FLOW: discharge, emit, issue, drain, rush; EMPTY: spill, splash; RAIN: stream, flood, drench

**poverty** *n.* DESTITUTION: indigence, want, privation, insolvency; LACK: shortage, inadequacy, scarcity

**power** *n.* STRENGTH: vigor, stamina; AUTHORITY: jurisdiction, dominion, dominance, control, sway,

sovereignty, suprem-
acy; **FORCE:** compul-
sion, coercion, du-
ress; **ENERGY:** poten-
tial, dynamism
**powerful** *adj.* mighty,
omnipotent, influen-
tial, potent, forceful,
compelling
**powerless** *adj.* helpless, feeble, weak, im-
potent, infirm
**practical** *adj.* useful,
feasible, workable,
rational, utilitarian,
serviceable, effective
**practically** *adv.* virtu-
ally, nearly, almost
**practice** *n.* **CUSTOM:**
usage; **METHOD:**
mode, manner, fash-
ion; **REPETITION:** exercise, rehearsal
**practice** *v.* drill, train,
exercise, rehearse
**practiced** *adj.* skilled,
able, experienced
**pragmatic** *adj.* logical,
sensible, practical,
realistic
**praise** *v.* commend,
applaud, acclaim, en-
dorse, eulogize, com-
pliment, celebrate,
honor, glorify, extol

**prance** *v.* strut, caper,
cavort, frisk, gambol,
dance
**prank** *n.* trick, antic,
game, escapade, ca-
per, joke
**pray** *v.* ask, petition,
plead, beseech, beg,
implore
**prayer** *n.* appeal, request, petition, plea,
entreaty,
**preach** *v.* lecture,
teach, sermonize, dis-
course, exhort, mor-
alize, talk, harangue,
inform, address
**preacher** *n.* missionary, parson, evangel-
ist, minister
**preamble** *n.* preface,
prelude, introduction
**precarious** *adj.* un-
certain, unsafe, risky,
doubtful, dubious,
dangerous, unstable
**precaution** *n.* care,
prudence, anticipa-
tion, forethought, re-
gard, foresight
**precede** *v.* lead, ante-
date, preface, intro-
duce, herald
**precedence** *n.* preference, priority

**preceding** *adj.* foregoing, former, previous, earlier

**precious** *adj.* BELOVED: cherished, prized; VALUABLE: costly, expensive; REFINED: delicate, dainty

**precipice** *n.* cliff, crag, bluff, hill, mountain

**precipitate** *v.* cause, accelerate, press, hasten, speed

**precipitous** *adj.* sheer, steep, sharp, abrupt

**precise** *adj.* exact, accurate, careful

**precision** *n.* exactness, correctness, accuracy

**preconception** *n.* prejudice, bias, assumption

**predecessor** *n.* forerunner, antecedent, ancestor

**predicament** *n.* difficulty, strait, plight, scrape, circumstance, mess, pinch, crisis

**predict** *v.* foretell, prophesy, prognosticate, divine

**predominance** *n.* dominance, supremacy, control

**predominant** *adj.* SUPREME: almighty, powerful; FIRST: transcendent, surpassing, superlative, principal

**preeminent** *adj.* distinguished, eminent, outstanding

**preface** *v.* introduce, commence, precede, begin

**preference** *n.* choice, election, option, selection, pick

**preferred** *adj.* chosen, selected, favored

**prehistoric** *adj.* ancient, primitive, antiquated, old

**prejudice** *n.* bias, inclination, partiality

**prejudiced** *adj.* predisposed, opinionated, partisan, narrow, intolerant, parochial, provincial

**preliminary** *adj.* preparatory, preceding, introductory

**prelude** *n.* introduction, preamble, prologue, preface

**premature** *adj.* rash, precipitate, untimely, early

**premise** *n.* supposition, assumption, proposition

**premium** *adj.* excellent, select, prime, superior

**premium** *n.* reward, prize, remuneration, bonus

**premonition** *n.* foreboding, portent, sign, warning

**preoccupied** *adj.* distracted, absorbed, engrossed, disturbed, troubled,

**preparation** *n.* **READYING:** rehearsal, anticipation, build–up; **PREPAREDNESS:** readiness, fitness, training, education; **MIXTURE:** compound, medicine, poultice

**prepare** *v.* **READY:** fix, fabricate, devise, anticipate, plan, arrange, make; **OUTFIT:** equip; **COOK:** concoct

**prepossessing** *adj.* winning, captivating, charming

**prerequisite** *n.* requirement, necessity, essential

**prerogative** *n.* privilege, advantage, exemption, right

**prescription** *n.* remedy, formula, medicine

**presence** *n.* **ATTENDANCE:** occupancy, residence, inhabitancy; **PROXIMITY:** nearness, closeness; **DEMEANOR:** appearance, behavior, carriage

**present** *adj.* now, existing, contemporary, immediate, instant, today, nowadays, already, current

**present** *n.* gift, grant, donation, offering

**present** *v.* **EXHIBIT:** do, act, perform; **BESTOW:** give, grant, confer donate, proffer, offer

**presentable** *adj.* proper, satisfactory, attractive

**presently**, *adv.* soon, directly, shortly, immediately

**preservation** *n.* protection, conservation, keeping, storage, curing, refrigeration

**preserve** *v.* **GUARD:** protect, shield; **KEEP:** process, cure

**preside** *v.* superintend, direct, lead, manage

**press** *n.* haste, urgency, rush, confusion, strain

**pressing** *adj.* important, urgent, demanding

**pressure** *n.* **TENSION:** burden, stress, squeeze; **PERSUASION:** compulsion, coercion

**pressure** *v.* press, compel, constrain, urge, persuade

**prestige** *n.* influence, reputation, esteem

**presume** *v.* believe, consider, suppose, assume

**presumption** *n.* **ASSUMPTION:** conjecture, supposition; **IMPUDENCE:** audacity, arrogance, effrontery

**pretend** *v.* feign, affect, imitate, simulate, represent

**pretense** *n.* simulation, fabrication, imitation; deception, affectation, subterfuge, pretext

**pretentious** *adj.* presumptuous, arrogant, pompous

**pretty** *adj.* **PLEASANT:** delightful, cheerful, pleasing; **ATTRACTIVE:** comely, lovely, beautiful;

**prevalent** *adj.* prevailing, widespread, common

**prevent** *v.* preclude, block, stop, thwart, halt, impede, check, frustrate, obstruct, inhibit, restrain

**previous** *adj.* former, antecedent, prior, preceding

**prey** *v.* hunt, spoil, pillage, loot, victimize

**price** *n.* expense, cost, worth, payment

**price** *v.* appraise, assess, rate, value

**priceless** *adj.* invaluable, inestimable, valuable

**prick** *v.* pierce, stick, cut, hurt, puncture

**prickly** *adj.* thorny, pointed, spiny, sharp

**pride** *n.* egotism, haughtiness, disdain, condescension

**prim** *adj.* exact, stiff, formal, demure, decorous, polite

**primary** *adj.* **EARLIEST:** primitive, first, original; **FUNDAMENTAL:** elemental, basic; **PRINCIPAL:** chief, prime, main

**primitive** *adj.* **SIMPLE:** rough, rude, fundamental; **ANCIENT:** primeval, old, beginning, uncivilized

**primp** *v.* dress, prepare, paint, powder

**princely** *adj.* lavish, sumptuous, luxurious, expensive, handsome, rich

**principal** *adj.* chief, leading, first, main, foremost, preeminent, dominant, prevailing

**principle** *n.* **FUNDAMENTAL:** law, origin, source, postulate; **BELIEF:** opinion, teaching, faith

**prior** *adj.* before, antecedent, foregoing, preceding

**priority** *n.* preference, precedence, advantage

**prisoner** *n.* captive, convict, detainee, hostage

**privacy** *n.* seclusion, solitude, isolation, aloofness, separation, concealment, secrecy

**private** *adj.* personal, separate, secluded, clandestine

**privilege** *n.* right, perquisite, prerogative, concession

**prize** *n.* reward, premium, bonus, booty, plunder, loot, award, medal, trophy, crown

**probable** *adj.* likely, seeming, presumable, feasible

**problem** *n.* **DIFFICULTY:** dilemma, quandary, obstacle; **QUESTION:** query, intricacy, enigma, puzzle

**procedure** *n.* fashion, mode, method, system, order

**proceed** *v.* progress, continue, advance

**proceeding** *n.* performance, undertaking, venture, happening, operation, procedure, exercise

**proceeds** *n.* gain, interest, yield, return

**process** *n.* means, manner, method

**process** *v.* treat, ready, concoct, prepare

**prod** *v.* provoke, crowd, shove, push

**produce** *v.* **CREATE:** originate, devise, conceive, design, compose, invent; **MAKE:** assemble, construct, manufacture; **CAUSE:** effect, occasion

**product** *n.* result, output, outcome

**productive** *adj.* rich, fruitful, prolific, fertile

**profanity** *n.* irreverence, abuse, cursing, swearing

**profession** *n.* **CAREER:** occupation, calling, avocation, vocation; **DECLARATION:** avowal, vow, oath

**professional** *adj.* skillful, expert, adept, able, qualified

**professor** *n.* teacher, educator, instructor, lecturer

**proficiency** *n.* skill, knowledge, ability

**proficient** *adj.* adept, expert, skilled, able

**profit** *n.* gain, return, proceeds

**profitable** *adj.* lucrative, beneficial, advantageous

**profound** *adj.* **SCHOLARLY:** learned, sagacious, intellectual; **HEARTFELT:** great, intense

**program** *n.* **SCHEDULE:** agenda, curriculum, calendar, plan, outline; **ENTERTAINMENT:** performance, show

**progress** *n.* headway, impetus, improvement, advancement, development, growth

**progressive** *adj.* tolerant, lenient, open-minded

**prohibit** *v.* forbid, interdict, obstruct, prevent, ban

**project** *n.* plan, scheme, outline, design

**projection** *n.* **BULGE:** prominence, protuberance; **FORECAST:** prognostication, prediction, guess

**prolong** *v.* lengthen, extend, increase

**prominent** *adj.* FAMOUS: notable, distinguished, leading; CONSPICUOUS: striking, noticeable

**promiscuous** *adj.* indiscriminate, unrestricted, lewd

**promise** *n.* agreement, pact, covenant, contract

**promise** *v.* pledge, declare, vow, swear, profess, guarantee, warrant, insure, underwrite, subscribe

**promising** *adj.* likely, encouraging, hopeful

**promote** *v.* further, encourage, help, aid, assist, support, back, champion, advocate, bolster, nourish, nurture, subsidize, boost, advance

**prompt** *adj.* timely, precise, punctual

**prompt** *v.* instigate, arouse, inspire, incite, urge

**prone** *adj.* disposed, inclined, predisposed, likely

**pronounced** *adj.* noticeable, clear, definite, obvious

**pronouncement** *n.* report, declaration, statement

**proof** *n.* verification, confirmation, corroboration, substantiation, testimony

**propensity** *n.* talent, capacity, ability

**proper** *adj.* decent, conventional, decorous, prudish, prim

**property** *n.* possessions, belongings, assets, holdings

**prophecy** *n.* prediction, forecast, prognostication

**prophesy** *v.* foretell, predict, divine

**prophet** *n.* seer, oracle, soothsayer, astrologer

**propitious** *adj.* auspicious, encouraging, promising

**proponent** *n.* defender, advocate, champion

**proposal** *n.* OFFER: overture, proposition, suggestion, PLAN: scheme, program, prospectus

**propose** v. offer, recommend, submit, volunteer

**proposition** n. offer, scheme, project, plan

**propriety** n. accordance, compatibility, congruity, modesty, dignity, pleasantness

**prospect** n. expectation, promise, outlook, possibility

**prospective** adj. proposed, promised, planned

**prosper** v. flourish, thrive, flower, succeed

**protect** v. shelter, shield, guard, preserve, defend

**protection** n. shield, screen, shelter, defense, security

**protector** n. champion, defender, patron, sponsor, benefactor, supporter, advocate

**protest** n. rally, demonstration, dissent

**protest** v. object, demur, disagree, oppose

**proud** adj. DIGNIFIED: stately, lordly; EGOTISTICAL: vain, haughty, arrogant

**prove** v. demonstrate, substantiate, authenticate, corroborate, validate, confirm

**provide** v. furnish, equip, outfit, stock, supply

**provincial** adj. narrow, backward, rude, unpolished

**provision** v. requirement, stipulation, prerequisite

**provisional** adj. transient, passing, temporary

**provoke** v. VEX: irritate, aggravate, bother; INCITE: stir, rouse, arouse; CAUSE: make, produce, begin

**prowl** v. slink, lurk, rove, sneak

**proxy** n. agent, broker, representative, delegate

**prudent** adj. CAREFUL: cautious, circumspect, wary, discreet; PRACTICAL: sensible, wise, discerning

**pry** v. snoop, spy, nose, inquire, meddle

**pseudo** adj. imitation, quasi, sham, false

**publication** *n.* broadcasting, announcement, advisement, disclosure

**publicize** *n.* announce, broadcast, promulgate

**publish** *v.* **DISTRIBUTE:** print, issue; **ADVERTISE:** announce, promulgate, proclaim

**pull** *n.* **TOW:** drag, haul; **INFLUENCE:** power, authority

**pulpy** *adj.* soft, smooth, thick, fleshy

**pulse** *n.* beating, pulsation, vibration

**pun** *n.* witticism, quip, joke

**punch** *v.* **HIT:** thrust, blow, strike, knock; **PERFORATE:** pierce, puncture, bore, penetrate, prick

**punctual** *adj.* prompt, precise, exact, meticulous

**puncture** *v.* pierce, prick, perforate, penetrate

**punish** *v.* correct, discipline, chasten, reprove, penalize, fine, incarcerate, chastise

**puny** *adj.* small, feeble, inferior, diminutive, weak

**purchase** *v.* obtain, acquire, buy

**pure** *adj.* **CLEAN:** immaculate, germ–free, sterilized, sanitary, refined; **UNMIXED:** unadulterated, undiluted, simple, clear; **CHASTE:** virginal, celibate; **ABSOLUTE:** sheer, utter, complete

**purge** *v.* cleanse, evacuate, eliminate

**purpose** *n.* aim, intention, end, goal, mission, objective, expectation, intent, aspiration

**pursue** *v.* chase, seek, hound, track, stalk

**push** *n.* shove, drive, exertion, straining, inducement, impact, blow, pressure

**push** *v.* **PRESS:** thrust, shove, ram, jostle, elbow; **PROMOTE:** advance, launch, start, sell

**put** *v.* **PLACE:** set, plant, lodge, situate, deposit

**putrid** *adj.* rotten, corrupt, putrefied, decayed

**puzzle** *v.* **PERPLEX:** obscure, bewilder, complicate, confuse; **WONDER:** marvel, surprise, astonish

**puzzling** *adj.* obscure, uncertain, ambiguous, mystifying, difficult, perplexing, abstruse, hard

**quaint** *adj.* strange, odd, fanciful, cute, whimsical

**quake** *v.* tremble, shrink, cower, shake

**qualified** *adj.* **LIMITED:** conditional, confined, restricted; **COMPETENT:** adequate, equipped, able

**quality** *n.* **ATTRIBUTE:** trait, endowment, condition, property; **CHARACTER:** nature, essence; **GRADE:** class, merit, worth, excellence, variety, rank

**qualm** *n.* scruple, doubt, uncertainty

**quantity** *n.* amount, number, measure

**quarrel** *v.* dispute, wrangle, clash, contend, squabble, disagree, bicker, contest, argue, feud, oppose

**quarrelsome** *adj.* factious, irritable, pugnacious, contentious, cantankerous

**queasy** *adj.* squeamish, sick, uneasy, uncomfortable

**queer** *adj.* odd, peculiar, strange, curious

**question** *v.* **ASK:** inquire, interrogate, petition, solicit, quiz, probe, investigate; **DOUBT:** challenge, dispute

**questionable** *adj.* **CONTROVERSIAL:** vague, unsettled, debatable, ambiguous, indefinite; **DUBIOUS:** disreputable, notorious, suspicious

**quick** *adj.* **RAPID:** swift, fleet, fast; **IMMEDIATE:** instantaneous, prompt; **HASTY:** impetuous, quick–tempered, rash; **ALERT:** ready, sharp, vigorous, active

**quicken** v. HASTEN: speed, hurry, accelerate, move, EXPEDITE: urge, promote

**quiet** adj. silent, calm, peaceful, hushed, reserved, muffled, reticent, noiseless, still

**quiet** n. calm, tranquillity, relaxation, peace, repose; silence, hush, stillness

**quip** n. retort, remark, jest, repartee, banter

**quirk** n. whim, caprice, fancy, peculiarity

**quit** v. ABANDON: surrender, renounce, relinquish; CEASE: discontinue, halt, desist, stop; LEAVE: go, depart, vacate, resign

**quiver** v. vibrate, shudder, tremble

**quiz** v. question, examine, test, query

**quote** v. EXCERPT: extract, say, repeat; PRICE: request, demand, value

**rabid** adj. FANATICAL: obsessed, zealous; INSANE: raging, deranged, mad

**race** v. hurry, run, tear, bustle, fly, dash, sprint

**racket** n. UPROAR: clatter, disturbance, din; CONSPIRACY: scheme, corruption, crime, theft

**racketeer** n. criminal, extortionist, trickster

**radial** adj. branched, outspread, spreading

**radiant** adj. shining, luminous, radiating, bright

**radiate** v. spread, diffuse, disperse, disseminate

**radiation** n. fallout, pollution, radioactivity, heat

**radical** adj. EXTREME: progressive, militant, seditious, riotous, rebellious, revolutionary, heretical; FUNDAMENTAL: original, primitive, native, organic

**raffle** n. lottery, sweepstakes, pool

**raft** n. flatboat, barge, float, catamaran, boat

**rag** n. cloth, remnant, wiper, shred

**rage** *n.* **FURY:** frenzy, tantrum, uproar, storm, outburst; **FAD:** fashion, style, mode, vogue, craze, mania

**rage** *v.* rave, splutter, scream, rant, bluster, storm

**ragged** *adj.* tattered, frayed, threadbare, frazzled

**raid** *n.* attack, invasion, foray, assault

**rain** *v.* pour, drizzle, shower, sprinkle, mist

**raise** *v.* **LIFT:** elevate, hoist, boost; **REAR:** breed, cultivate, produce; **ERECT:** construct, build

**rake** *n.* **RASCAL:** lecher, drunkard, scoundrel

**rally** *n.* gathering, meeting, session

**ram** *v.* butt, bump, collide, thrust, drive

**ramble** *v.* **SAUNTER:** stroll, roam, wander; **DRIFT:** stray, diverge, meander, digress

**ramp** *n.* incline, slope, grade, hill, inclination

**rampant** *adj.* raging, violent, turbulent, tumultuous, unruly

**rancid** *adj.* unpleasant, tainted, stale, rotten

**random** *adj.* aimless, haphazard, casual, unpredictable

**range** *n.* **SCOPE:** extent, area, expanse; **MOUNTAINS:** highlands; **DISTANCE:** reach, span, projection

**range** *v.* **VARY:** differ, fluctuate, diverge; **TRAVERSE:** wander, ramble, explore, traverse

**rank** *adj.* foul, smelly, fetid, putrid, stinking, rancid, offensive, noxious, gamy, disgusting, malodorous

**rank** *n.* **ROW:** column, file, string, line; **EMINENCE:** position, distinction, standing, status, ancestry

**rank** *v.* **ARRANGE:** assign, order; **EVALUATE:** judge, fix, valuate, classify

**ransack** *v.* **SEARCH:** rummage, scour, seek; **LOOT:** pillage, plunder, ravish, strip, rifle

**rant** *v.* rave, fume, rail, rage, yell

**rap** *n.* knock, thump, slap, blow

**rapid** *adj.* accelerated, swift, speedy, hurried

**rapt** *adj.* awed, transported, entranced, enchanted

**rapture** *n.* delight, ecstasy, pleasure, satisfaction

**rare** *adj.* UNCOMMON: exceptional, singular, extraordinary, unusual; SCARCE: expensive, precious; CHOICE: select, superlative, excellent

**rascal** *n.* scoundrel, rogue, rake, knave, shyster, cad, scalawag, reprobate, miscreant

**rash** *adj.* hasty, impetuous, impulsive, foolish, heedless, foolhardy, brash

**rate** *v.* rank, judge, evaluate, grade

**ratify** *v.* substantiate, endorse, approve, sanction

**rating** *n.* grade, class, degree, rank

**ration** *n.* allowance, allotment, portion, quota, share

**rational** *adj.* LOGICAL: stable, thoughtful, sensible, impartial, objective, sober; REASONABLE: intelligent, sensible, wise; SANE: normal, lucid, responsible

**rattle** *v.* disconcert, bother, unnerve, confuse, disturb, embarrass

**raucous** *adj.* hoarse, harsh, loud, gruff, rough

**ravage** *v.* pillage, devastate, despoil, plunder, sack

**rave** *v.* TALK: babble, gabble, jabber; RAGE: storm, splutter, rail, rant

**ravel** *v.* untwist, disentangle, unsnarl, free, loosen

**ravenous** *adj.* voracious, starved, hungry

**ravine** *n.* hollow, gully, gorge, canyon, gulch, valley, gap, chasm, abyss, break, crevice, crevasse

**raw** *adj.* **UNFINISHED:** natural, crude, rough; **UNTRAINED:** immature; **COLD:** biting, windy, bleak

**reach** *n.* compass, range, scope, grasp, stretch, extension, orbit, horizon, gamut, ability, limit, extent

**reach** *v.* **EXTEND:** span, encompass, overtake; stretch, strain, seize; **ARRIVE:** gain, enter

**react** *v.* respond, reciprocate, behave, answer

**reaction** *n.* response, rejoinder, repercussion

**read** *v.* **UNDERSTAND:** comprehend, perceive, apprehend, grasp, learn; **INTERPRET:** decipher, explain, expound, construe

**readable** *adj.* **LEGIBLE:** distinct, comprehensible, decipherable; **INTERESTING:** absorbing, fascinating, engrossing, entertaining, engaging, stimulating

**readily** *adv.* quickly, promptly, eagerly, willingly

**reading** *n.* **EXCERPT:** passage, quotation; **INTERPRETATION:** translation, commentary

**ready** *adj.* **PREPARED:** alert, handy, expectant; **ENTHUSIASTIC:** eager, willing, ardent, zealous

**real** *adj.* **GENUINE:** authentic, original; **EXISTING:** actual, substantive, tangible

**realism** *n.* authenticity, naturalness, actuality, reality

**realization** *n.* understanding, comprehension, consciousness, awareness

**realize** *v.* **FULFILL:** complete, accomplish; **UNDERSTAND:** recognize, apprehend, discern; **OBTAIN:** receive get

**realm** *n.* kingdom, province, domain

**rear** *n.* back, hindmost, tail, posterior, rump, butt

**reason** *n.* **JUDGMENT:** intelligence, sanity; **LOGIC:** rationalism, analysis; **MOTIVE:** rationale, intent, aim; **MIND:** brain, mentality, intellect

**reason** *v.* **THINK:** reflect, deliberate, contemplate; **ASSUME:** suppose, gather, conclude; **DISCUSS:** persuade, argue, contend, debate

**reasonable** *adj.* **RATIONAL:** sane, conscious, sensible, unbiased; **JUST:** fair, right, honest; **LIKELY:** feasible, sound, plausible; **MODERATE:** inexpensive, fair, cheap

**reassure** *v.* console, comfort, encourage, guarantee

**rebel** *n.* revolutionary, agitator, insurgent, seditionist, malcontent, dissenter, renegade, radical

**rebel** *v.* rise, revolt, resist, mutiny, riot, oppose

**rebellion** *n.* insurrection, revolt, revolution

**rebound** *v.* recoil, reflect, ricochet, bounce

**rebuke** *v.* chide, reprove, reprimand

**recede** *v.* retreat, ebb, abate, decline, lessen, decrease

**receipt** *n.* **ACQUISITION:** receiving, acceptance, arrival; **VOUCHER:** acknowledgment, notice

**receive** *v.* **ACCEPT:** inherit, acquire, obtain, secure; **EXPERIENCE:** undergo, suffer; **WELCOME:** accommodate, accept, greet

**recent** *adj.* modern, fresh, novel, contemporary, late

**receptacle** *n.* repository, holder, container

**reception** *n.* gathering, party, soiree, entertainment

**receptive** *adj.* alert, sensitive, perceptive, observant

**recess** *n.* **ALCOVE:** nook, cell, cubicle; **SUSPENSION:** intermission, interlude

**recipe** *n.* formula, compound, instructions, directions

**recite** *v.* dramatize, enact, interpret, soliloquize, narrate, recount, portray

**reckless** *adj.* heedless, thoughtless, rash

**reckon** *v.* consider, evaluate, estimate

**reclaim** *v.* recover, redeem, regain, mend

**recognition** *n.* acknowledgment, verification, appreciation, esteem, regard, honor

**recognize** *v.* **RECALL:** distinguish, place, remember, perceive; **ACKNOWLEDGE:** appreciate, realize

**recoil** *v.* shrink, retreat, bounce, spring

**recommend** *v.* commend, endorse, suggest, prescribe, advise

**reconcile** *v.* **ADJUST:** adapt, arrange, regulate; **HARMONIZE:** pacify, mitigate, mediate, intercede

**reconciliation** *n.* conciliation, adjustment, agreement

**record** *n.* document, manuscript, account, history, disk

**record** *v.* write, transcribe, catalogue, tabulate, chronicle

**recover** *v.* **SALVAGE:** redeem, rescue, reclaim; **RALLY:** convalesce, heal, mend, revive, recuperate

**recreation** *n.* pastime, amusement

**recuperate** *v.* recover, convalesce, heal

**recur** *v.* return, reappear, happen, repeat

**redecorate** *v.* refurbish, refresh, restore, recondition, remodel, renovate, revamp

**redeem** *v.* **RECOVER:** repay, purchase, atone, compensate; **SAVE:** liberate, free, deliver, rescue

**redemption** *n.* regeneration, salvation, rebirth, rescue

**redress** *n.* compensation, reparation

**reduce** *v.* **LESSEN:** dilute, diminish, decrease, lower; **DEFEAT:** conquer, overcome, subdue; **HUMBLE:** degrade, demote, abase, humiliate

**redundant** *adj.* superfluous, wordy, verbose, dull

**refine** *v.* purify, filter, strain, clean, improve, better, clarify

**refined** *adj.* genteel, cultivated, elegant, gracious, mannerly, courteous, polite

**refinement** *n.* **CULTURE:** sophistication, breeding, enlightenment, scholarship; **POLITENESS:** polish, manners, tact, civility, affability

**reflect** *v.* ponder, contemplate, concentrate, weigh, consider, think

**reflection** *n.* thought, consideration, contemplation, deliberation, meditation

**reform** *n.* reformation, betterment, improvement

**reform** *v.* revise, redeem, rectify, rehabilitate, remedy, restore, rebuild, reclaim, regenerate, amend, correct

**refrain** *v.* avoid, cease, forbear, abstain

**refresh** *v.* invigorate, renew, replenish, restore

**refuge** *n.* shelter, sanctuary, retreat, haven

**refugee** *n.* exile, expatriate, fugitive, foundling, alien, outcast

**refund** *n.* return, reimbursement, compensation, remuneration, repayment, rebate

**refuse** *n.* rubbish, leavings, remains, residue, trash

**refuse** *v.* reject, decline, rebuff, spurn, deny

**refute** *v.* disprove, answer, deny

**regain** *v.* recapture, retrieve, reacquire, recover

**regard** *n.* **LOOK:** gaze, glance; **OPINION:** estimation, appreciation, affection, admiration

**regard** *v.* **OBSERVE:** notice, mark; **CONSIDER;** view, think; **RESPECT:** esteem, value, admire

**region** *n.* territory, area, realm, locale, domain, sphere

**regress** v. backslide, relapse, revert, retreat, sink

**regret** n. **REMORSE:** repentance, misgiving, qualm; **GRIEF:** pain, anxiety, sorrow

**regret** v. mourn, lament, rue, repent, grieve, sorrow

**regular** adj. **ORDERLY:** methodical, precise, systematic, organized, consistent, rhythmic, periodic, measured; **CUSTOMARY:** conventional, usual;

**regularly** adv. customarily, habitually, usually, commonly, ordinarily, normally

**regulate** v. **CONTROL:** rule, legislate, direct, govern; **ADJUST:** standardize, adapt, rectify, correct

**regulation** n. rule, law, statute, ordinance

**rehabilitate** v. restore, reinstate, reestablish

**reinforce** v. buttress, strengthen, support

**reject** v. **REFUSE:** repudiate, renounce, deny; **DISCARD:** expel

**rejoice** v. exult, enjoy, revel, celebrate

**rejoinder** n. answer, reply, rebuttal, refutation

**rejuvenate** v. reinvigorate, refresh

**relapse** v. backslide, revert, regress, deteriorate, degenerate

**relate** v. **TELL:** recount, recite, retell, describe, report; **CONNECT:** associate, correlate, compare

**related** adj. associated, linked, affiliated, akin, parallel, correlated, similar

**relax** v. slacken, repose, recline, unbend, rest

**relaxed** adj. untroubled, carefree, comfortable

**relay** n. communicate, transmit, carry, deliver, send

**release** v. liberate, acquit, loose, free

**relent** v. soften, comply, relax, yield

**relentless** adj. unmerciful, vindictive, hard, ruthless

**relevance** *n.* connection, pertinence, importance

**relevant** *adj.* pertinent, pertaining, applicable, related, concerning, connected

**reliable** *adj.* unimpeachable, trustworthy, reputable, irrefutable, incontestable, dependable

**reliance** *n.* confidence, hope, faith, trust, dependence

**relic** *n.* vestige, trace, heirloom, antique, keepsake, memento, curiosity, token

**relief** *n.* **SOFTENING:** alleviation, comforting; **AID:** assistance, support, help, succor; **RELAXATION:** comfort, contentment, restfulness

**relieve** *v.* **REPLACE:** discharge, dismiss; **LESSEN:** ease, alleviate, allay, lighten, mitigate

**religion** *n.* **FAITH:** belief, persuasion, theology, doctrine, communion, piety

**religious** *adj.* **DEVOUT:** pious, sanctimonious, reverential; **SCRUPULOUS:** methodical, thorough

**reluctance** *n.* unwillingness, disinclination, qualm, hesitation, doubt

**remain** *v.* **STAY:** inhabit, stop, settle; **ENDURE:** prevail, continue; **SURVIVE:** outlive, outlast

**remainder** *n.* residue, remains, remnant, dregs, surplus, leavings, excess, scrap, fragment, salvage

**remark** *v.* say, state, speak, mention

**remarkable** *adj.* exceptional, extraordinary, unusual

**remedy** *v.* help, aid, heal, counteract, repair, cure

**remember** *v.* **RECALL:** recollect, reminisce; **MEMORIZE:** learn, master, retain

**remembrance** *n.* **GIFT:** reward, token; **MEMORY:** recollection, recognition, reminder

**remind** *v.* hint, mention, prompt, prod, stress, emphasize, note, warn

**remit** *v.* transmit, pay, tender, forward

**remnant** *n.* remainder, residue, dregs, leavings

**remodel** *v.* renovate, refurbish, redecorate, modernize

**remorse** *n.* anguish, guilt, compunction, contrition, regret

**remote** *adj.* **DISTANT:** removed, secluded, isolated; **ANCIENT:** aged, old; **SEPARATED:** unrelated, irrelevant

**removal** *n.* dismissal, discharge, expulsion, exile, deportation, banishment, elimination, ejection

**rend** *v.* tear, burst, rip, sever, sunder, break

**rendition** *n.* interpretation, translation, version

**renew** *v.* refresh, regenerate, rehabilitate, restore, freshen

**renounce** *v.* disown, disavow, deny

**renovate** *v.* remake, rehabilitate, renew

**rent** *n.* **LEASE:** lend, sublet; **HIRE:** charter, engage

**reorganize** *v.* renovate, regenerate, reconstruct

**repair** *v.* restore, fix, correct, refurbish, mend

**reparation** *n.* amends, compensation, indemnity, retribution

**repay** *v.* **REIMBURSE:** recompense, refund, indemnify, compensate; **RETALIATE:** reciprocate, revenge

**repeal** *v.* revoke, abrogate, annul, abolish, cancel

**repeat** *v.* iterate, echo, recite, recapitulate

**repel** *v.* **REBUFF:** resist, oppose, repulse; **OFFEND:** revolt, disgust; **REJECT:** disown, dismiss, refuse

**repentance** *n.* sorrow, remorse, self–reproach, regret

**repentant** *adj.* penitent, regretful, contrite, sorry

**repetition** *n.* recurrence, duplication, renewal, reiteration, wordiness

**repetitious** *adj.* boring, wordy, repeating, dull

**replace** *v.* substitute, supplant, restore, reinstate

**replenish** *v.* refill, restock, renew

**replica** *n.* copy, likeness, model, duplicate, imitation

**reply** *v.* answer, retort, rejoin, return

**report** *v.* narrate, recount, inform, advise, relate, tell

**reporter** *n.* journalist, newsman, correspondent

**represent** *v.* **DEPICT:** render, portray, enact, symbolize, describe; **IMITATE:** substitute, impersonate

**representative** *n.* emissary, deputy, agent, delegate, congressman, deputy, diplomat

**repress** *v.* check, restrain, control, curb, hinder

**reprieve** *n.* delay, respite, suspension

**reprimand** *v.* reprove, rebuke, chide, reproach, denounce, criticize, scold

**reproach** *v.* censure, upbraid, condemn, scold, blame

**reproduce** *v.* **COPY:** duplicate; **REPEAT:** recreate, re–enact, relive, mirror, echo; **MULTIPLY:** procreate, breed, propagate

**repudiate** *v.* reject, retract, repeal, revoke, abandon

**repulse** *v.* resist, repel, rebuff, spurn, snub

**repulsive** *adj.* offensive, disgusting: odious, forbidding

**reputable** *adj.* distinguished, celebrated, honorable, trustworthy, honest, worthy, brave, noble

**reputation** *n.* character, honor, standing, prestige, prominence, eminence, notoriety

**request** *v.* ask, solicit, beseech, entreat, sue, beg

**require** *v.* **NEED:** want; **DEMAND:** exact, expect

**requirement** *n.* **NEED:** necessity, demand; **PREREQUISITE:** condition, stipulation, provision, qualification;

**rescue** *v.* **SAVE:** recover, redeem, salvage, retrieve; **FREE:** liberate, release

**research** *n.* analysis, experimentation, examination, study

**resemblance** *n.* likeness, correspondence, coincidence, similarity

**resentment** *n.* annoyance, irritation, anger

**reserve** *n.* **SECURITY:** savings, insurance, resources, provisions, assets, hoard; **CALM:** caution, restraint, reticence, inhibition, demureness

**reserve** *v.* retain, keep, possess, hold

**reserved** *adj.* **BOOKED:** saved, claimed, held; **WITHHELD:** preserved, conserved; **RESTRAINED:** composed, sedate, collected, serene, placid

**reside** *v.* dwell, live, stay, lodge, occupy

**residence** *n.* habitation, quarters, apartment, home

**residue** *n.* remainder, leavings, scraps

**resign** *v.* **RELINQUISH:** yield, surrender, capitulate, abandon, submit; **QUIT:** retire, leave

**resigned** *adj.* quiet, peaceable, docile, submissive, yielding, relinquishing, obedient, passive

**resilient** *adj.* rebounding, elastic, springy, flexible

**resist** *v.* oppose, endure, bear, persist, suffer, abide, persevere, last, repel

**resolute** *adj.* constant, determined, steadfast, firm

**resolution** *n.* **DETERMINATION:** fortitude, perseverance, resolve; **PROPOSAL:** recommendation, declaration

**resolve** *v.* decide, determine, conclude

**resource** *n.* reserve, support, stratagem, means

**resourceful** *adj.* ingenious, capable, active, intelligent

**resources** *n.* means, money, riches, assets, capital, property, reserve, wealth

**respect** *n.* regard, relation, esteem, honor, admiration

**respectable** *adj.* presentable, tolerable, passable, virtuous, honorable

**respectful** *adj.* deferential, courteous, reverent, attending, venerating, deferring, polite

**respite** *n.* delay, postponement, reprieve, pause, delay

**respond** *v.* reply, rejoin, acknowledge

**response** *n.* reply, rejoinder, acknowledgment, answer

**responsibility** *n.* **STABILITY:** loyalty, faithfulness, competence, honesty; **DUTY:** obligation, trust

**responsible** *adj.* **ACCOUNTABLE:** liable, obligated, bound, answerable, obliged, pledged; **ABLE:** reliable, capable, dependable, competent

**rest** *n.* **REPOSE:** quiet, slumber, relaxation, doze, nap, respite; **REMAINDER:** residue, surplus, balance, remnant; **CESSATION:** intermission, interval, inactivity, pause

**restful** *adj.* tranquil, calm, peaceful, quiet, serene, soothing, relaxing, refreshing

**restless** *adj.* fidgety, jumpy, nervous, uneasy, agitated, unsettled, restive, impatient, jittery

**restore** *v.* **RETURN:** replace; **RECREATE:** revive, recover, renew; **REBUILD:** reconstruct, rehabilitate, repair; **HEAL:** refresh, cure

**restrain** *v.* curb, bridle, rein, regulate, muzzle, inhibit, deter, hamper, restrict, gag, limit, contain, check

**restraint** *n.* **SELF-CONTROL:** reserve, reticence, forbearance, abstinence, abstention; **LIMITATION:** hindrance, restriction, impediment

**restrict** *v.* limit, circumscribe, contract, shorten

**restricted** *adj.* limited, confined, hampered, bridled, blocked, decreased, barred, diminished, reduced

**result** *n.* consequence, outcome, aftermath, upshot, settlement, determination, payoff, end

**retain** *v.* **HOLD:** grasp, clutch; **REMEMBER:** recall, recollect, recognize; **EMPLOY:** engage, maintain, hire

**retaliate** *v.* repay, requite, return, revenge

**retard** *v.* hinder, postpone, delay, impede

**retire** *v.* **LEAVE:** withdraw, part, retreat; **REST:** sleep; **RESIGN:** relinquish

**retort** *n.* reply, counter, response, answer

**retort** *v.* reply, rejoin, answer

**retraction** *n.* denial, revocation

**retreat** *n.* refuge, sanctuary, port, haven, resort

**retreat** *v.* withdraw, depart, backtrack, reverse, leave

**retribution** *n.* punishment, reprisal, retaliation

**retrieve** *v.* recover, regain, reclaim

**return** *n.* **HOMECOMING:** arrival, reappearance; **RESTORATION:** restitution, recompense; **PROCEEDS:** profit, income, results, gain, revenue, yield, interest

**return** *v.* **REAPPEAR:** recur, repeat, revive, rebound; **REINSTATE:** restore, replace; **ANSWER:** reply, respond, retort; **REPAY:** reimburse, recompense, refund; **YIELD:** interest, profit

**reveal** *v.* disclose, publish, betray, announce, declare

**revenge** n. retaliation, reprisal, retribution

**revenue** n. income, return, earnings, proceeds, yield, receipts, profits

**reverence** n. veneration, respect, admiration, regard, esteem, adoration, praise

**reverse** n. **OPPOSITE:** converse, contrary; **DEFEAT:** downfall, annihilation

**review** v. correct, criticize, revise, inspect, examine, analyze

**revise** v. improve, correct, reconsider, rewrite, edit

**revival** n. renewal, rebirth, resurrection, restoration, freshening, awakening

**revive** v. enliven, refresh, renew, resuscitate, invigorate; freshen, rouse, arouse, strengthen

**revoke** v. annul, reverse, recall, retract, cancel

**revolt** n. rebellion, uprising, mutiny, revolution

**revolting** adj. awful, loathsome, repulsive, offensive

**revolutionary** adj. **REBELLIOUS:** mutinous, insurgent, subversive; **NOVEL:** new, unusual, advanced, forward

**revolve** v. roll, spin, rotate, twirl, turn

**reward** n. **PAYMENT:** compensation, remuneration, pay, recompense; **PRIZE:** premium, bonus, award

**rhythmic** adj. measured, regular, balanced

**rich** adj. **WEALTHY:** moneyed, affluent; **SUMPTUOUS:** luxurious, magnificent, resplendent, lavish, ornate, splendid, elegant; **FERTILE:** lush, fruitful, luxuriant

**riches** n. wealth, fortune, possessions, money

**rid** v. clear, relieve, shed, free

**riddle** n. enigma, puzzle, dilemma, complexity

**ride** *n.* excursion, drive, trip, transportation, journey

**rider** *n.* addition, codicil, addendum, appendix, amendment, supplement

**ridicule** *v.* mock, gibe, scoff, sneer, taunt, mimic, deride, scorn, caricature, satirize

**ridiculous** *adj.* absurd, ludicrous, preposterous, funny, unusual

**right** *adj.* **CORRECT:** precise, accurate, exact, factual, true, valid; **JUST:** lawful, legitimate, honest, fair

**right** *n.* **PREROGATIVE:** immunity, exemption, license; **JUSTICE:** equity, fairness

**right** *v.* correct, repair, restore, remedy, rectify, mend

**righteous** *adj.* **VIRTUOUS:** just, honorable, exemplary, impartial, noble, trustworthy, ethical; **RELIGIOUS:** devout, pious, saintly, angelic, devoted, reverent, spiritual, holy

**rightful** *adj.* proper, just, honest, fair, legal

**rigid** *adj.* **STIFF:** unyielding, inflexible, solid, firm; **STRICT:** exact, rigorous, severe; **FIXED:** set, unmoving, definite, determined

**rigorous** *adj.* harsh, austere, uncompromising, severe

**rim** *n.* margin, edge, border, verge, brim, lip, brink

**rind** *n.* covering, skin, peel, hull, shell

**ring** *n.* **CIRCLE:** circlet, girdle, rim; **JEWELRY:** band, signet, bracelet; **GROUP:** party, bloc, faction, group, gang, band; **SOUND:** clangor, jangle

**rinse** *v.* cleanse, clean, flush, dip, soak, wash

**riot** *n.* uproar, tumult, confusion, disorder, disturbance, protest

**rip** *v.* divide, tear, cut, rend, split, cleave, rive, shred

**ripe** *adj.* matured, grown, developed

**ripen** *v.* develop, evolve, advance, grow

**rise** *v.* ASCEND: mount, climb, scale; IMPROVE: prosper, flourish, thrive; HEIGHTEN: enlarge, grow, extend, raise; SWELL: inflate, billow, bulge; BEGIN: spring, emanate, issue

**risk** *n.* DANGER: hazard, peril, jeopardy; CHANCE: contingency, prospect, uncertainty

**risky** *adj.* perilous, precarious, hazardous, dangerous

**rite** *n.* ceremony, observance, service, ritual, custom

**rival** *n.* competitor, antagonist, opponent

**rivalry** *n.* competition, contention, opposition, dispute

**roam** *v.* ramble, range, meander, saunter, traipse

**rob** *v.* burglarize, plunder, defraud, cheat, pilfer, purloin, filch, pillage, sack, loot

**robbery** *n.* burglary, larceny, thievery

**robust** *adj.* vigorous, husky, hale, hearty, sound

**rock** *v.* totter, sway, reel, quake, tremble

**rogue** *n.* knave, outlaw, miscreant, criminal

**roll** *n.* ROTATION: turn, revolution; LIST: register, index, record;

**roll** *v.* rotate, circle, turn, revolve, spin

**romantic** *adj.* poetic, fanciful, chivalrous, courtly

**room** *n.* SPACE: vastness, sweep, extent; OPENING: place, vacancy; QUARTERS: lodgings, apartment

**roomer** *n.* lodger, occupant, dweller, renter, tenant

**rooted** *adj.* grounded, based, fixed, firm

**rosy** *adj.* promising, optimistic, favorable, cheerful

**rot** *n.* DECAY: decomposition, corruption, disintegration, NONSENSE: trash, silliness, foolishness

**rotate** *v.* turn, twist, wheel, revolve, move

**rotation** *n.* turn, circumrotation, circle, revolution

**rotten** *adj.* **SPOILED:** putrefying, decaying, rancid; **UNSOUND:** defective, impaired, weak; **CORRUPT:** contaminated, polluted, tainted, defiled, dirty

**rough** *adj.* **UNEVEN:** irregular, bumpy, jagged, coarse; **SEVERE:** harsh, strict, stern; **CRUDE:** boorish, uncivil, rude, uncultivated; **TURBULENT:** stormy, tumultuous; **UNFINISHED:** incomplete, imperfect; **APPROXIMATE:** inexact, unprecise, uncertain

**round** *adj.* **SPHERICAL:** circular, globular, cylindrical; **CURVED:** arched, rounded, bowed, curled

**rouse** *v.* **WAKEN:** arouse, raise, awaken; **STIMULATE:** urge, stir, provoke, animate, excite

**routine** *adj.* usual, customary, conventional, habitual

**rove** *v.* walk, meander, wander, roam

**row** *n.* line, series, order, file

**rowdy** *adj.* noisy, rebellious, mischievous, unruly

**royal** *adj.* **REGAL:** imperial, sovereign, noble; **STATELY:** dignified, majestic, aristocratic, courtly, lordly, imposing, resplendent

**rub** *v.* stroke, smooth, scrape, scour, polish

**rubbish** *n.* waste, debris, litter, trash

**rude** *adj.* **BOORISH:** loutish, brutish, uncouth, vulgar, ribald; **HARSH:** gruff, abusive, brazen, audacious, hostile, rough, insensitive; **COARSE:** rough, unrefined, crude, unpolished; **PRIMITIVE:** ignorant, uncivilized, barbarous

**ruffle** *v.* **DISARRANGE:** rumple, tousle; **ANGER:** irritate, fret, bother, agitate

**rugged** *adj.* **ROUGH:** uneven, hilly, broken, mountainous;

**STRONG:** vigorous, hale, sturdy, hardy, healthy

**ruin** *v.* **DESTROY:** demolish, wreck, ravage; **BANKRUPT:** impoverish, beggar

**rule** *v.* govern, control, dictate, manage, regulate

**rumor** *n.* report, gossip, tidings, hearsay

**rumple** *v.* wrinkle, crumple, crush, fold

**run** *n.* **SPRINT:** pace, amble, gallop, canter, lope, trot, dart, rush, dash, flight, escape, race, scamper, tear, whisk; **SERIES:** continuity, succession, sequence; **COURSE:** way, route, field, track

**run** *v.* **FLOW:** pour, tumble, drop, melt; **RUSH:** hurry, scurry, scramble, scamper, dash, speed, scuttle; **FUNCTION:** move, work, go; **MANAGE:** control, govern; **CONTINUE:** last, persevere

**rupture** *v.* break, burst, crack, tear

**rural** *adj.* country, rustic, agrarian, suburban

**rush** *n.* haste, dash, charge, hurry

**rut** *n.* **GROOVE:** hollow, trench, furrow, track; **HABIT:** routine, custom, course, practice

**ruthless** *adj.* cruel, savage, brutal, merciless, fiendish, unmerciful, ferocious, vengeful, barbarous

**sabotage** *v.* subvert, undermine, attack, destroy

**sacrifice** *n.* **OFFERING:** tribute, atonement; **LOSS:** discount, deduction, reduction

**sacrifice** *v.* forfeit, forgo, relinquish, yield, renounce

**sad** *adj.* **UNHAPPY:** downcast, gloomy, sorrowful, glum, dispirited, depressed, melancholy, blue; **PITIABLE:** disheartening, discouraging, dreary, disquieting

**safe** *adj.* **SECURE:** protected, guarded,

shielded, sheltered; **INNOCENT:** innocuous, harmless; **RELIABLE:** trustworthy, dependable, competent

**safe** *n.* chest, strongbox, coffer, repository, vault, case

**salary** *n.* wages, recompense, pay

**sale** *n.* **COMMERCE:** traffic, barter, exchange, trade; **DEAL:** transaction, auction, purchase, disposal; **CLEARANCE:** bargain, reduction, unloading

**salute** *v.* greet, recognize, praise

**salvage** *v.* save, retrieve, recover, regain

**salvation** *n.* deliverance, liberation, emancipation, rescue, safeguard, assurance

**same** *adj.* equivalent, identical, corresponding, equal

**sanction** *v.* approve, confirm, authorize, countenance

**sanctuary** *n.* **CHURCH:** shrine, temple; **SHELTER:** refuge, asylum, haven

**sane** *adj.* rational, normal, lucid, sober, sound, balanced, sensible, reasonable, wise

**sap** *n.* **FLUID:** secretion, essence, liquid; **DUPE:** dolt, gull, simpleton, fool

**sarcastic** *adj.* scornful, mocking, ironical, satirical, taunting, derisive, sneering, snickering, cynical

**satire** *n.* irony, sarcasm, mockery, ridicule, caricature

**satisfaction** *n.* **GRATIFICATION:** fulfillment, achievement; **COMFORT:** pleasure, contentment, serenity

**satisfy** *v.* please, delight, amuse, entertain, gladden, gratify, indulge, humor, fascinate, fill

**saturate** *v.* soak, drench, steep, immerse

**savage** *adj.* **PRIMITIVE:** crude, simple; **CRUEL:** barbarous, inhuman, brutal; **WILD:** untamed, uncivilized, uncultured

**save** *v.* **DELIVER:** rescue, extricate, liberate, ransom, redeem; **HOARD:** collect, store, accumulate, gather; **PRESERVE:** conserve, keep

**savor** *v.* partake, enjoy, relish, appreciate, like

**say** *v.* utter, speak, state, announce, declare, assert

**saying** *n.* aphorism, maxim, proverb, adage

**scaffold** *n.* platform, gallows, framework, structure

**scald** *v.* burn, steam, char, blanch, parboil

**scale** *v.* **MOUNT:** climb, ascend, surmount; **MEASURE:** compare, balance, compute

**scamper** *v.* hasten, speed, hurry, run

**scan** *v.* examine, scrutinize, browse, consider, look

**scandal** *n.* gossip, slander, defamation

**scanty** *adj.* scarce, meager, small, inadequate, thin, skimpy, sparse, diminutive

**scarcity** *n.* deficiency, inadequacy, insufficiency, lack

**scare** *v.* panic, terrify, alarm, frighten

**scatter** *v.* **DISPERSE:** disband, spread; **DIFFUSE:** dispel, dissipate, distribute

**scene** *n.* spectacle, view, display

**scenic** *adj.* beautiful, spectacular, dramatic

**scent** *v.* smell, odor, fragrance

**scheme** *v.* plan, contrive, intrigue, devise

**scholarly** *adj.* erudite, studious, learned

**schooling** *n.* education, learning, nurture, discipline

**scientific** *adj.* **LOGICAL:** deductive, methodical, sound; **ACCURATE:** precise, exact, clear, objective;

**scoff** *v.* mock, deride, jeer, ridicule

**scold** *v.* chide, admonish, rebuke, censure, reprove, reprimand, criticize, chasten

**scoot** *v.* run, dart, speed, hasten, hurry

**scope** *n.* range, reach, field, extent

**scorching** *adj.* fiery, searing, sweltering, burning, hot

**score** *v.* ORCHESTRATE: arrange, adapt; PROCURE: get, secure

**scorn** *v.* refuse, despise, disdain

**scornful** *adj.* contemptuous, disdainful, haughty

**scoundrel** *n.* rogue, scamp, villain, rascal

**scowl** *v.* frown, glower, disapprove, grimace

**scramble** *v.* MIX: combine, blend, beat; CLIMB: clamber, push, struggle

**scrap** *n.* TRASH: junk, waste, cuttings, chips; BIT: fragment, particle, piece, morsel; FIGHT: quarrel, brawl, squabble

**scrape** *v.* rub, abrade, scour, rasp

**scratch** *v.* wound, hurt, cut, mark, scar

**scrawl** *v.* write, scribble, scratch, doodle

**scrawny** *adj.* lean, lanky, gaunt, thin

**scream** *v.* shriek, screech, squeal, cry

**screen** *v.* HIDE: veil, conceal, mask, shelter; CHOOSE: select, eliminate

**scrub** *v.* rub, cleanse, scour, clean, wash

**scrupulous** *adj.* exact, punctilious, exacting, careful

**scrutinize** *v.* examine, view, study, stare, watch

**scrutiny** *n.* analysis, inspection, examination

**sealed** *adj.* secured, fixed, firm, tight

**seam** *n.* joint, union, stitching, closure, suture

**search** *v.* seek, examine, rummage, hunt, quest

**seasonal** *adj.* periodically, biennial, annual, yearly

**seasoned** *adj.* SPICY: tangy, sharp, aromatic; EXPERIENCED: established, settled, mature, able

**secede** *v.* withdraw, retract, leave, retreat

**seclude** *v.* screen, conceal, cover, hide

**seclusion** *n.* solitude, aloofness, privacy, retirement

**secondary** *adj.* MINOR: inconsiderable, petty, small, trivial, unimportant; DERIVED: dependent, subsequent, subsidiary, subordinate

**secrecy** *n.* concealment, hiding, seclusion, privacy, mystery, dark, darkness, isolation, reticence, stealth

**secret** *adj.* unknown, mysterious, arcane, cryptic, occult, mystical, veiled, obscure, shrouded, hidden, concealed, clandestine, underhanded, stealthy

**secretary** *n.* ASSISTANT: clerk, typist, stenographer, correspondent; OFFICER: director, executive

**secrete** *v.* HIDE: conceal, cover, disguise; EMIT: discharge, produce, exude

**secretive** *adj.* reticent, taciturn, undercover, reserved

**secure** *adj.* SAFE: guarded, defended; SELF–CONFIDENT: assured, determined, confident

**secure** *v.* FASTEN: bind, tighten; OBTAIN: get, achieve, acquire, grasp

**security** *n.* guarantee, token, pawn, pledge, collateral, bail, warranty, agreement, covenant, hostage

**sediment** *n.* dregs, silt, grounds, residue

**see** *v.* PERCEIVE: observe, regard, view, gaze, detect, notice, contemplate; UNDERSTAND: comprehend, discern, recognize; WITNESS: observe, regard

**seek** *v.* search, delve, dig, ransack, look, sniff, prowl

**seem** *v.* appear, look, resemble, show

**seep** *v.* percolate, trickle, leak, flow, drain

**segment** *n.* part, portion, section, fragment, division

**segregate** *v.* separate, isolate, sever, divide

**seize** *v.* **GRASP:** take, catch, grab, clutch, snatch; **CAPTURE:** conquer, overwhelm, apprehend, arrest; **UNDERSTAND:** comprehend, perceive

**seizure** *n.* spasm, spell, convulsion

**seldom** *adv.* rarely, infrequently, occasionally, uncommonly, scarcely, hardly

**select** *v.* pick, decide, elect, choose

**selective** *adj.* discriminating, judicious, particular

**self–conscious** *n.* unsure, uncertain, shy, doubtful

**self–control** *n.* poise, restraint, reserve, discretion, stability, dignity, constraint

**self–esteem** *n.* pride, vanity, egotism

**self–evident** *n.* obvious, plain, visible, apparent

**self–restraint** *n.* patience, endurance, control

**sell** *v.* market, vend, barter, trade, exchange, bargain, peddle, retail, wholesale, contract, retail

**seller** *n.* dealer, salesman, tradesman, retailer, agent, vender, merchant, auctioneer, shopkeeper, peddler, trader, storekeeper, marketer

**semblance** *n.* resemblance, aspect, appearance

**send** *v.* **DISPATCH:** convey, ship, post, convey; **BROADCAST:** relay, transmit

**senile** *adj.* aged, infirm, feeble, old, sick

**senior** *adj.* older, elder, higher, superior

**seniority** *n.* standing, ranking, station

**sensation** *n.* consciousness, perception, feeling

**sensational** *adj.* **FASCINATING:** exciting, marvelous, incredible, impressive;

**MELODRAMATIC:** exaggerated, excessive, emotional

**sense** *n.* **SENSATION:** feeling, touch, sight, hearing, taste, smell; **REASONABLENESS:** judgment, discretion, fairness; **INTELLECT:** perception, reason, cleverness, thought; **INSIGHT:** tact, understanding, discernment

**senseless** *adj.* ridiculous, silly, foolish, illogical, stupid

**sensible** *adj.* reasonable, prudent, perceptive, careful, aware, capable, rational, intelligent

**sensitive** *adj.* **TENDER:** delicate, sore, painful; **TOUCHY:** tense, nervous, irritable, unstable

**sensitivity** *n.* awareness, delicacy, feelings, sympathy

**sensuality** *n.* appetite, ardor, desire, emotion

**sensuous** *adj.* passionate, physical, exciting, sensual

**sentence** *n.* judgment, decree, punishment, verdict

**sentiment** *n.* feeling, emotion, opinion, thought

**sentimental** *adj.* emotional, tender, romantic, idealistic, visionary, affected

**sentry** *n.* sentinel, protector, watchmen

**separate** *v.* **ISOLATE:** divide, seclude; **DEPART:** leave

**separated** *adj.* disconnected, severed, removed, disjointed, scattered

**sequence** *n.* **SUCCESSION:** order, continuity, progression, flow; **ARRANGEMENT:** distribution, classification; **SERIES:** chain, string, array

**serene** *adj.* calm, unruffled, tranquil, composed, sedate, placid

**serious** *adj.* **GRAVE:** solemn, pressing; **THOUGHTFUL:** earnest, somber, sincere

**sermon** *n.* discourse, lesson, lecture

**serve** *v.* help, aid, assist, attend

**service** *v.* maintain, sustain, repair

**session** *n.* sitting, assembly, gathering

**set** *adj.* FIRM: stable, settled, fixed, rigid; DETERMINED: steadfast, decided

**set** *n.* COLLECTION: assemblage, assortment; GROUP: clique, circle, faction

**set** *v.* ESTABLISH: anchor, fix, install; JELL: solidify, harden, congeal; PLACE: put, plant, situate

**setting** *n.* environment, surroundings, mounting, backdrop, frame, context

**settle** *v.* PROVE: establish, verify; FINISH: end, achieve; LOCATE: reside, dwell, colonize

**settlement** *n.* AGREEMENT: covenant, compact, contract; COMPENSATION: remuneration, reimbursement

**sever** *v.* separate, part, split, cleave, cut

**several** *adj.* some, sundry, various, numerous, many

**severe** *adj.* exacting, inflexible, harsh, oppressive, cruel, rigid, rigorous, difficult, oppressive, relentless

**sew** *v.* join, fasten, stitch, tack, bind, piece, baste

**shabby** *adj.* threadbare, worn, ragged, faded, seedy

**shade** *n.* DARKNESS: blackness, shadow; TINT: color, brilliance, saturation, hue; VARIATION: difference, hint, suggestion; SCREEN: shelter, covering, curtain

**shake** *n.* tremble, shiver, pulsation, movement

**shaken** *adj.* unnerved, upset, overcome, excited

**shaky** *adj.* INFIRM: trembling, unsteady, tottering, unstable; UNRELIABLE: uncertain, questionable

**shallow** *adj.* **SLIGHT:** inconsiderable, superficial; **SILLY:** trifling, inane, frivolous, petty, foolish

**sham** *adj.* pretended, false, misleading, untrue

**shame** *v.* humiliate, mortify, dishonor, disgrace

**shameful** *adj.* **IMMODEST:** immoral, debauched, degraded, indecent, lewd, vulgar; **DISHONORABLE:** scandalous, disreputable, outrageous, infamous

**shameless** *adj.* brazen, bold, forward, rude, lewd

**shape** *v.* **CAST:** mold, form; **DEVELOP:** grow, adapt, become

**shape** *n.* **FORM:** contour, configuration; **PATTERN:** frame, mold; **CONDITION:** fitness, health

**share** *v.* **DIVIDE:** allot, apportion; **PARTAKE:** participate, receive; **GIVE:** yield, bestow, accord

**sharp** *adj.* **EDGED:** honed, cutting, keen; **CLEVER:** astute, intelligent; **DISTINCT:** explicit, clear, definite; **INTENSE:** piercing, shrill; **STYLISH:** chic, fashionable

**shatter** *v.* break, sliver, split, burst

**shears** *n.* clippers, cutters, snips, scissors

**sheath** *n.* scabbard, case, covering

**shed** *n.* shelter, hut, outbuilding, lean–to, woodshed

**shed** *v.* drop, molt, slough, discard, exude, emit

**sheer** *adj.* **ABRUPT:** steep, precipitous, perpendicular; **THIN:** transparent, delicate, fine

**shelter** *n.* protection, refuge, haven, sanctuary

**shelter** *v.* cover, defend, screen, hide, conceal, harbor, protect, shield, safeguard, surround, enclose

**shine** *v.* **RADIATE:** glitter, sparkle, twinkle, glimmer, glow, blaze; **REFLECT:** glisten, gleam, mirror; **POLISH:** scour, brush, burnish, wax

**ship** *v.* transport, send, consign

**shock** *v.* **STARTLE:** astound, disturb; **OFFEND:** disgust, outrage, horrify, abash, dismay; **JAR:** rock, jolt

**shocking** *adj.* repulsive, revolting, offensive

**shoddy** *adj.* cheap, flimsy, tacky, inferior, poor

**shore** *n.* coast, beach, seaside, bank

**short** *adj.* **CONCISE:** brief, condensed; **ABRUPT:** curt, inconsiderate, rude, testy; **DEFICIENT:** inadequate substandard

**shortage** *n.* lack, deficiency, dearth

**shove** *v.* push, nudge, jostle, press

**show** *v.* display, explain, indicate, reveal, demonstrate

**show** *n.* **PRODUCTION:** play, ceremony; **DISPLAY:** appearance, plausibility, pretext

**shower** *n.* rainfall, sprinkle, drizzle, mist

**shred** *n.* strip, fragment, splinter, rag

**shred** *v.* cut, mince, grate, tear

**shrew** *n.* scold, nag, harridan

**shrewd** *adj.* cunning, sharp, keen, intelligent, perceptive, sly, canny, crafty, cagey

**shriek** *v.* scream, yell, shout, howl, squawk

**shrill** *adj.* piercing, sharp, harsh

**shrine** *n.* temple, altar, church, sanctuary

**shrink** *v.* **CONTRACT:** shrivel, constrict, lessen; **RECOIL:** cringe, wince, retreat, withdraw

**shrivel** *v.* wither, shrink, decrease

**shudder** *v.* tremble, shake, shiver, quiver

**shun** *v.* avoid, ignore, eschew, evade

**shut** *v.* close, bar, secure, fasten, enclose

**shy** *adj.* timid, reserved, distrustful, suspicious

**sick** *adj.* ill, diseased, infected, afflicted, queasy, nauseous, feeble, unhealthy

**side** *n.* EDGE: border; FACTION: team, party

**siege** *n.* attack, assault, onslaught, blockade

**sieve** *v.* strain, purify, filter

**sift** *v.* separate, strain, filter, screen

**sigh** *n.* moan, groan, gasp, cry

**sight** *n.* view, spectacle, scene, display, show, vision

**sign** *n.* SYMPTOM: indication, hint, clue, suggestion; EMBLEM: badge

**sign** *v.* GESTURE: indicate, signal; ENDORSE: confirm, acknowledge, initial, autograph

**signal** *v.* signify, motion, gesture, wave

**significant** *adj.* important, notable, momentous, symbolic, meaningful

**signify** *v.* mean, indicate, communicate, denote, imply, intimate, portend

**silence** *n.* serenity, hush, tranquillity, quiet

**silence** *v.* hush, still, quiet, muzzle, stifle, suppress

**silent** *adj.* quiet, hushed, still, reserved, dormant

**silly** *adj.* foolish, imprudent, ridiculous, absurd, inane, frivolous

**similar** *adj.* resembling, like, comparable, related

**similitude** *n.* resemblance, likeness

**simple** *adj.* unaffected plain clear, unadorned, uncomplicated, bare, innocent, artless

**simplify** *v.* clarify, explain, elucidate, interpret

**simulate** *v.* feign, fake, pretend, disguise, fabricate

**simultaneous** *adj.* concurrent, coexisting

**sin** *v.* transgress, misbehave, offend, trespass

**sincere** *adj.* honest, genuine, earnest, faithful

**single** *adj.* individual, lone

**singular** *adj.* unique, unusual, remarkable, individual

**sinister** *adj.* ominous, menacing, base, bad, evil

**sink** *v.* submerge, depress, fall, slump, lower, droop

**sip** *v.* drink, imbibe, taste, sample, savor

**sit** *v.* **PERCH:** seat, squat; **MEET** convene, assemble

**site** *n.* location, place, spot, position

**situation** *n.* circumstances, predicament, state, job, profession, trade, status, station, rank

**size** *n.* bulk, magnitude, extent, mass, dimensions

**skeleton** *n.* bones, framework, outline, structure

**skeptic** *n.* doubter, cynic, unbeliever, agnostic

**skeptical** *adj.* doubtful, cynical, incredulous

**sketch** *v.* draw, outline, design, plan, draft, picture

**skid** *v.* slip, slide, swerve, veer, glide

**skill** *n.* **DEXTERITY:** ability, expertise, competence, talent; **OCCUPATION:** craft, vocation, trade, job

**skillful** *adj.* adept, adroit, proficient, accomplished

**skin** *v.* strip, peel, husk, scale, scalp

**skinny** *adj.* thin, lean, bony, gaunt, emaciated

**skirmish** *n.* scuffle, scrimmage, engagement, combat

**skirt** *v.* circumvent, bypass, detour, sidestep

**skittish** *adj.* jumpy, nervous, fidgety, timid, bashful

**skulk** *v.* sneak, lurk, prowl

**slab** *n*. hunk, block, chunk

**slack** *adj*. lax, loose, lazy, indolent, sluggish, slow

**slacken** *v*. decrease, abate, diminish

**slander** *n*. gossip, libel, scandal, misrepresentation

**slander** *v*. malign, vilify, besmirch, disparage

**slang** *n*. jargon, lingo, dialect, colloquialism

**slant** *n*. slope, incline, grade, inclination, bent

**slant** *v*. LEAN: angle, tilt; DISTORT: misrepresent, color

**slap** *v*. smack, strike, hit, spank, cuff, buffet

**slaughter** *n*. slaying, bloodshed, carnage, massacre

**slay** *v*. kill, murder, butcher, destroy, annihilate

**sleek** *adj*. smooth, glossy, glassy, shiny, neat

**sleep** *v*. slumber, rest, doze, snooze, nod, nap

**sleepy** *adj*. drowsy, tired, sluggish

**slender** *adj*. thin, slim, slight, spare, fragile, flimsy

**slight** *adj*. TRIVIAL: trifling, insignificant, petty, unimportant, superficial; DELICATE, dainty, flimsy, slender, fragile, frail, insubstantial

**slight** *v*. disregard, insult, snub, neglect, overlook

**slim** *adj*. slender slight trifling, dainty, slender

**slime** *n*. mire, muck, mud, ooze

**sling** *v*. hurl, throw, chuck, pitch, launch

**slink** *v*. skulk, cower, creep, lurk, sneak, steal, prowl

**slip** *n*. error, mistake, blunder, indiscretion

**slip** *v*. slide, totter, stumble, fall

**slipshod** *adj*. slovenly, careless, sloppy, untidy

**slit** *v*. cut, gash, slash, rip, slice, split, tear, pierce

**sloppy** *adj.* careless, lax, untidy, messy, disorderly

**slope** *n.* incline, grade, slant, inclination

**slouch** *v.* slump, droop, bend, stoop

**slovenly** *adj.* messy, careless, sloppy, disorderly, disheveled, bedraggled, untidy, slipshod

**slow** *adj.* LEISURELY: gradual, deliberate, lethargic; DENSE: dull, stupid

**sluggish** *adj.* languid, lethargic, indolent, slothful

**slumber** *v.* sleep, rest, nap, doze, snooze

**slump** *n.* decrease, drop, depression, setback, decline

**sly** *adj.* cunning, wily, deceitful, deceptive, tricky, artful, shifty, evasive, shrewd, elusive, clever, calculating, treacherous

**small** *adj.* SELFISH: stingy, mean, petty; INCONSEQUENTIAL: little, insignificant, trivial, unimportant

**smart** *adj.* CLEVER: intelligent, keen, penetrating, alert, bright; STYLISH: sharp, dashing, neat, elegant

**smash** *v.* break, shatter, crush, pound, destroy, wreck, demolish, ruin

**smear** *v.* SLANDER: libel, sully, slur; SMUDGE: daub, plaster, spread, apply

**smell** *n.* odor, aroma, fragrance, scent, stench, stink

**smile** *v.* grin, smirk, beam, laugh

**smirk** *n.* sneer, leer, grimace

**smoky** *adj.* hazy, foggy, smoggy, dingy, frosted, filmy

**smooth** *adj.* EVEN: level, flat, flush, polished, sleek, uniform; SUAVE: glib, polite, courteous

**smother** *v.* suffocate, stifle, asphyxiate, strangle, subdue, suppress

**smudge** *n.* smear, blot, blur, stain, blemish, streak

**smug** *adj.* conceited, egotistical, satisfied

**smutty** *adj.* pornographic, lewd, indecent, obscene, vulgar, suggestive, raunchy

**snare** *v.* catch, entangle, trap, trick, lure

**snatch** *v.* grab, pluck, seize, steal, filch, swipe, take

**sneak** *v.* lurk, prowl, creep, slink, steal, skulk

**sneer** *v.* criticize, deride, ridicule, scoff, gibe, taunt

**snide** *adj.* underhanded, sarcastic, derogatory, insinuating, vicious, nasty, mean, malicious

**snip** *v.* clip, pare, cut, lop, nip, slice, slit

**snivel** *v.* weep, whine, bawl, bemoan, blubber

**snobbery** *n.* contempt, arrogance, insolence

**snobbish** *adj.* condescending, patronizing

**snub** *n.* insult, affront, slight, slur, rebuke

**snug** *adj.* comfortable, cozy, secure, safe

**snuggle** *v.* cuddle, nestle, nuzzle, burrow, hug

**soak** *v.* steep, saturate, douse, permeate, infuse

**sob** *v.* cry, moan, weep, wail, lament, whimper, bewail

**sober** *adj.* serious, solemn, subdued, restrained, sedate, composed, rational, reasonable, sound, somber

**social** *adj.* genial, pleasant, polite, civil, pleasant

**society** *n.* **ORGANIZATION:** fellowship, association, brotherhood, fraternity, club; **CULTURE:** community, civilization, people, nation

**soft** *adj.* malleable, pliant, yielding, fluffy

**sojourn** *n.* stay, visit, stopover, vacation, abide

**solace** *v.* comfort, console, soothe, cheer, relieve, alleviate, assuage, allay, soften, mitigate

**sole** *adj.* one, single, lone, exclusive, individual, unique, unshared

**solemn** *adj.* sacred, grave, serious, grim, imposing, thoughtful, dignified, somber

**solemnize** *v.* commemorate, celebrate, honor, hallow

**solicit** *v.* supplicate, beg, implore, urge, request, ask, inquire, question, proposition

**solicitation** *n.* request, petition, appeal

**solicitor** *n.* attorney, petitioner, supplicant

**solicitous** *adj.* concerned, anxious, heedful, kind, devoted, tender, loving, thoughtful

**solid** *adj.* whole, unbroken, firm, substantial, sound, hard, stable, dense, stout

**solidify** *v.* harden, crystallize, set, coagulate, congeal

**solitary** *adj.* single, sole, individual, singular, isolated, lonely, remote, separate

**solitude** *n.* isolation, seclusion, privacy

**solution** *n.* answer, resolution, conclusion, explanation, settlement

**solve** *v.* answer, resolve, explain, decipher, decode

**somber** *adj.* dull, gloomy, dark, dim, drab, dismal, depressing, dreary, melancholy

**sonorous** *adj.* resonant, reverberating, vibrant

**sooty** *adj.* blackened, dirty, grimy, dingy, filthy

**soothe** *v.* calm, comfort, ease, quiet, refresh, soften, alleviate, assuage, mitigate, pacify

**soothsayer** *n.* prognosticator, diviner, oracle, prophet, astrologer, seer, mystic

**sophisticated** *adj.* worldly, refined, cultured

**sorcery** *n.* magic, witchcraft, alchemy, enchantment

**sordid** *adj.* vile, dirty, squalid, foul, low, base, abject

**sore** *adj.* sensitive, raw, tender, painful, inflamed

**sorrow** *n.* grief, affliction, anguish, remorse, misery, sadness, woe, trouble, affliction

**sorrow** *v.* grieve, mourn, weep, lament, deplore

**sorry** *adj.* regretful, repentant, apologetic

**sort** *v.* order, arrange, classify, distribute, assort

**soul** *n.* spirit, essence, ghost, being

**sound** *adj.* safe, whole, healthy, strong, complete, vigorous, stable, sensible, rational, sane, hale

**sound** *n.* tone, noise, vibration, resonance, intonation

**source** *n.* origin, beginning, inception, cause, root

**souvenir** *n.* keepsake, token, memento, relic, trophy

**sow** *v.* scatter, disseminate, disperse, plant

**space** *n.* room, area, gap, expanse, distance, interval

**spacious** *adj.* roomy, capacious, large, ample, commodious, vast, huge, voluminous, extensive

**span** *n.* distance, measure, length, extent, stretch

**span** *v.* cross, traverse, reach, connect, link, bridge

**spare** *adj.* LEAN: thin, gaunt, slight, emaciated; EXTRA: excess, additional

**sparkle** *v.* glitter, gleam, twinkle, glisten, shine

**sparse** *adj.* meager, inadequate, scanty, thin, spare

**spasm** *n.* convulsion, fit, contortion, seizure

**spatter** *v.* splash, slosh, spray, shower, speckle

**speak** *v* talk, articulate, say, utter, lecture, address

**special** *adj.* specific, certain, particular, designated, unique, distinctive, uncommon, unusual

**specialist** *n.* expert, professional, authority

**specie** *n.* coin, money, currency

**species** *n.* type, kind, class, breed, variety, category

**specific** *adj.* precise, particular, distinct, explicit

**specify** *v.* stipulate, designate, cite, name, define

**specimen** *n.* sample, example, model, type, pattern

**specious** *adj.* deceptive, misleading, false

**speck** *n.* bit, particle, trace, grain, iota

**spectacle** *n.* sight, show, demonstration, wonder

**spectacular** *adj.* amazing, marvelous, impressive, sensational, dramatic, splendid, striking, fabulous

**spectator** *n.* onlooker, observer, witness, bystander

**specter** *n.* ghost, spook, spirit, phantom, apparition

**spectrum** *n.* range, scale, sweep, extent

**speculate** *v.* **CONSIDER:** theorize, contemplate, consider, infer; **RISK:** gamble, venture, chance

**speech** *n.* language, oration, communication

**speed** *v.* hasten, hurry, expedite, precipitate

**speedy** *adj.* quick, fast, hasty, brisk, swift, hurried

**spend** *v.* give, waste, disburse, dissipate, deplete

**sphere** *n.* **GLOBE:**, orb, shell, planet; **DOMAIN:** province realm

**spill** *v.* slop, splash, drop, flow

**spin** *v.* turn, rotate, twirl, whirl, gyrate

**spindle** *n.* shaft, beam, axle, arbor

**spirit** *n.* **GHOST:** apparition, phantom,

specter; **VITALITY:** vivacity, vigor, zeal, ardor; **SIGNIFICANCE:** sense, meaning

**spite** n. malice, malevolence, rancor

**spiteful** adj. vindictive, malicious, cruel, malevolent

**splash** v. spatter, douse, spray, swash

**spleen** n. anger, petulance, wrath, rancor

**splendid** adj. grand, magnificent, impressive, dazzling

**splendor** n. glory, magnificence, grandeur

**splice** v. join, implant, unite, graft

**splinter** v. crumble, shatter, break, fracture, smash

**split** v. divide, sever, break, separate, cleave

**spoil** v. decay, ruin, damage, decompose, putrefy

**sponsor** n. patron, mentor, supporter, backer

**spontaneous** adj. impromptu, impulsive, natural

**sporadic** adj. occasional, infrequent, scattered

**spot** n. **STAIN:** blot, blemish; **LOCATION:** locale, site

**spout** v. pour, discharge, emit, flow, spill, gush

**sprawl** v. recline, lounge, relax, slouch

**sprightly** adj. lively, frisky, nimble, animated, agile

**spring** v. bound, leap, issue, jump, hop, vault

**sprinkle** v. disperse, distribute, scatter, spatter

**sprint** v. run, race, zip, dash, tear

**sprout** v. germinate, bud, burgeon, grow, develop

**spry** adj. nimble, agile, active, vigorous, animated, brisk, lively, quick, energetic

**spur** v. urge, incite, induce, provoke, goad, press

**spurious** adj. false, fake, deceptive, phony, feigned

**spurn** *v.* reject, shun, slight, snub, scorn, disdain

**spurt** *v.* burst, gush, spout, issue, spring

**spy** *v.* see, discover, glimpse

**squabble** *v.* wrangle, quarrel, bicker, argue, feud

**squalid** *adj.* filthy, foul, dirty, unclean, seedy

**squalor** *n.* filth, poverty, misery

**squander** *v.* waste, dissipate, expend, lavish, misuse

**square** *adj.* fair, just, honest, straight, level, true

**squeamish** *adj.* queasy, modest, prudish, finicky

**squeeze** *v.* compress, crush, squash, press

**squelch** *v.* subdue, crush, squash, suppress, thwart

**squirm** *v.* wriggle, writhe, fidget, twist, shift

**stab** *n.* wound, cut, puncture, thrust

**stabilize** *v.* steady, secure, brace, poise

**stable** *adj.* fixed, firm, steady, sturdy, enduring, perpetual, steadfast, sound, reliable, solid

**staff** *n.* personnel, employees, crew, cast

**stage** *n.* platform, dais, scaffold

**stagger** *v.* WEAVE: falter, waver; ASTONISH: astound, amaze, dumbfound, shock, surprise

**stagnant** *adj.* inert, stale, dirty, filthy, fetid

**stagnate** *v.* decay, rot, decompose, taint

**staid** *adj.* steady, sober, sedate, quiet, solemn

**stale** *adj.* dry, trite, common, dull, humdrum

**stalk** *v.* hunt, track, chase, pursue

**stall** *v.* delay, obstruct, hamper, hinder, impede

**stalwart** *adj.* stout, sturdy, strong, rugged, robust, vigorous, bold, gallant, steadfast, formidable

**stamina** *n.* endurance, strength, vigor, vitality, power

**stammer** *v.* sputter, falter, stumble, hesitate, stutter

**stand** *n.* position, attitude, belief, opinion

**stand** *v.* endure, resist, oppose, confront, withstand

**standard** *n.* **MODEL:** measure, gauge, example; **BANNER:** symbol, flag, pennant

**staple** *adj.* basic, necessary, essential, fundamental

**stare** *v.* gaze, gawk, gape, glare, watch

**stark** *adj.* simple, desolate, dreary, grim, harsh

**start** *n.* beginning, onset, origin, outset, initiation

**start** *v.* initiate, begin, commence, establish

**startle** *v.* surprise, alarm, scare, frighten, disturb

**state** *n.* condition, situation, status, circumstance, position, standing, station

**state** *v.* recite, declare, pronounce, assert, affirm

**statement** *n.* declaration, allegation, assertion, remark, report, account

**stately** *adj.* majestic, dignified, regal, elegant, grand

**static** *adj.* immobile, stationary, fixed, rigid

**station** *n.* rank, standing, position

**stationary** *adj.* fixed, static, permanent, rooted, stable

**statue** *n.* sculpture, bust, image, icon, figurine

**stature** *n.* height, bulk, build, status, standing

**status** *n.* state, condition, position, rank, standing

**statute** *n.* law, decree, act, bill, rule, ordinance, edict

**stay** *n.* prop, support, brace, prop

**stay** *v.* remain, continue, wait, linger, pause, detain, hinder, suspend, curb

**steadfast** *adj.* resolute, unwavering, constant, faithful, dependable, firm

**steal** *v.* rob, thieve, filch, pilfer, swindle, embezzle

**steep** *adj.* precipitous, sheer, abrupt

**steeple** *n.* spire, tower, minaret

**steer** *v.* guide, direct, pilot, conduct, lead, navigate

**stellar** *adj.* remarkable, phenomenal, outstanding

**stereotype** *v.* classify, categorize, typecast, label

**sterling** *adj.* genuine, flawless, noble, perfect, excellent, superior, exceptional

**stern** *adj.* severe, rigid, hard, strict, austere, rigorous

**stiff** *adj.* rigid, formal, inflexible, firm, stubborn, obstinate, unyielding, formal, uncompromising, severe

**stiffen** *v.* harden, congeal, thicken, coagulate

**stifle** *v.* suppress, repress, restrain, stop

**stigma** *n.* disgrace, shame, blemish, infamy, blot, stain

**stigmatize** *v.* disgrace, discredit, dishonor, defame, taint, shame, brand, humiliate

**still** *adj.* silent, motionless, inert, stationary, calm, serene, hushed, tranquil

**still** *v.* silence, hush, calm, soothe, stop, stall, arrest

**stilted** *adj.* awkward, affected, unnatural, strained, contrived, artificial, labored, stiff

**stimulate** *v.* excite, arouse, rouse, activate, provoke

**stingy** *adj.* niggardly, miserly, tight, close-fisted

**stint** *v.* limit, confine, restrict, restrain

**stipulate** *v.* specify, determine, designate, indicate

**stipulation** *n.* prerequisite, condition, qualification, term, requirement, clause

**stir** *n.* tumult, bustle, excitement, commotion, disorder, uproar, furor, agitation, fuss

**stir** *v.* agitate, rouse, excite, incite, provoke, stimulate

**stock** *v.* store, supply, hoard, equip, fill, furnish

**stockpile** *n.* reserve, supply, deposit, hoard, store

**stoic** *n.* impassive, apathetic, indifferent, nonchalant, composed, poised

**stolid** *adj.* impassive, unemotional, dispassionate, indifferent, imperturbable

**stoop** *v.* bend, bow, crouch

**stop** *v.* halt, end, terminate, discontinue, arrest, restrain, hinder, impede, prevent, thwart

**store** *v.* hoard, gather, collect, stash, stockpile

**storm** *n.* tempest, blizzard, gale, squall, commotion, turmoil, outbreak, disturbance

**stormy** *adj.* tempestuous, wild, blustering, tumultuous, raging, turbulent, boisterous

**story** *n.* TALE: anecdote, yarn, parable, fable, legend, report, account; LEVEL: floor, landing

**stout** *adj.* PLUMP: portly, heavy, bulky, corpulent; RESOLUTE: brave, courageous, bold, fearless, dauntless, hardy, indomitable, strong, robust

**straggler** *n.* dawdler, lingerer, laggard, slowpoke

**straight** *adj.* direct, honest, fair, just, virtuous, open

**straighten** *v.* adjust, align, rectify, correct

**strain** *n.* effort, exertion, force, pressure, anxiety, stress

**strait** *n.* difficulty, distress, predicament, plight

**strange** *adj.* unusual, abnormal, bizarre, peculiar, outlandish, extraordinary, unfamiliar

**stranger** *n.* foreigner, alien, outsider

**stratagem** *n.* trick, deception, ruse, wile, scheme, plan, contrivance, device

**strategy** *n.* tactics, scheme, system, approach

**stray** *v.* wander, drift, roam, deviate, digress

**stream** *n.* flow, emit, issue, pour, run

**streamer** *n.* flag, banner, pennant, standard, ensign

**strength** *n.* power, force, might

**strengthen** *v.* fortify, reinforce, restore, invigorate

**strenuous** *adj.* vigorous, spirited, laborious

**stress** *n.* emphasis, weight, significance, accent

**stretch** *n.* expanse, range, reach, extent

**strew** *v.* scatter, spread, disseminate, broadcast

**strict** *adj.* demanding, exacting, rigid, inflexible

**strident** *adj.* raucous, shrill, harsh, piercing, grating

**strife** *n.* conflict, fight, discord, clash

**strike** *v.* HIT: slap, cuff; UNEARTH: find, uncover

**stringent** *adj.* strict, harsh, severe

**stripling** *n.* youth, child, lad, lass, youngster

**strive** *v.* endeavor, attempt, compete, contend

**stroll** *v.* walk, saunter, meander, wander, roam

**strong** *adj.* muscular, potent, solid, impregnable

**struggle** *n.* battle, clash, conflict, exertion, endeavor

**struggle** *v.* grapple, contend, strive, toil, labor

**stubborn** *adj.* obstinate, headstrong, stiff, resolute, inflexible, intractable

**student** *n.* pupil, scholar, disciple, apprentice

**study** *v.* investigate, analyze, scrutinize, examine, ponder, consider, reflect

**stun** *v.* shock, confound, amaze, astonish, astound, bewilder, stupefy

**stupendous** *adj.* amazing, astounding, marvelous, extraordinary, incredible, spectacular, wondrous

**stupid** *adj.* dull, boring, tedious, vapid, tiresome, foolish, absurd, inane, senseless

**stupor** *n.* daze, trance, numbness, lethargy

**sturdy** *adj.* robust, rugged, stalwart, strong, strapping, muscular, firm, indomitable, stout

**stutter** *v.* stammer, stumble, falter

**stylish** *adj.* fashionable, chic, smart, modish

**suave** *adj.* sophisticated, smooth, cultured, worldly

**subdue** *v.* defeat, conquer, overpower, tame

**subjective** *adj.* biased, prejudiced, individual

**subjugate** *v.* conquer, enslave, subdue, defeat

**sublime** *adj.* lofty, inspiring, imposing, majestic

**submerge** *v.* immerse, engulf, plunge, sink

**submission** *n.* surrender, resignation, compliance

**submit** *v.* ACCEDE: comply, obey; SUGGEST: volunteer, propose, present, tender

**subordinate** *adj.* inferior, lower, junior, subservient

**subscribe** *v.* support, donate, authorize, sanction

**subsequent** *adj.* following, ensuing, succeeding, later

**subservient** *adj.* subordinate, servile, deferential

**subside** *v.* decline, dwindle, diminish, lessen, wane

**subsidize** *v.* support, sponsor, fund, back

**subsidy** *n.* endowment, allowance, grant, bequest

**substance** *n.* object, element, essence, basis, meaning, import, gist, significance

**substantial** *adj.* plentiful, abundant, ample, considerable, wealthy affluent, influential, valuable

**substantiate** *v.* verify, authenticate, confirm, validate, prove, corroborate, attest

**substitute** *adj.* alternative, surrogate, tentative

**subterfuge** *n.* ploy, scheme, stratagem, device, expedient, deceit, deception

**subtle** *adj.* delicate, understated, refined, elusive, deceptive, inferred, insinuated, artful, insidious

**subtract** *v.* deduct, decrease, diminish, lessen, lower

**succeed** *v.* **FLOURISH:** thrive, prevail, triumph; **REPLACE:** supersede

**success** *n.* achievement, mastery, victory, attainment

**successful** *adj.* triumphant, flourishing, thriving

**succession** *n.* sequence, order, continuation

**succinct** *adj.* brief, concise, terse, abbreviated

**succor** *n.* aid, help, sustenance, assistance

**succumb** *v.* submit, concede, relent, capitulate, collapse, fail

**sudden** *adj.* abrupt, quick, unexpected, impromptu

**suffer** *v.* endure, tolerate, bear, undergo, agonize

**sufficient** *adj.* plenty, ample, enough

**suffuse** *v.* saturate, pervade, soak, impregnate

**suggest** *v.* propose, submit, imply, insinuate

**suit** *v.* satisfy, please, gratify, shape, accommodate

**suitor** *n.* wooer, admirer, gallant, beau

**sulk** *v.* pout, scowl, frown, glower

**sullen** *adj.* moody, morose, gloomy, somber

**sully** *v.* shame, dishonor, stain, taint, tarnish, blemish, defile, corrupt, besmirch

**sultry** *adj.* sweltering, muggy, humid, sticky

**summary** *n.* condensation, digest, abridgment, brief

**summit** *n.* peak, pinnacle, apex, crown, culmination

**summon** *v.* call, invite, invoke, request, petition

**sumptuous** *adj.* luxurious, elegant, lavish, opulent

**sundry** *adj.* various, several, divers

**superb** *adj.* outstanding, exquisite, grand, magnificent, luxurious

**supersede** *v.* replace, supplant, succeed

**supervise** *v.* superintend, chaperon, manage, control

**supervision** *n.* management, guidance, surveillance

**supplant** *v.* replace, displace, succeed, supersede

**supple** *adj.* elastic, pliable, limber

**supplement** *n.* addition, subsidiary, extension

**supplement** *v.* augment, enhance, fortify

**supplicate** *v.* implore, beseech, beg, entreat

**supply** *v.* equip, stock, replenish

**support** *n.* **AID:** assistance, help, relief, succor; **BRACE:** prop, column, buttress, strut

**suppose** *v.* assume, infer, presume, believe, think

**suppress** *v.* **OVERPOWER:** repress, curb, quell, crush; **CONCEAL:** bury, cover

**supreme** *adj.* preeminent, superior, greatest

**supremacy** *n.* dominion, dominance, preeminence

**sure** *adj.* trusty, reliable, infallible, certain, safe, solid, precise, accurate, unerring, inevitable

**surface** *n.* rise, appear, emerge

**surge** *v.* gush, rush, pour, rise, heave

**surly** *adj.* cantankerous, rude, irritable, sullen, hostile

**surmise** *v.* speculate, guess, infer, imagine, suppose

**surmount** *v.* conquer, transcend, hurdle, overcome

**surpass** *v.* exceed, transcend, excel

**surplus** *n.* excess, abundance, remainder, residue

**surprise** *n.* astonishment, amazement, shock, wonder

**surprise** *v.* astound, bewilder, dumbfound, startle

**surrender** *v.* submit, abandon, capitulate, yield

**surreptitious** *adj.* furtive, clandestine, stealthy

**surrogate** *adj.* substitute, backup, alternative

**surround** *v.* encompass, enclose, circle

**survey** *v.* scrutinize, scan, examine, inspect, observe

**survive** *v.* endure, persist, remain, continue

**suspect** *v.* **DISTRUST:** mistrust, doubt; **BELIEVE:** suppose, imagine, conjecture

**suspend** *v.* postpone, delay, defer, interrupt

**suspense** *n.* apprehension, anxiety

**suspension** *n.* delay, deferment, postponement

**suspicion** *n.* skepticism, misgiving, mistrust, cynicism, notion, impression

**suspicious** *adj.* **DUBIOUS:** shady, untrustworthy, doubtful; **WARY:** skeptical

**sustenance** *n.* food, nourishment, provisions

**swagger** *v.* strut, prance, boast, brag, gloat

**swallow** *v.* drink, eat, gulp, consume, devour

**swamp** *n.* bayou, marsh, mire, morass, slough

**swarm** *n.* horde, mass, flock, multitude, host

**sway** *n.* dominion, dominance, control, influence

**swear** *v.* **PROMISE:** declare, testify, affirm; **BLASPHEME:** damn, curse

**sweet** *adj.* luscious, aromatic, fragrant, clean, fresh, melodious, harmonious

**swell** *v.* increase, inflate, bloat, bulge, grow

**swift** *adj.* fast, rapid, expeditious, fleet, prompt, quick

**swig** *v.* drink, swallow, quaff, gulp, guzzle

**swindle** *v.* trick, deceive, dupe, defraud, victimize

**swing** *v.* hang, dangle, flap, oscillate, wave

**switch** *v.* swap, trade, exchange, replace, substitute

**sycophant** *n.* flatterer, flunky, parasite, toady

**symbol** *n.* character, letter, numeral, representation

**symbolize** *v.* signify, connote, mean, represent

**sympathetic** *adj.* considerate, compassionate

**sympathize** *v.* commiserate, console, pity

**sympathy** *n.* compassion, understanding, warmth, consolation, solace, comfort

**symptom** *n.* clue, trait, characteristic, feature, sign

**synchronize** *v.* accommodate, adjust, attune

**syndicate** *n.* coalition, alliance, company, association

**syndicate** *v.* affiliate, connect, consolidate, merge

**synopsis** *n.* summary, abridgment, condensation

**system** *n.* strategy, plan, scheme, method

**systematic** *adj.* methodical, orderly, precise, regular

**tabloid** *n.* newspaper, periodical, publication

**taboo** *adj.* forbidden, banned, prohibited

**tacit** *adj.* implied, understood, assumed, inferred

**taciturn** *adj.* reserved, quiet

**tact** *n.* subtlety, discretion, finesse, style

**tactics** *n.* scheme, stratagem, procedure, system

**tailor** *v.* customize, adapt, adjust

**taint** *v.* corrupt, infect, defile, contaminate

**take** *v.* obtain, get, procure, seize, grasp, capture, adopt, select, accept, choose, pick

**tale** *n.* YARN: narrative, account; FALSEHOOD: fib, lie

**talent** *n.* aptitude, genius, gift

**talisman** *n.* amulet, charm

**talk** *n.* conversation, dialogue, speech

**talk** *v.* converse, speak, discuss, gossip

**talkative** *adj.* loquacious, chatty, garrulous, gabby

**tall** *adj.* towering, high, big, rangy, lanky

**tally** *n.* count, reckoning, sum, calculation

**tame** *adj.* docile, gentle, obedient

**tamper** *v.* change, alter, meddle, damage

**tangible** *adj.* material, corporeal, tactile, discernible, evident, actual, real, genuine

**tantalize** *v.* tease, provoke, torment, frustrate, vex

**tantamount** *adj.* equivalent, parallel, identical

**tape** *n.* bind, wrap, seal, mend

**tarnish** *n.* blemish, blot, stain, taint

**tarnish** *v.* defame, disgrace embarrass

**tarry** *v.* stall, linger, loiter, dally, dawdle, stay

**task** *n.* job, labor, assignment, duty, chore

**taste** *n.* partiality, liking, bias, preference

**taste** *v.* sample, try, sip, savor, relish

**taunt** *v.* insult, jeer, mock, provoke

**tavern** *n.* bar, saloon, pub, cafe, inn, lodge, hostelry

**tax** *n.* levy, assessment, tariff, toll, duty, obligation

**teach** *v.* instruct, inform, train, enlighten, guide

**tear** *v.* rip, split, sever, cleave, rend

**tease** *v.* annoy, taunt, torment, harass, irritate, vex

**technique** *n.* **METHOD:** procedure, system, approach, methodology; **ABILITY:** skill, aptitude, knack

**tedious** *adj.* monotonous, tiresome, dull, boring

**tell** *v.* recount, describe, report, speak, mention, explain, reveal, declare, divulge

**temper** *n.* disposition, temperament, humor, composure, poise

**temper** *v.* soothe, pacify, calm, mollify

**temperament** *n.* disposition, attitude, mood, emotion

**temperance** *n.* restraint, sobriety, abstinence

**temperate** *adj.* calm, composed, cool, reasonable

**tempestuous** *adj.* stormy, raging, tumultuous

**temporary** *adj.* transitory, fleeting, interim

**tenable** *adj.* defensible, justifiable

**tenacious** *adj.* resolute, persistent, obstinate

**tenant** *n.* renter, leaseholder, inhabitant

**tend** *v.* guard, protect, keep, manage

**tendency** *n.* inclination, partiality, bias, penchant

**tender** *adj.* **DELICATE:** fragile, frail; **COMPASSIONATE:** sympathetic, kindhearted considerate

**tenet** *n.* belief, conviction, dogma, creed, doctrine

**tenor** *n.* drift, trend, tone, course

**tense** *adj.* taut, nervous, strained, agitated, drawn

**tension** *n.* pressure, strain, stress, unease

**tentative** *adj.* provisional, probationary, experimental, indefinite

**tenuous** *adj.* fine, narrow, insubstantial, flimsy, feeble

**terminal** *adj.* boundary, limit, extremity

**terminate** *v.* complete, conclude, eliminate, cancel

**termination** *n.* close, finish, cessation, completion

**terminology** *n.* vocabulary, language, jargon

**terminus** *n.* extremity, objective, conclusion

**terrible** *adj.* frightful, appalling, dreadful, horrible, horrendous, disastrous, disturbing, extreme

**terrific** *adj.* splendid, marvelous, wonderful, outstanding, super

**terrify** *v.* terrorize, appall, paralyze, horrify, frighten

**territory** *n.* area, region, dominion

**terror** *n.* fright, horror, alarm, dismay, consternation

**terse** *adj.* brief, succinct, concise, precise, curt

**test** *n.* inspection, experiment, examination, quiz

**testify** *v.* swear, certify, demonstrate, indicate, argue

**testimony** *n.* statement, declaration, confirmation, testament, affidavit

**testy** *adj.* irritable, cranky, grouchy, edgy, short–tempered, touchy, peevish

**thank** *v.* acknowledge, appreciate, recognize, credit

**thaw** *v.* warm, melt, dissolve, liquefy

**theft** *n.* burglary, robbery, thievery, looting

**theology** *n.* religion, faith, belief, scripture, dogma, convictions, creed

**theorem** *n.* principle, hypothesis, postulate, premise

**theory** *n.* conjecture, speculation, rationale, explanation, view, conception, outlook

**theoretical** *adj.* abstract, academic, hypothetical

**theorize** *v.* speculate, postulate, presume, suppose

**therapeutic** *adj.* restorative, curative, recuperative, remedial, corrective

**thesis** *n.* opinion, contention, argument, assumption, assertion, hypothesis

**thick** *adj.* abundant, dense, packed, crowded

**thicken** *v.* jell, congeal, stiffen, harden, intensify

**thin** *adj.* lean, gaunt, scanty, meager

**thin** *v.* dilute, weaken, reduce

**think** *v.* contemplate meditate, consider, remember, recall, recollect, believe, suppose

**thirst** *n.* longing, desire, yearning, eagerness

**thorough** *adj.* total, meticulous, precise, painstaking

**thoroughfare** *n.* artery, highway, expressway, boulevard, concourse, freeway

**thought** *v.* concept, conviction, notion, opinion, theory, hypothesis, supposition

**thoughtful** *adj.* considerate, caring, attentive, concerned, discreet, tender

**threadbare** *adj.* worn, shabby, tattered, frayed, seedy

**threat** *n.* risk, hazard, danger, jeopardy, menace

**threaten** *v.* endanger, menace, terrorize, scare

**threshold** *n.* start, beginning, outset, commencement

**thrift** *n.* economy, husbandry, conservation

**thrifty** *adj.* frugal, sparing, provident

**thrill** *n.* excitement, stimulation

**thrill** *v.* delight, electrify, rouse

**thrive** *v.* flourish, succeed, increase, grow

**throb** *v.* pulse, pound, thump, pulsate

**throng** *n.* mass, multitude, horde, swarm, host, assemblage, crowd

**through** *adj.* completed, done, finished

**throw** *v.* fling, hurl, pitch, heave, toss

**thrust** *v.* shove, plunge, jab, push

**tidings** *n.* news, information, gossip

**tidy** *adj.* neat, orderly, spruce, trim

**tie** *n.* **ROPE:** band, strap, cord, **NECKTIE:** bow, scarf, cravat, choker, **CONNECTION:** relation, bond, link, knot, **STANDOFF:** draw, deadlock, stalemate

**tie** *v.* fasten, secure attach, connect, join, link

**tier** *n.* line, row, array, bank

**tiff** *n.* quarrel, dispute, disagreement, scrap, spat

**tighten** *v.* squeeze, compress, constrict, clench

**tilt** *n.* tip, list, slant, incline, slope, angle, pitch

**time** *n.* **AGE:** epoch, generation, cycle; **INTERVAL:** duration, span; **RHYTHM:** tempo, beat, cadence

**timely** *adj.* auspicious, propitious, favorable, prompt

**timetable** *n.* schedule, program, calendar, agenda

**timid** *adj.* shy, retiring, fearful, withdrawn, reticent, indecisive, vacillating

**timorous** *adj.* timid, fearful, apprehensive, anxious, scared, afraid

**tinge** *n.* trace, hint, trifle, dab, nuance

**tinker** *v.* dabble, putter, potter, trifle

**tiny** *adj.* small, diminutive, minute, microscopic

**tip** *n.* PEAK: pinnacle, summit; GRATUITY: compensation, consideration; ADVICE: pointer, hint, clue

**tirade** *n.* harangue, denunciation, outburst

**tire** *v.* exhaust, fatigue, drain, irk, bore

**title** *n.* DESIGNATION: name, appellation, epithet; CLAIM: interest, holding, ownership

**titter** *v.* laugh, giggle, snicker, chuckle

**toil** *v.* labor, work, strive, slave, sweat

**token** *adj.* nominal, superficial, minimal

**token** *n.* sign, emblem, mark

**tolerable** *adj.* ENDURABLE: bearable, sufferable; ADEQUATE: decent, average

**tolerance** *n.* forbearance, impartiality, magnanimity

**tolerant** *adj.* unprejudiced, moderate

**tolerate** *v.* SUFFER: abide, accept, bear; ALLOW: oblige, indulge

**tomb** *n.* grave, vault, crypt, sepulcher, mausoleum

**tool** *n.* implement, appliance, gadget, utensil

**top** *n.* pinnacle, crest, summit, zenith, crown

**topical** *adj.* local, isolated, provincial, regional

**topple** *v.* fall, tumble, collapse, overturn, upset

**torment** *n.* anguish, suffering, distress, misery

**torment** *v.* distress, vex, afflict, annoy, tease, harass, irritate, pester, provoke, needle

**torpid** *adj.* inactive, inert, lethargic, sluggish, motionless, dormant, hibernating

**torpor** *n.* idleness, inactivity, indolence, sluggishness

**torrent** *n.* cloudburst, deluge, flood

**tortuous** *adj.* winding serpentine, twisted, snaky, crooked, bent

**toss** *v.* throw, fling, pitch, cast, hurl, chuck

**total** *adj.* entire, utter, whole, gross

**totter** *v.* stumble, falter, weave, reel, lurch

**tough** *adj.* rugged, hardy, sturdy, durable, hardy, unyielding, incorrigible

**tourist** *n.* visitor, sightseer, wayfarer

**tournament** *n.* competition, rivalry, contest, match

**tousle** *v.* dishevel, disarray, ruffle, muss

**tout** *v.* vaunt, plug, promote, herald, extol

**town** *n.* community, municipality, village, hamlet

**toxic** *adj.* poisonous, deadly, lethal, virulent

**trace** *n.* vestige, indication, hint

**track** *v.* hunt, trail, pursue, trace

**tractable** *adj.* docile, compliant, pliable, flexible

**trade** *n.* vocation, profession, livelihood, craft

**trade** *v.* exchange, swap, barter, buy, sell

**tragedy** *n.* disaster, calamity, catastrophe, affliction, suffering, tribulation

**tragic** *adj.* disastrous, dreadful, distressing

**train** *v.* tutor, teach, enlighten, inform, instruct, educate, guide

**trait** *n.* characteristic, quality, property, attribute, mannerism, habit

**tramp** *n.* hobo, vagabond, vagrant, gypsy

**tramp** *v.* roam, rove, hike, tromp, march

**tranquil** *adj.* peaceful, serene, placid, still, pleasant

**tranquillity** *n.* quiet, calm, serenity

**transform** *v.* alter, transfigure, convert, commute

**transgress** *n.* infringe, violate, trespass

**transient** *adj.* brief, transitory, passing, fleeting

**translate** *v.* reword, explain, interpret, decipher

**translucent** *adj.* transparent, clear

**transmit** *v.* transfer, send, convey, dispatch

**transparent** *adj.* lucid, translucent, diaphanous, clear, sheer

**transpose** *v.* switch, swap, exchange, transfer

**trap** *n.* snare, trick, stratagem, maneuver, artifice

**traumatic** *adj.* alarming, upsetting, frightful

**travel** *v.* journey, tour, roam, expedition, excursion

**travesty** *n.* parody, satire, spoof burlesque, lampoon, caricature, farce

**treacherous** *adj.* unfaithful, deceitful, deceptive, insidious, disloyal, treasonous, difficult, unstable

**treatise** *n.* dissertation, thesis, essay, discourse

**treaty** *n.* agreement, settlement, covenant, pact

**tremble** *v.* shiver, quiver, shake

**tremendous** *adj.* colossal, huge, immense

**tribulation** *n.* distress, suffering, hardship

**tribute** *n.* accolade, homage, recognition, applause

**trick** *n.* deception, artifice, ruse

**trim** *adj.* neat, orderly, tidy, groomed, natty

**trinket** *n.* bauble, adornment, decoration, ornament

**trip** *n.* voyage, excursion, jaunt, pilgrimage

**trite** *adj.* ordinary, commonplace, hackneyed, stale

**triumph** *v.* prevail, conquer, overwhelm, overpower

**trivial** *adj.* insignificant, inconsequential, unimportant, irrelevant, frivolous

**troll** *v.* goblin, gremlin, hobgoblin, demon

**trophy** *n.* award, citation, medal

**trot** *v.* canter, jog, lope, amble

**trouble** *n.* calamity, distress, misfortune, tribulation

**trouble** *v.* distress, harass, harry, irritate, pester

**troublesome** *adj.* pesky, bothersome, trying, perplexing, galling, burdensome, disturbing

**trough** *n.* channel, furrow, rut, crater, ditch

**truce** *n.* armistice, reprieve, amnesty

**truculent** *adj.* fierce, mean, malevolent, pugnacious, belligerent, contentious, hostile

**true** *adj.* real, genuine, truthful, undistorted, authentic, just, honest, faithful, reliable

**trunk** *n.* chest, strongbox, coffer, case

**trust** *n.* confidence, dependence, reliance, faith

**try** *v.* endeavor, strive, test, examine

**tryst** *n.* meeting, rendezvous, assignation

**tumble** *v.* fall, slip, descend, decline, drop

**tumor** *n.* growth, cyst, polyp, melanoma, sarcoma

**tumult** *n.* disorder, commotion, turmoil, melee, agitation

**tumultuous** *adj.* riotous, violent, restive, uneasy, boisterous, disorderly, obstreperous

**turbulent** *adj.* violent, blustery, disorderly

**turbulence** *n.* commotion, excitement, uproar, tumult, disturbance

**turmoil** *n.* chaos, commotion, disorder, tumult, turbulence, uproar

**turn** *v.* **ROTATE:** spin, gyrate; **CONVERT:** transform, change, alter, transmute,

**turpitude** *n.* depravity, baseness, perversion, vileness, evil, sinfulness, corruption

**tutor** *n.* instructor, trainer, teacher

**tweak** *v.* nip, pinch, grasp, squeeze, twist

**twine** *n.* rope, cord, strand, string, braid

**twinge** *n.* twitch, tingle, spasm, crick, stitch, throb

**twinkle** *v.* shimmer, glitter, flicker, glint, glimmer

**twirl** *v.* twist, gyrate, turn, rotate, pivot

**type** *n.* kind, class, breed, group, family, genus

**typical** *adj.* characteristic, representative, ideal

**typify** *v.* represent, personify, epitomize, exemplify

**tyrannical** *adj.* oppressive, despotic, arbitrary, domineering, unjust, cruel

**tyro** *n.* amateur, novice, apprentice, neophyte

**ubiquity** *n.* prevalence, pervasiveness, commonness, omnipresence, universality

**ugly** *adj.* homely, unsightly, displeasing, monstrous, objectionable, nasty

**ulcer** *n.* abscess, infection, boil

**ulterior** *adj.* concealed, shrouded, obscured

**ultimate** *adj.* extreme, final, decisive, concluding, eventual, maximum, utmost, preeminent

**ultimatum** *n.* warning, mandate, demand, order

**unaffected** *adj.* NATURAL: simple, sincere, genuine, real, artless; UNMOVED: indifferent, unemotional, unresponsive, disinterested

**unassuming** *adj.* modest, unpretentious, humble, simple, plain, diffident

**unauthorized** *adj.* unsanctioned, prohibited, illicit, forbidden, banned

**unbalanced** *adj.* unstable, maladjusted, biased, untrustworthy, treacherous

**unbearable** *adj.* intolerable, insufferable, obnoxious

**unbecoming** *adj.* inappropriate, unsuitable, indecent, unseemly, rough, improper, unfit

**unbiased** *adj.* impartial, objective, neutral, unprejudiced, tolerant, disinterested

**unbounded** *adj.* IMMENSE: endless, vast; UNCONFINED: free, unbridled, unfettered

**uncanny** *adj.* strange, odd, weird, mysterious, eerie

**unceasing** *adj.* continual, incessant, chronic, perpetual, persistent

**uncivilized** *adj.* primitive, barbarous, crude, uncouth

**unclean** *adj.* dirty, grimy, soiled, squalid, foul, vile, impure, defiled, adulterated, profaned

**uncommon** *adj.* exceptional, extraordinary, unique, remarkable, rare, scarce

**uncompromising** *adj.* obstinate, inflexible, unyielding, immovable, steadfast,

**unconditional** *adj.* absolute, certain, unrestricted

**unconscionable** *adj.* unscrupulous, unprincipled, wicked, wanton, dishonest, unholy

**unconscious** *adj.* senseless, oblivious, benumbed

**uncouth** *adj.* rude, ill-mannered, vulgar, crass

**uncover** *v.* reveal, expose, disclose, unearth

**undaunted** *adj.* fearless, courageous, valiant, intrepid, audacious

**underestimate** *v.* misjudge, miscalculate, slight

**undergo** *v.* endure, tolerate, suffer, bear, abide

**underhanded** *adj.* sly, furtive, deceitful, dishonest, traitorous, unscrupulous

**undermine** *v.* weaken, erode, corrode, decay, threaten

**underrate** *v.* devaluate, lessen, downgrade, depreciate

**understand** *v.* comprehend, grasp, perceive, discern, interpret, hear, accept, conclude

**understanding** *adj.* sympathetic, accepting, tolerant

**understanding** *n.* comprehension, grasp, awareness

**undervalue** *v.* minimize, cheapen, misjudge, belittle, discredit, underrate

**underwrite** *v.* guarantee, support, endorse

**undetermined** *adj.* dubious, obscure, enigmatic, doubtful, unsettled

**undo** *v.* cancel, efface, erase, expunge, obliterate

**undress** *n.* disrobe, undrape, shed, peel

**undulate** *v.* wave, surge, heave, flap, pulsate, billow

**unduly** *adj.* excessively, inordinately, exceedingly

**undying** *adj.* eternal, permanent, everlasting, unceasing

**uneasy** *adj.* restless, perplexed, troubled, apprehensive, fidgety, nervous, jittery, uncomfortable

**unencumbered** *adj.* free, unobstructed, unhampered, unhindered, unfettered

**unequal** *adj.* disparate, unlike, uneven, odd

**unequaled** *adj.* incomparable, matchless, unparalleled, distinct, peerless, special

**unequivocal** *adj.* definite, unmistakable, incontestable, evident, absolute, explicit, clear, plain

**unerring** *adj.* accurate, exact, precise, perfect, correct, definite, unfailing, infallible

**uneven** *adj.* jagged, coarse, rugged, serrated, intermittent, spasmodic, irregular, rough

**unfailing** *adj.* certain, absolute, sure, reliable, surefire, dependable

**unfair** *adj.* unjust, prejudiced, discriminatory, biased, inequitable, despotic, wrongful, arbitrary

**unfaltering** *adj.* steadfast, resolute, untiring, unfailing, unflagging, tireless, persistent, firm

**unfathomable** *adj.* incomprehensible, enigmatic, mysterious, inscrutable, profound, baffling, puzzling

**unfeeling** *adj.* callous, merciless, unsympathetic, cold-hearted, hard, brutal, cruel

**unfeigned** *adj.* genuine, real, natural, unaffected, truthful, candid, sincere

**unflagging** *adj.* tireless, unrelenting, persisting, assiduous, devoted, consistent

**unfold** *v.* evolve, reveal, show, unravel, unearth, resolve, open, extend, expand

**unfortunate** *adj.* unlucky, inept, hapless, doomed, cursed, ill-fated

**unfounded** *adj.* baseless, groundless, unsupported, unsound, erroneous, untrue

**unfurl** *v.* unfold, open, uncoil, extend

**ungovernable** *adj.* uncontrollable, headstrong, unruly

**unguarded** *adj.* open, undefended, unprotected, incautious

**unguent** *n.* ointment, salve, lotion, balm, poultice, dressing

**uniform** *adj.* regular, routine, normal, unwavering, invariable, consistent, steady

**uniformity** *n.* regularity, similarity, accord, order, concord

**unify** *v.* combine, integrate, consolidate, compact, concentrate, arrange, blend, integrate, synthesize

**unimpeachable** *adj.* irrefutable, obvious, unassailable, conclusive, adequate

**unintentional** *adj.* involuntary, accidental, inadvertent, unconscious, unplanned

**union** *n.* coalition, merger, alliance, association, confederacy, order, league, brotherhood, society, matrimony

**unique** *adj.* singular, particular, peerless, unrivaled, unequaled, matchless, unusual, uncommon, odd, peculiar, rare

**unit** *n.* element, constituent, component, part, section, piece, member

**unite** *v.* combine, join, link, couple, connect, associate, incorporate, blend, consolidate, compound, fuse, weld, marry, join

**unity** *n.* union, harmony, agreement, concert, unison, concord, rapport, congruity

**universal** *adj.* general, widespread, extensive, entire, whole, sweeping

**universe** *n.* cosmos, world, totality

**unjust** *adj.* unfair, partial, prejudiced, biased, inequitable, shabby, undeserved, unjustified, unmerited

**unkempt** *adj.* disorderly, disheveled, untidy, messy, tousled

**unkind** *adj.* cruel, harsh, unfeeling, callous, cold-hearted, hard, brutal, heartless

**unlettered** *adj.* untaught, ignorant, uneducated, illiterate, unenlightened, untutored

**unlike** *adj.* different, dissimilar, incompatible, mismatched, disparate, divergent, diverse

**unlimited** *adj.* boundless, infinite, immense, vast, extensive, endless, unconstrained, unrestricted, total, complete, totalitarian

**unmanageable** *adj.* ungovernable, unruly,

difficult, uncooperative, stubborn, obstinate, balky, rebellious, uncontrollable, wild, irrepressible

**unmoved** *adj.* determined, decided, solid, unshaken, unaffected, collected, firm, steadfast, indifferent, resolute, unemotional

**unnerve** *v.* upset, unsettle, fluster, disarm, discourage, aggravate, disconcert, trouble, rattle

**unparalleled** *adj.* uncommon, rare, singular, unequaled, unrivaled, unique, peerless, matchless

**unprecedented** *adj.* unparalleled, unique, unequal, unusual, uncommon, untoward

**unprincipled** *adj.* amoral, corrupt, unethical, wanton, unscrupulous, dishonest

**unqualified** *adj.* incompetent, unskilled, unable, inept, untrained, unsatisfactory, unsuitable, incapable, ineligible

**unravel** *v.* explain, elucidate, clarify, justify, resolve, interpret, solve, untangle, unwind, disengage

**unremitting** *n.* constant, ceaseless, endless, incessant, constant, perpetual, unending, continuous,

**unrest** *n.* agitation, disquiet, trouble, disturbance, bickering, crisis, turbulence

**unscathed** *adj.* unharmed, safe, unimpaired, sound, uninjured

**unseemly** *adj.* indecent, improper, unbecoming, inappropriate, wrong, incorrect,

**unsettle** *v.* confuse, disturb, upset, perturb, bother, trouble, fluster, ruffle, rattle

**unsightly** *adj.* unattractive, homely, plain, disagreeable, repulsive, hideous

**unsophisticated** *adj.* naive, provincial, callow, unrefined, simple, coarse, crude, harsh, vulgar, artless, guileless, ingenuous, natural, genuine

**unspeakable** *adj.* unutterable, indescribable, astonishing, incredible, offensive, abusive, nasty, repulsive, coarse, odious, ineffable

**untiring** *adj.* inexhaustible, constant, powerful, resolute, strong, unflagging

**unveil** *v.* reveal, show, expose, divulge, announce

**upbraid** *v.* censure, scold, chide, admonish, reproach, reprove, berate, condemn

**upheaval** *n.* eruption, earthquake, volcano, blowup, outbreak, explosion, outburst

**uphold** *v.* maintain, support, champion, sustain, endorse, sanction, bolster, help

**uppermost** *adj.* topmost, foremost, highest, predominant, supreme, loftiest

**upright** *adj.* upstanding, honest, good,

outstanding, moral, ethical, principled, just, righteous, pure, true

**uprising** *n.* revolt, insurrection, rebellion, revolution, demonstration, skirmish

**uproar** *n.* disturbance, clamor, commotion, fracas, furor, hubbub, melee

**uproarious** *adj.* hilarious, funny, noisy, tumultuous, turbulent, frenzied, confused, disorderly

**uproot** *v.* remove, transport, liquidate, excavate, extirpate, eradicate, eliminate, dislodge

**upset** *adj.* irritated, worried, uneasy, disturbed, troubled, aggravated, concerned, perturbed, unsettled, disconcerted

**upset** *v.* capsize, overturn, upend, topple, founder, invert, flip

**upshot** *n.* outcome, consequence, conclusion, result

**upstart** *n.* opportunist, pretender, snob, phony, fraud, rogue, impostor

**urban** *adj.* city, metropolitan, municipal

**urbane** *adj.* suave, poised, polished, refined, elegant, gracious, courteous

**urchin** *n.* waif, stray, foundling, orphan, ragamuffin, child, infant

**urge** *n.* drive, desire, impulse, craving, passion, push, influence, stimulus, impulse

**urge** *v.* drive, impel, press, spur, incite, goad, stimulate, implore, beg, beseech, entreat, persuade, induce, advise, advocate, recommend

**urgent** *adj.* pressing, compelling, demanding, driving, forcing, imperative, anxious, insistent, earnest

**urgency** *n.* seriousness, need, insistence, gravity, exigency, emergency, crisis, necessity

**usable** *adj.* useful, employable, applicable, functional

**usage** *n.* custom, practice, acceptance, convention, habit, fashion, form

**use** *n.* application, help, habit, custom

**use** *v.* employ, utilize, operate, apply, exploit

**useful** *adj.* beneficial, helpful, serviceable, effective, practical, functional, handy

**usual** *adj.* common, customary, familiar

**usurp** *v.* capture, commandeer, appropriate, assume

**utensil** *n.* instrument, device, implement, gadget

**utility** *n.* usefulness, value, advantage

**utilize** *v.* use, employ, exploit, operate

**utmost** *adj.* ultimate, maximum, maximal, entire, greatest, undiminished, unlimited

**utopian** *adj.* idealistic, ideological, visionary, perfect, ideal, fanciful, theoretical

**utter** *adj.* complete, entire, total, unconditional, unqualified, thorough

**utter** *v.* speak, articulate, vocalize, voice, say, remark, express, proclaim, state

**utterance** *n.* assertion, declaration, enunciation, proclamation, pronouncement

**vacant** *adj.* empty, uninhabited, abandoned, deserted, expressionless, vacuous, vapid

**vacate** *v.* leave, abandon, depart, quit

**vacation** *n.* holiday, furlough, respite, sabbatical

**vaccinate** *v.* immunize, inoculate, inject

**vacillate** *v.* waver, hesitate, fluctuate, alternate, sway

**vacuum** *n.* void, emptiness, vacuity, nothingness

**vagary** *n.* caprice, whim, urge, notion, impulse, fancy, quirk, eccentricity

**vagrant** *n.* beggar, tramp, hobo, idler, loafer, rascal

**vague** *adj.* obscure, indistinct, indefinite, imprecise, unspecified, uncertain, loose, unclear

**vain** *adj.* **FUTILE:** unavailing, fruitless, ineffective, inefficient, hollow; **CONCEITED:** egotistical, arrogant, proud, narcissistic

**valet** *n.* manservant, attendant, butler, steward

**valiant** *adj.* valorous, brave, bold, courageous, intrepid, stouthearted, fearless, chivalrous

**valid** *adj.* logical, well-founded, sensible, sound, convincing, authoritative, legal, lawful

**valley** *n.* glen, dale, hollow, basin, lowland, vale

**valor** *n.* bravery, courage, boldness, spirit

**valorous** *adj.* brave, valiant, courageous, fearless

**valuable** *adj.* expensive, precious, rare, priceless, useful, beneficial, profitable, serviceable

**value** *n.* worth, importance, cost, price, significance

**value** *v.* appraise, assess, estimate, evaluate, judge, reckon, weigh, consider, rate

**vandalism** *n.* defacement, damage, mutilation, disfiguration, marring, spoiling

**vanguard** *n.* forefront, leaders, precursors, spearhead

**vanish** *v.* disappear, depart, evaporate, fade, dissolve

**vanity** *n.* conceit, pretension, self–esteem, pride, folly

**vanquish** *v.* conquer, overwhelm, subdue, overpower, defeat, suppress, quell, subjugate, quash, crush

**vapid** *adj.* dull, lifeless, insipid, uninteresting, tiresome, spiritless, vacuous, prosaic, mundane

**vapor** *n.* fog, haze, mist, gas, smog, condensation

**vaporize** *v.* evaporate, vanish, dissolve, disappear

**variable** *adj.* fluctuating, inconstant, wavering

**variance** *n.* difference, divergence, discrepancy, incongruity, disagreement, discord

**variation** *n.* alteration, modification, deviation, difference, discrepancy, diversity, dissimilarity, irregularity, inequality, aberration, departure

**variety** *n.* category, group, classification, division

**various** *adj.* miscellaneous, assorted, divers, diverse, diversified, varied, sundry

**varnish** *v.* embellish, disguise, mask, veil, falsify

**vary** *v.* change, alter, modify, diversify, deviate, differ, fluctuate, alternate

**vast** *adj.* boundless,

large, limitless, unbounded, extensive, immense, widespread

**vat** *n.* container, keg, barrel, cask, tub

**vault** *n.* crypt, tomb, mausoleum, sepulcher

**vault** *v.* jump, hurdle, bound, leap, spring

**vaunt** *v.* boast, gloat, brag, strut, swagger, flaunt

**veer** *v.* swerve, deviate, diverge, curve, deflect

**vehement** *adj.* fervent, impassioned

**vehemence** *n.* ardor, eagerness, energy, enthusiasm, passion, zeal, spirit

**vehicle** *n.* conveyance, transportation, medium, means, agency, instrumentality

**veil** *v.* conceal, mask, cover, shroud, cloud, obscure

**velocity** *n.* speed, swiftness, dispatch, quickness

**venal** *adj.* corrupt, unscrupulous, treacherous, mercenary, dishonorable, corruptible

**vend** *v.* sell, merchandise, market, retail

**veneer** *n.* facing, cover, coating, surfacing

**venerable** *adj.* esteemed, revered, distinguished, honorable, ancient, respected

**venerate** *v.* admire, worship, revere, esteem, respect

**vengeance** *n.* revenge, retaliation, retribution

**vengeful** *adj.* vindictive, unforgiving, unrelenting, spiteful, rancorous, malicious

**venial** *adj.* excusable, justifiable, forgivable

**venom** *n.* bitterness, virulence, malice anger, contempt, spitefulness, malevolence, hate

**vent** *v.* express, air, assert, verbalize, articulate, expound, release, unleash, discharge

**venture** *n.* undertaking, enterprise, investment, speculation, endeavor, attempt

**venture** *v.* chance, wager, risk, gamble, hazard, dare, plunge, imperil, jeopardize, endanger, hazard

**veracious** *adj.* truthful, accurate, precise, honest, sincere, trustworthy, righteous

**veracity** *n.* truth honesty, sincerity, accuracy, precision, exactness, correctness

**verandah** *n.* terrace, porch, deck, patio, courtyard

**verbal** *adj.* oral, spoken, stated

**verbose** *adj.* wordy, windy, loquacious, tedious, garrulous, talkative, chatty

**verdant** *adj.* green, flourishing, thriving, dense, lush

**verdict** *n.* decision, judgment, ruling, finding, adjudication, decree, determination, sentence

**verify** *v.* confirm, prove, authenticate, corroborate, substantiate, validate

**verification** *n.* evidence, proof, validation, documentation, support, confirmation

**veritable** *adj.* real, genuine, actual, positive, true, virtual, authentic

**vernacular** *adj.* native, indigenous, regional, informal, colloquial, everyday, ordinary, familiar

**vernacular** *n.* dialect, argot, jargon, idiom

**versatile** *adj.* flexible, pliable, adaptable, tractable, docile, pliant, yielding

**versatility** *n.* flexibility, pliancy, agility, compliance, adaptability, amenity, amiability

**versed** *adj.* experienced, seasoned, competent, adept, capable, skilled, practiced, trained

**version** *n.* rendition, interpretation, rendition

**vertical** *adj.* erect, upright, perpendicular, plumb

**vestibule** *n.* foyer, hallway, entry, lobby

**vestige** *n.* trace, indication, shred, fragment, remainder, hint, suggestion

**veteran** *adj.* experienced, skilled, seasoned, versed

**veto** *v.* reject, discard, eliminate, refuse, void, nullify, invalidate, forbid, dismiss

**vex** *v.* annoy, harass, irk, bother, disturb, irritate, plague, torment, agitate

**viaduct** *n.* bridge, overpass, trestle

**vibrate** *v.* shake, flutter, tremble, quiver, undulate, fluctuate, oscillate, reverberate

**vicarious** *adj.* substituted, delegated, sympathetic

**vice** *n.* wickedness, corruption, evil, depravity, immorality, depravity, iniquity, malignancy

**vicinity** *n* area, locality, neighborhood, environment, proximity, nearness

**vicious** *adj.* base, degenerate, vile, depraved, reprehensible, malicious, malevolent, malignant, unruly

**victim** *n.* casualty, dupe, gull, prey

**victor** *n.* winner, champion, conqueror

**victory** *n.* triumph, conquest, success, achievement

**victorious** *adj.* triumphant, successful

**vie** *v.* compete, oppose, contend, clash, rival, strive

**view** *n.* scene, sight, spectacle, vision, glimpse, aspect, object, purpose, intention, description, notion, opinion, judgment, assessment

**view** *v.* observe, regard, behold, survey, witness, inspect, examine, study, scrutinize

**vigil** *n.* watchfulness, wakefulness, surveillance

**vigilant** *adj.* watchful, alert, observant, attentive, careful, wary

**vigor** *n.* vitality, stamina, strength power, potency, energy, endurance, soundness

**vile** *adj.* evil depraved, wretched, repulsive, contemptible, revolting, disgusting, offensive, vulgar

**vilify** *v.* malign, slander, slur, defame

**village** *n.* town, community, hamlet, municipality

**villain** *n.* miscreant, cad, rascal, rogue, scoundrel

**vindicate** *v.* exonerate, acquit, absolve, clear, defend, justify, support, uphold, corroborate, assert

**vindictive** *adj.* vengeful, spiteful, unforgiving

**vintage** *adj.* classic, choice, old, excellent

**violate** *v.* breach, infringe, transgress, trespass

**violation** *n.* transgression infringement, breach, defilement, debasement, assault, outrage

**violent** *adj.* intense, fierce, furious, rough, vicious, brutal, barbarous, savage, fierce

**virgin** *n.* pure, undefiled, unsullied, unadulterated, unmixed, fresh, unspoiled

**virile** *adj.* vibrant, strong, forceful, vigorous, robust

**virtue** *n.* integrity, temperance, purity, decency

**virtuous** *adj.* moral, ethical, honest, noble, right, pure, chaste

**virulent** *adj.* LETHAL: malignant, venomous, poisonous; HATEFUL: bitter, malicious, antagonistic

**virus** *n.* infection, disease, germ, microbe

**visa** *n.* endorsement, permit, authorization

**visage** *n.* countenance, appearance, aspect

**viscous** *adj.* sticky, thick, sticky, gummy

**visible** *adj.* discernible, perceptible, perceivable, obvious, apparent, clear, evident, conspicuous

**visibility** *n.* distinctness, perceptibility, prominence

**vision** *n.* **PERCEPTION:** sight, understanding, discernment, intuition; **CONCEPT:** image, imagination, view, **HALLUCINATION:** apparition, ghost, phantom

**visit** *n.* call, appointment, interview, talk, sojourn

**visitor** *n.* guest, caller, company

**visor** *n.* shield, sunshade, bill, peak

**vista** *n.* view, perspective, prospect, outlook

**visual** *adj.* visible, perceptible, obvious; ocular

**vital** *adj.* **ESSENTIAL:** necessary, important, critical, requisite; **VIGOROUS:** lively, energetic, active

**vivacious** *adj.* lively, animated, brisk, spirited, sprightly, energetic, spry

**vivid** *adj.* **BRIGHT:** shining, intense, lucid, lively, spirited, energetic, vivacious, realistic, picturesque, distinct, graphic, striking, clear, discernible

**vocabulary** *n.* lexicon, glossary, dictionary

**vocal** *adj.* **UTTERED:** spoken, oral, articulated, expressed, verbalized; **OUTSPOKEN:** open, honest, assertive, candid, blunt

**vocation** *n.* occupation, trade, profession, business, pursuit, calling

**vociferous** *adj.* noisy, boisterous, uproarious, blatant

**vogue** *n.* fashion, style, custom, trend, fad, popularity

**voice** *n.* expression, utterance, assertion, declaration, preference, opinion, say, vote, view

**void** *adj.* useless, empty, barren, destitute, vacant, abandoned, unoccupied

**void** *n.* nothingness, emptiness, space, vacuum

**volatile** *adj.* explosive, unstable, fickle, erratic, passing, transient, frivolous

**volition** *n.* will, choosing, preference, choice, election, discretion, determination

**voluble** *adj.* talkative, loquacious, fluent, articulate, verbose, wordy, garrulous

**volume** *n.* EDITION: book, manuscript; MASS: size, magnitude, bulk; LOUDNESS: intensity, strength

**voluntary** *adj.* willing, disposed, inclined, prone, deliberate, intended, intentional, planned, willful

**volunteer** *v.* offer, extend, render, submit, proffer, tender, propose, suggest, recommend

**voluptuous** *adj.* sensual, indulgent, carnal, erotic, lustful, licentious

**voracious** *adj* greedy, insatiable, ravenous, hungry, rapacious, grasping

**vote** *v.* elect, choose, enact, legislate, select, decide

**vouch** *v.* certify, attest, swear, state, assure

**vow** *n.* promise, pledge, covenant, contract

**vow** *v.* swear, promise, assure, attest, certify, affirm

**voyage** *n.* journey, excursion, trip, tour

**vulgar** *adj.* coarse tasteless, gross, crude, unrefined

**vulgarity** *n* obscenity, rudeness, indelicacy, coarseness, crassness, impropriety, immodesty

**vulnerable** *adj.* unprotected, unguarded, defenseless, exposed, susceptible, unsafe

**waft** *v.* float, hover, drift, skim flit flutter

**wage** *v.* conduct, undertake, pursue

**wages** *n.* pay, compensation, stipend, remuneration

**wager** *v.* bet, stake, risk, gamble, speculate, hazard

**waif** *n.* stray, foundling, orphan, urchin, ragamuffin

**wail** *v.* lament, bemoan, sob, whine, mourn

**wait** *v.* abide, delay, linger, remain, tarry, stay

**waive** *v.* forgo, sacrifice, relinquish, renounce, resign, postpone, defer

**wake** *v.* arouse, rise, awaken, stir, rouse, call, prod, activate, provoke, stimulate, motivate, kindle

**walk** *n.* path, lane, passageway, promenade

**wan** *adj.* pallid, sickly, pale, pasty, ashen, blanched

**wand** *n.* baton, staff, stick, scepter

**wander** *v.* roam, drift, ramble, meander, rove, range, stroll, saunter, digress, stray, shift, veer

**wane** *v.* diminish, subside, abate, decline, weaken, dwindle, decrease, fade, sink, fail

**want** *n.* **NECESSITY:** requirement, demand, lack, deficiency, inadequacy, **POVERTY:** impoverishment, indigence, privation, need

**want** *v.* desire, crave, covet, fancy

**wanton** *adj.* **MALICIOUS:** hateful, spiteful, unruly, willful, reckless; **LEWD:** lascivious, lustful, dissolute

**ward** *n.* **DEPENDENT:** child, minor, orphan; **DISTRICT:** territory, precinct, parish

**warden** *n.* guard, jailer, guardian, caretaker, custodian, watchman

**warm** *adj.* gracious, amiable, pleasant, kind, intimate, amicable, sympathetic, close

**warn** *v.* caution, advise, admonish, counsel, forewarn, alert, inform, apprise

**warrant** *n.* guarantee, insurance, assurance, pledge, certificate, authorization, commission, license, permit, order, writ

**warrant** *v.* certify, approve, authorize, sanction

**wary** *adj.* alert, cautious, circumspect, vigilant, watchful

**wash** *v.* clean, cleanse, scrub, swab, bathe

**waste** *n.* **DEVASTATION:** ruin, blight, destruction; **TRASH:** garbage, debris, refuse, rubbish; **SQUANDER:** consume, expend, misuse, dissipate

**watch** *v.* observe, view, see, regard, scrutinize, inspect, guard, patrol, protect

**watchful** *adj.* vigilant, alert, careful, mindful, attentive, observant, wary

**waterlogged** *adj.* soaked, sodden, sopping, saturated

**waver** *v.* fluctuate, vacillate, hesitate

**wax** *v.* increase, grow, enlarge, expand, flourish

**way** *n.* method, style, technique, system

**waylay** *v.* ambush, assail, lurk, trap

**weak** *adj.* delicate, dainty, feeble, puny, infirm, powerless, flimsy, slight, wobbly

**wealth** *n.* riches, affluence, assets, abundance

**wear** *n.* deterioration, erosion, fraying, fatigue

**weary** *adj.* tired, exhausted, drained, fatigued, spent

**weary** *v.* harass, annoy, bother, badger, pester, irk, vex, distress, harry, torment

**weep** *v.* cry, sob, whimper, bawl, moan, wail, lament

**weigh** *v.* consider, contemplate, ponder, study

**weight** *n.* **MASS:** density, heft, heaviness, tonnage; **SIGNIFICANCE:** import, importance, gravity, consequence, influence

**weird** *adj.* mysterious, eerie, spooky, uncanny, unnatural, ghostly, puzzling, arcane

**welcome** *adj.* appreciated, desirable, delightful

**welcome** *v.* greet, salute, hail, embrace

**weld** *v.* join, connect, bind, bond

**well** *adj.* healthy, strong, hardy, robust, fit, sound

**wet** *v.* soak, drench, saturate, dampen, douse

**wheedle** *v.* coax, wangle, entreat, appeal, beg, cajole

**whereabouts** *n.* location, position, situation, locale, place, spot, site

**whet** *v.* sharpen, hone, strop, file, grind

**whim** *n.* impulse, inclination, urge, impulse, desire, craving, caprice, whimsy, notion, fancy, quirk

**whimper** *v.* cry, whine, sniffle, snivel, weep

**whimsical** *adj.* capricious, fanciful, playful, impulsive

**whine** *v.* cry, complain, grumble, snivel, whimper

**whip** *v.* beat, lash, flog, scourge, switch, punish

**whirl** *n.* revolve, rotate, spin, gyrate

**whittle** *v.* form, fashion, sculpt, carve, chisel, shape

**whole** *adj.* entire, unbroken, undivided, complete

**wholesome** *adj.* nourishing, healthy, nutritious, beneficial, advantageous, good

**whoop** *v.* holler, howl, shout, cheer, scream, yell

**wicked** *adj.* evil, depraved, immoral, nefarious

**wide** *adj.* extensive, comprehensive, universal

**widen** *v.* broaden, increase, expand, extend, spread, extend, enlarge, augment, stretch

**width** *n.* breadth, expanse, amplitude, scope

**wield** *v.* handle, utilize, operate, use, control, manage

**wild** *adj.* untamed, uncivilized, unrestrained

**will** *n.* **COMMAND:** decree, order, bidding, **DECISION:** choice, determination, **DESIRE:** purpose, pleasure, fancy, wish

**will** *v.* **COMMAND:** order, decree, proclaim, direct; **BEQUEATH:** grant, give, leave

**willful** *adj.* **DELIBERATE:** intended, meant, voluntary, willed; **STUBBORN:** obstinate, headstrong, inflexible, adamant, resolute

**wilt** *v.* droop, wither, shrivel, decay, slump

**wily** *adj.* deceitful, artful, cunning, sly, crafty, treacherous

**win** *v.* **TRIUMPH:** prevail; **ACHIEVE:** secure, persuade, influence, convert

**wind** *v.* curve, twist, swerve, snake, meander, curl, twist, twine, encircle

**windfall** *n.* blessing, godsend, boon, bonanza

**winning** *adj.* **ENGAGING:** captivating, charming, pleasant, likable, dazzling, winsome; **VICTORIOUS:** triumphant, conquering, successful

**winnings** *n.* accumulation, profits, gain

**winnow** *v.* sift, separate, sieve, extract

**winsome** *adj.* winning, beautiful, charming, captivating, lovely, cute, comely, engaging, delightful

**wisdom** *n.* sagacity, understanding, discretion, insight, tact, diplomacy, intelligence, knowledge

**wise** *adj.* intelligent, scholarly, learned, educated, sagacious, rational, sensible, prudent, insightful, discerning, smart

**wish** *n.* desire, craving, inclination, aspiration, goal

**wish** *v.* **CRAVE:** yearn, want, need; **DIRECT:** order, bid, instruct; **REQUEST:** beg, , entreat, solicit

**wistful** *adj.* melancholy, sentimental, nostalgic, plaintive

**wit** *n.* intellect, reason, sagacity, sense, wisdom

**witch** *n.* sorceress, enchantress, hag, crone

**witchcraft** *n.* sorcery, wizardry, divination

**withdraw** *v.* retract, revoke, recant

**wither** *v.* shrivel, wilt, shrink, atrophy, languish

**withhold** *v.* repress, restrain, check, retain

**withstand** *v.* oppose, defy, confront, resist, endure

**witness** *n.* spectator, bystander, onlooker, eyewitness

**witness** *v.* observe, see, watch, perceive, notice

**witticism** *n.* quip, jest, pun, gag, joke, wisecrack

**witty** *adj.* humorous, amusing, bright, keen, droll

**wizard** *n.* magician, conjurer, soothsayer, sorcerer

**wizened** *adj.* withered, shriveled, dry, dehydrated

**woe** *n.* sorrow, anguish, grief, misery, agony

**woeful** *adj.* mournful, sad, sorrowful, doleful

**wonder** *n.* amazement, astonishment, awe

**wonder** *v.* **QUESTION:** ponder, speculate, doubt; **MARVEL:** gape, stare

**wonderful** *adj.* extraordinary, marvelous, astounding, awesome, remarkable, startling, excellent, superb

**wondrous** *adj.* amazing, astonishing, striking, astounding, extraordinary, miraculous

**word** *n.* pledge, promise, guarantee, assurance

**work** *n.* labor, enterprise, undertaking, profession, business, occupation

**work** *v.* labor, toil, accomplish, perform, produce

**world** *n.* earth, globe, planet, realm, sphere, domain, kingdom, province, environment

**worldly** *adj.* sophisticated, urbane, suave

**worry** *n.* anxiety, apprehension, fear, disquiet, misgiving, uneasiness

**worry** *v.* FRET: care, fuss; IRRITATE: torment, bother, disturb, harass, trouble, pester, plague

**worship** *n.* adoration, devotion, reverence, veneration

**worship** *v.* esteem, revere, venerate, glorify, respect

**worst** *adj.* poorest, lowest

**worth** *n.* value, importance, quality, excellence

**worthy** *adj.* deserving, commendable, estimable, noble, excellent, exemplary

**wound** *v.* injure, harm, hurt, lacerate

**wrap** *v.* enfold, envelop, swathe, bandage, swaddle

**wrath** *n.* anger, fury, ire, irritation, resentment

**wreak** *v.* perpetrate, do, perform, commit

**wreath** *n.* garland, bouquet, decoration

**wreathe** *v.* curl, entwine, encircle

**wreck** *v.* destroy, demolish, ruin, shatter, spoil, raze

**wreckage** *n.* remains, debris, wreck, flotsam

**wretch** *n.* miscreant, rogue, villain, rascal, brute

**wretched** *adj.* miserable, woeful, dejected, depressed, forlorn, unhappy, contemptible, pitiful, sorry, vile

**wriggle** *v.* wiggle, squirm, writhe, worm, twist

**wrinkle** *n.* fold, crease, pucker, furrow, ridge

**writ** *n.* law, decree, order, edict

**write** *v.* inscribe, scrawl, sign, compose, record

**writing** *n.* penmanship, hand, lettering, calligraphy

**writhe** *v.* squirm, contort, agonize, thrash, flail

**wrong** *adj.* immoral, evil, false, inaccurate, improper

**wrong** *v.* harm, abuse, oppress, maltreat, dishonor

**wrongful** *adj.* unlawful, criminal, illegal, illicit

**yard** *n.* tract, area, enclosure, patch, courtyard, lot, plot, square

**yardstick** *n.* measure, guide, gauge, scale, model, norm, standard

**yarn** *n.* tale, anecdote, alibi, fabrication

**yearning** *n.* longing, craving, desire, want, wish

**yell** *v.* cheer, root, shout, call, holler, scream

**yellow** *adj.* cowardly, timid, scared, timorous, craven

**yen** *n.* longing, yearning, desire, urge, craving

**yield** *v.* surrender, abdicate, cede, concede, resign, grant, acquiesce, give

**yoke** *n.* couple, harness, join, link, attach, connect

**young** *adj.* immature, juvenile, adolescent, youthful, inexperienced, green

**youth** *n.* immaturity, adolescence, minority

**zany** *adj.* crazy, funny, silly, nonsensical, wacky

**zeal** *n.* enthusiasm, fervor, passion, spirit, ardor

**zealot** *n.* fanatic, devotee, partisan

**zealous** *adj.* enthusiastic, eager, fervent, passionate, spirited, ardent, earnest

**zenith** *n.* top, peak, crest, elevation

**zephyr** *n.* breeze, draft, wind

**zest** *n.* relish, enthusiasm, gusto, enjoyment, delight